Contents

ESSENTIAL INFORMATION TECHNOLOGY

Also in the HarperCollins Essential Series

Essential Accountancy and Finance
Bijon Kar

Essential Business Studies
Stephen Barnes

Essential Government and Politics
Jim Cordell

Essential Marketing
Tony Proctor

Essential Mechanics
Owen Elbourn

Essential Practical Psychology
Keith Maglennon

Essential Psychology
G. C. Davenport

Series Editor: Roger Gomm

ESSENTIAL
INFORMATION TECHNOLOGY

A. A. Berk

Collins Educational
An imprint of HarperCollins*Publishers*

Published by Collins Educational
An Imprint of HarperCollins*Publishers*
77–85 Fulham Palace Road
Hammersmith
London W6 8JB

First published in 1995

British Library Cataloguing-in-Publication Data
A catalogue record for this book is available from the British Library

Edited by Patricia Briggs
Cover design by Ridgeway Associates

ISBN 0–00–322368–X

Typeset by Create Publishing Services Ltd, Bath.
Printed by Scotprint, Musselburgh.

Foreword

Every book in the Essential Series is designed carefully to put you in control of your own learning.

When using this book, you will not only cover the key elements of your course but you will also benefit from the author's use of modern learning techniques, with the result that you will make the best possible use of your time.

This book includes the following features.

- An introductory section at the beginning of each chapter, which focuses your attention on its contents and which tells you exactly what you should have learned by the end of the chapter. These are your 'learning objectives'.

- A listing of key terms at the beginning of the chapter. This alerts you to the important words in the vocabulary of the subject. You should know what each means by the end of the chapter.

- End of chapter reviews which give you a synopsis of the most important points you should have learned.

- Notes in the margin of the text, where the author takes the role of a tutor: picking out key ideas, highlighting important concepts.

- Sideflashes in the margin which help you to locate or relocate important ideas when using the book for reference.

- Activities which allow you to learn by applying the ideas in the text.

- Study skills advice which give you suggestions for organizing your study and improving your learning.

Learning is not easy; nobody learns without effort. However, if you use this book effectively, you will not only succeed in your course and assessment, but you will also enjoy the experience of learning.

Author's preface

Few subjects are as wide-ranging in their effect as those of information technology and computing. We are all touched, more or less strongly, by the effects of this still embryonic subject. This book attempts to provide a technically complete description of the main subjects that you should meet if you wish to study this field.

Not all the chapters and sections will be relevant to a particular course. Those which are not directly applicable to you should be used as reference to provide an understanding of the terms and products which you will come across in magazines, and in your career in general.

As always, I am most indebted to the professional and courteous attitude of the publisher and associated staff which has made the task of preparing this book both pleasurable and efficient. I am particularly grateful to the Essential-Series editor, Roger Gomm, for his hard work on the layout, his many useful suggestions and his continuous encouragement. My thanks are also due to Hwfa Jones of Wirral Metropolitan College for his good nature in reading large quantities of text, and providing me with some excellent comment.

Naturally, I have as always picked and chosen from the many suggestions and comments which people have been good enough to offer, and as such I am exclusively responsible for mistakes, omissions and anything else which may be found wanting in this text.

Finally, and by no means least, I once again give my deepest thanks to my wife and two children for their continuous backing of this work, and also to my father for his usual proofreading and many technical discussions.

Dr A.A.Berk

 # How to use this book

Chapter objectives

By the end of this chapter you should have:

▮ matched the contents of this book to the syllabus you are following

▮ considered how you are going to arrange hands-on practical experience to reinforce what you learn from the boo

▮ considered ways of applying the ideas of information technology to the process of study

▮ identified the key dates in your course

▮ considered the best ways of organizing study time.

HOW TO USE THIS BOOK

If you are reading this book it is probable that you are following a course in information technology, computing or something similar. This book has been written to provide you with a good grounding in these areas. However, courses in computing and information technology are very variable, and for your own course this book might provide too much in some respects and too little in others. Your first task then is to ask yourself how this book relates to the course you are following.

 Whatever course you are following, your tutor should have given you a detailed syllabus, i.e. a listing of the topics the course will cover. If you haven't been given one, then you have every right to demand one. Take the syllabus for your course and use it with the Contents list for this book to see how far the topics match: you will probably also have to look at individual chapters from time to time. Write the chapter numbers on the side of the syllabus if you like. Try to identify:

• where there is a good match between the book and the syllabus

• where the syllabus contains topics which are missing from the book. You will have to find alternative sources for these

• where the book contains topics which are not on the syllabus, or seems to deal with them in greater detail than you need. In these cases, there is no reason why you

▶ Whenever you see this logo it is an indication that there is an activity for you to complete.

► Without knowing the syllabus you are following, study is like making a journey to an unknown destination without a map.

should not use these sections of the book, but you will give them a lower priority than other sections.

This activity will have given you a good idea of what the book contains but it should also have given you a fairly clear overview of the syllabus you are following.

Reading and practical experience

There is a limit to how much you can learn about computing and information technology by reading a book. Equally there is a limit on how much you can learn about these topics just through hands-on experience. We couldn't write a book for you giving you practical hands-on activities to do because hardware and software differ so much. If we had tried to do this, we would have written a book which might have been excellent for people with some kinds of hardware and software, and useless for others.

► The more opportunities you can make for 'hands-on' experience, the more real the text of this book will become.

Opportunities for hands-on experience

If you are going to gain the maximum benefit from this book it is essential that you arrange practical experience for yourself. For example when the text is about wordprocessing, then it would be a good idea to read it alongside whatever wordprocessing package you have access to, and then try the wordprocessing program; and when the text describes the physical properties of a printer interface, it would be worth looking at the back of a printer to see what the sockets really look like.

► Using manuals.

For your own use of hardware and programs you will need to use the various manuals which go with them: their 'dedicated paperware'. These will also be useful in providing you with concrete and more detailed examples of layouts and procedures which you can add to those in the book.

 Make a list of the information technology devices which you have access to. Do this by drawing up a sheet of paper with two vertical columns. In the first column list the device, and in the second any useful sources of information. For example, if you have access to a wordprocessor, then there may be a tutor program on disk and there will certainly be a manual and other documents to guide users. Spread your net widely. You almost certainly have access to a telephone, so what about the information you can obtain from banks about armchair banking?

File this list and add to it while you use the book.

Computer magazines and catalogues

► Magazines and catalogues.

There are many computer magazines which will provide you with a continuous stream of information both on the established and the latest hardware and software. We strongly recommend that you either purchase one of these, or identify whether one is available in your library; and remember to look at it periodically. Select a magazine which is not tied to a particular make of computer or software house. You need a magazine which will give you unbiased reviews of different models, programs and applications. In these magazines you will also find advertisements from suppliers of hardware or software. They often produce free and very informative catalogues. Remember that catalogues are advertising material, so avoid the hype, but read the more detailed specifications.

Science magazines, such as *New Scientist*, are worth looking at from time to time for the news they give about the most recent developments in computing and computer applications. Most of the 'heavy' daily papers have a weekly or occasional information technology supplement.

► You might like to consider developing a scrapbook of cuttings from catalogues, computer magazines and science magazines. Using a database program to index the material would be a worthwhile exercise in information technology skills.

Information technology and your other studies

You are probably studying subjects other than information technology, and even if you are not, you will have other interests. Make a point of applying what you learn about information technology to your other interests. For example, if you are also studying biology, then look out for the way in which computers are used in biological and medical research. If you are studying a business subject, then the application of information technology to business is a central topic.

Using information technologies as study aids

Since you are studying information technology, it is worth trying as far as possible to use an information technology approach to your study. Three applications come immediately to mind: personal organizer programs for managing time, wordprocessing for making notes, writing essays and assignments, and databases for storing and retrieving information. You can learn more about databases later in the book. However, you probably know already that computer databases are somewhat like card indexes, but that computerization makes it easy and quick to select cards in any of a large number of combinations you care to specify. Like card indexes, however, computer databases are better for storing smaller rather than larger amounts of information. So, for example, you would not want to use a database to store all you know about wordprocessors, but you might like to use one to store references to your notes on wordprocessing (what they are, and where they are) and references to books and articles about wordprocessing. If you have access to a personal database, we strongly recommend that you use it, first as an opportunity for designing a computer application, and second as a study aid to store and retrieve information which is important to you.

► At the beginning of each chapter of the book after this one there is a listing of 'key terms'. These are the words you need to know the meaning of. Key terms, their definitions and the context in which they are used could be usefully stored with a database program.

From what you know already about information technology write down your own ideas about how its application might assist your study.

GETTING ORGANIZED FOR STUDY

The remarks above are particularly relevant to anyone studying information technology. However, there are also general guidelines which are relevant, whatever you are studying.

Your course

 Make sure you know the answers to the following questions.

- How long is your course, in hours per week, days per week and in total?

- What homework and course work will you have to do?

- What organization arranges for your assessment? How are you assessed? If by examination, what is the date of the examination? If by course assignments, when will you be briefed on these and when are the final deadlines?

Place

 Identify a location at home which is your study place and nothing else. With practice you will reach a point where the act of sitting in that chair, at that table, triggers the work response in you. This will not happen if you choose to work on the settee where you usually watch TV. As well as a quiet space for private study, you will also need to arrange access to information technology equipment. Apart from your personal equipment, identify:

▶ This might refer to access to a suite of wordprocessors in a college, or time using a friend's desk-top publishing program.

- Where can you have access to the equipment?

- When can you have access to it?

- Whose permission do you need to gain access?

- What kind of support and assistance will you get while you are using it?

If equipment is available on a self-access basis, then there will be times when there is more competition than others. Try to identify times when you can be fairly certain of access.

Time

 Draw up a calendar of crucial dates for your course of study: term dates, assignment deadlines, examination dates, etc. Use a personal organizer program by all means, but make sure a hard copy is the first page of your notes.

Here are some other matters you should consider in managing time.

- How will you fit study around your other commitments? You cannot simply add a course onto an already over-full life. You will have to reorganize your life to make time for study and make better use of the time you fritter away now.

- At what time of day do you work most effectively? Not *prefer* to work, but work *more effectively*. Experiment.

- For how long can you study effectively at a stretch? Practise and test your learning until you know the answer to this question. With book work, for most people the answer is 'about an hour'; then they need at least a short break. People often find that they can go on learning for longer when the activity is more practical: when learning to wordprocess, for example.

- For book work, private study for two hours every day is more likely to be effective than a ten-hour stint on Sunday, but for practical learning longer periods may be necessary.

- For each period of study set yourself realistic objectives. In this book every chapter starts with a set of targets or objectives. Use the chapter objectives to phase your study.

- Plan your study sessions and their objectives a week in advance. Things may not go exactly to plan, but at least you will know what you have to do to make up for lost time.

- When you have finished a chapter, look again at the chapter objectives. Ask yourself whether you have learned what you were supposed to learn. Make a list of the things you still don't seem to understand. Often just doing this clarifies matters. Then use the book again, or another book, or ask a friend or your tutor to help you sort out the remainder.

The next two chapters are introductory. They form a kind of platform from which you can approach the more detailed and advanced information in Chapters 4 to 13.

► **Now that you have completed this chapter, look back to the objectives at the beginning and check that you have accomplished each of them.**

2 Introduction to computer systems

Chapter objectives

By the time you have read this chapter, you will understand:

▌ how computers arose, and why they are important

▌ the meaning of 'binary' and 'digital' technology

▌ how to code information for computer use

▌ how the machine stores binary data

▌ the types and levels of computers in existence

▌ how computers are generally used

▌ the types of information which can be handled by computer

▌ how computers can be used to control everyday products

▌ the following key words: IT, hardware, software, data, program, binary, digital, variables, TRUE, FALSE, Boolean logic, BIT, computer, analogue, discrete, code, ASCII, EBCDIC, BYTE, NIBBLE, KB, MB, IC, VLSI, mainframe, mini, microcomputer, desktop, data processing, keyboard, screen.

Introduction

▶ This chapter and the next introduce you to the main jargon and concepts of computers and computing, and many of these subjects will be expanded upon fully in later chapters. Where appropriate, the subheadings below start with a reference to a later chapter so that you can see where the information presented is expanded. You should regard this present chapter, and the next, as a set of introductions to the later parts of the book.

As you will discover, the study of computers spans all areas of human endeavour. It takes you into the heart of organizations as large as the government of a country, or as small as your local corner sweet shop. It takes you to the controls of a complete spaceship, and the playing of video games. It reaches into the centre of most businesses and educational bodies, and gives you insight into the workings of every part of manufacturing industry. It covers, for instance, health care, sport, police work, advertising, psychology, even art. As an exercise, you might like to consider whether you can find any area which is truly free from the influence of the computer.

That is not to say you will find every firm and body fully computerized – there are many that are not – and new enterprises are starting up all the time. Your job, in the future, could well be to try to persuade such people to computerize. In order to do that, you have to know how computer systems work, and how they are applied. In a nutshell, these are the aims of any course you are following, and the aims of this book.

If you already have a grounding in IT, you may feel tempted to skip these first two chapters, but you should scan through and check you are familiar with all the information here. Later chapters will assume that you have read the first two.

We will start with a short history of computers, as this will give you an insight into the main components, jargon and applications of computer systems in a simple and logical manner.

EARLY HISTORY OF COMPUTERS

Pre-mechanical computers

The exact history of the computer depends upon the definition of 'computer'. For instance, if one simply takes the definition as 'any inanimate object which automatically provides answers to questions', then Stonehenge, on Salisbury Plain, might be argued to be a computer. Once a year, as it has done every year for the best part of 4,000 years, it automatically answers the question: 'Which day is the summer solstice?'. In fact, this monument probably answers many more questions on a regular basis, but unfortunately it is silent on the question: 'What was the main purpose of Stonehenge?'.

Figure 2.1 Stonehenge: a computer designed to answer the question: 'When is the summer solstice?' and perhaps other questions

To take this analogy further, Stonehenge could be said to be 'programmed'. After all, it was built with stones which were placed in a precise pattern, very much as we write programs for computers in precise patterns – it is the information locked up in that stone pattern which does the work. The physical stone might be called the computer's 'hardware' – the bit you can touch; the pattern and theory of the placement of the stones the 'software' – the part you cannot touch, but which controls the problem solving. And so on.

The history of the computer could become very diverse if the definition is made wide enough. Where would the 'abacus' come, or our own ten fingers and thumbs, for instance? However, to confine our study to the main elements, we should look at the history of number-based computing machines.

► At Stonehenge the stones are the hardware, and the pattern they are arranged in is the software.

The history of such devices spans a considerable period, and even includes a time when the mechanical technology was simply not sophisticated enough to realize the basic theory.

Mechanical calculators

The great seventeenth-century French mathematician, physicist and philosopher, Blaise Pascal, invented and built perhaps the first mechanical calculator. This machine was based on intermeshing gears which were constrained to pass rotational movements along the gear chain, and rotate numbered wheels on which the user could read off the final answer. He used the calculator to help his father perform additions for his business accounts. Pascal's name is immortalized in various places, but computing remembers him by naming a computer language after him – PASCAL.

▶ Blaise Pascal invented the first mechanical calculator. The computer language PASCAL is named after him.

Figure 2.2 Pascal's calculator

Developments of this basic invention remained on a level best described as that of a pure calculator, until a major leap was taken by Charles Babbage in the first half of the nineteenth century. His idea was to create a general computing machine which could, essentially, store data as well as a program to control the processes which the user wished performed. This would provide a flexible machine capable of being moulded to the user's wishes, thus solving general problems. The machine was called the 'analytical engine'.

In essence, Babbage's ideas, and those of his co-worker, Ada Augusta – the Countess of Lovelace – could have founded the main concepts of modern computing. These two discovered the concept of interfacing the machinery, or 'hardware' to the data and instructions or 'software' of computing. Ada Augusta is sometimes said to have been the first computer programmer, and her name is remembered, as with Pascal, by the name of a computer language – ADA.

▶ Babbage's analytic engine was too complicated for the engineers of the day, was never completed and was forgotten until the 1930s.

Figure 2.3 Babbage's engine

Unfortunately, the mechanical engineering of the day was simply not sophisticated enough to reproduce the complex machinery required for the task. The analytical engine was never completed, and Babbage was forgotten until his writings were rediscovered, by chance, in 1937.

In essence, Pascal and Babbage had the two major lateral thoughts which were required to produce the technology of today. The first was to harness machinery to perform repetitive calculative tasks, but with its processes (or software) fixed within the hardware and incapable of modification. The second was to produce a general machine, capable of storing and executing a program of instructions, and hence of solving any task required. This latter is often referred to as the 'stored program computer', where the software is flexible, and resides within the machine's memory, along with the data on which it will act.

▶ Babbage's collaborator, Ada Augusta, is remembered in the computer language called 'ADA'.

In order to realize the storing of data and programming, it became necessary to invent a language which could be used to code this information for the machine. Machines cannot be expected instantly to comprehend the full gamut and complexity of human language. In fact, machines need very simple languages, and anything which reduces the complex ways in which we talk and think to simple basic elements is useful for transferring to machinery – indeed, this is the principle at the heart of computer programming.

SOFTWARE – BINARY AND DIGITAL LOGIC

▶ See Chapter 6.

As with many fields, the early history of the computer was slow, and perhaps held back by the lack of parallel 'enabling' technologies, such as precision engineering, and the transition from mechanical to electronic machinery. In many scientific fields, too, theory predated practice. However, as the technology gradually evolved to produce computers, so the theory advanced at the same time.

▶ Boolean algebra is the basis of computer programming in binary.

In the mid-nineteenth century, George Boole, an English mathematician and logician, was founding a theory later called 'Boolean algebra' based upon the idea of simplifying the description of all problems to relationships between 'binary variables'.

A variable is an object which can take on any value. For instance, in ordinary algebra, the letter (or variable) X might be given the value '6'. Thus, the 'value' of X is said to be 6. Similarly, the value of, say, Y which is set equal to five times X would be 30. This might be written as:

$$X = 6$$

$$Y = 5X$$

Therefore Y = 30

Here, the multiplication sign is left out between '5' and 'X' so as not to confuse the notation.

In Boolean algebra, the 'binary' variables, as the name suggests, can simply take on one of two possible values or 'states'. These values are called 'TRUE' and 'FALSE', or '1' and '0'. The relationship between quantities which conform to these constraints forms the basis of all modern 'digital' computer technology and its languages.

▶ BIT is short for binary digit.

The 1 and 0 values are called 'binary digits', or BITs for short. Digital computers do not deal with the 'ordinary' numbers which we are used to, based on the digits 0 to 9, followed by 10s, 100s, 1,000s, etc. Digital computers deal only with 1 and 0, and strings of these. If one could look right into the inside of a working computer, and slow the process down to human speeds, all we would see would be 1s and 0s, in continuous streams, running throughout the machine.

Binary and analogue

The contrasting technology to digital computers is that of 'analogue' computers. These deal with continuously variable or 'analogue' quantities, as opposed to the 'discrete' binary quantities of digital technology. In this type of machine, for instance, two numbers which are to be multiplied might be converted into voltages proportional to those two values. These voltages are then fed into the inputs of an electronic (analogue) circuit. This combines the voltages in such a manner that the output line from the circuit is always proportional to the multiple of the inputs. The output gives the answer directly, and may be read by a voltmeter. There are many types of analogue circuit dealing with continuously variable quantities which combine and modify input voltages in set mathematical ways, and are thus used to produce answers to mathematical problems.

The big question which often arises with binary logic is how can the full range and richness of the whole of human activity be represented by just the humble 1 and 0? How can a machine present information in full colour, rich sound, and take in and present a whole planet of written data if it only has the 1 and the 0 to work with?

Codes

The answer lies in 'coding'. Simply stated, any character – a letter, a number, a punctuation mark, a coloured dot – can be represented by a string of BITs, i.e. 1s and 0s. There are internationally agreed codes for this representation. For instance, a computer expert would recognize the string of seven BITs 0110100 as the 'ASCII' code for the number '4', and 1000001 as ASCII for the upper case letter 'A'. ASCII stands for 'American Standard Code for Information Interchange'. It uses patterns of seven BITs to represent letters, numbers, special symbols such as punctuation marks, and various other items. However, to make storage and representation of the coding more compatible with current computer technology, the seven-BIT ASCII code usually has a leading zero tacked on to it to change it into eight BITs. As we shall see, a group of eight BITs has fundamental significance in modern computing.

▶ ASCII – American Standard Code for Information Interchange

There are various other coding systems which use different numbers of BITs, and completely different binary patterns for the characters. For instance, EBCDIC is an eight-BIT code which stands for 'Extended Binary Coded Decimal Indicator Code'. Such tables of code patterns can be chosen completely at random, as long as everyone agrees to abide by them.

As you can see, once you agree an artificial coding for each character in a human language, an entire book, for instance, can simply, though rather confusingly, be represented by a massively long sequence of BITs. To decode the 'book' into English, simply start at the very beginning splitting the BITs into groups of, say, eight BITs (depending upon the code used), and refer to the code table, letter by letter from start to finish. This, of course, is where computers come into their own. Here is a simple, repetitive task – perfect for an ultra-fast machine, incapable of boredom. For future reference, you should know that grouping BITs into strings of eight, known as BYTEs, is a convenient method of organization.

▶ A group of eight BITs is called a 'BYTE'. Other groupings of BITs are called 'words', and half a BYTE is called a NIBBLE (or NYBBLE).

 How many BITs and BYTEs would be needed to ASCII code the text on this page, assuming that the ASCII code has been extended with leading zeros to make each code take up eight BITs? (Don't forget the space between each word, and punctuation marks). This kind of exercise is needed continually in analysing problems for computer applications. As we shall see shortly, it indicates the memory capacity required by a system.

BITs and BYTEs

To see how much information can be held by the ASCII patterns of BITs, you should try to work out how many different patterns of 1s and 0s can be formed by a set of eight BITs. In other words, how many different characters can a single BYTE represent? To answer this question, note that, for instance, a single-BIT word can hold only two different patterns:

0 and 1

A two-BIT word can have 4 patterns:

00   01   10   and   11

 Can you see a general mathematical formula for working out how many different patterns can be produced from a group of any number of BITs?

If you have solved the problem above and played around with different numbers of BITs in groups, you should be able to see that numbers such as '64', '128' and so on are special in some way. In a similar manner the number '1,024' is special, and it happens to be near to 1,000. In general, the letter 'K' is used to denote thousands, and so it is in computing. In fact, to be exact, 'K' in computing denotes 1,024, but it is near enough to 1,000 for most purposes. If we wish to talk about the number of BYTEs needed to represent all the characters in a piece of text, such as a given large written report for instance, we might describe it as containing, say, a hundred thousand characters. As one BYTE is needed per character, we may say that it needs about 100K BYTEs to represent the report in full, character by character. In fact, 100K is not exactly 100,000 (it is actually 102,400) but in this case we are only estimating.

When we wish to represent a million, the term 'mega' (or simply 'M') is used. Again, the exact definition of 1M BYTE (often written 1 MB) is not exactly a million, but it is near enough to be useful as a unit of this order of size. You will understand the numbers involved here more accurately as you proceed, but for now remember that K and M are convenient ways of simplifying large numbers of BYTEs.

From the above, the answers to the last two problems are as follows. The number of BYTEs needed to code a page of text is simply the number of characters, including spaces etc., which are on the page – one BYTE per character – just count the characters. The number of BITs is simply eight times this – eight BITs per BYTE.

A single BIT has two possible patterns, or values: 0 and 1. A two-BIT number has four possible values: 00, 01, 10, 11. A three-BIT number has eight values, a four-BIT number has sixteen, and so on. Simply multiply by two each time. Thus, an eight-BIT number has $2 \times 2 \times 2 \ldots \times 2$ eight times, expressed alternatively as two to the power of eight, written as 2^8 (equal to 256), as the number of values possible. An N-BIT number has 2 to the Nth values – or 2 times itself N times.

► K equals 1,000, well, actually 1,024.

► M equals about 1,000,000

► Chapter 6 describes why groups of eight and sixteen BITs are special.

HARDWARE

In order to represent 1s and 0s inside a machine, the first machines were purely mechanical, and contained mechanical 'ON/OFF' switches. An ON/OFF switch is the most basic binary memory device. It can only take on one of two possible states – ON for 1, and OFF for 0, say. Its state must also be capable of being read by other devices – perhaps by attempting to pass an electric current through it – if ON, the current will pass, and it must be storing a 1, if OFF it will not, and clearly holds a 0. Millions of such devices can store a large amount of information, if the code can be read.

Initially, as BITs were processed, mechanical cogs and arms moved around, passing physical movements and positions from place to place within the machine. This, indeed, was the basis of Babbage's inventions.

At the same time, external data has to be able to be coded into BITs, and presented in a 'machine-readable' form. Many methods were used – but the concept of the punched hole appeared in the nineteenth century. The principle, essentially, is to present the computer with cards, or a continuous tape, punched with holes to represent 1s and 0s. Or to be exact, a 1 is represented by a hole in a given position, and a 0 by 'no hole'.

In the 1890 US census, Herman Hollerith used punched cards, probably inspired by the Jacquard loom's punched card system, to record information. An electromechanical reading system took in and counted the data. The punched card, and tape, endured until quite recently, and formed the basis of much of the input/output technology of this century. More immediate and accessible methods of communicating and holding data are used today, however.

As technology progressed, first vacuum tubes and then transistors began to be used for the ON/OFF switches which held and transported the 1s and 0s.

 Next time you are in a library, make a point of looking in the computer section to find a book which illustrates computers from, say, the 1970s. See if you can find pictures of machines which read holes in punched cards and tape. You should note how dated they appear, even though it is only a few years since they went out of fashion.

► See also Chapters 3, 4, 5 and 7.

► Nineteenth-century fairground organs were operated on a binary system using rolls of punched paper through which air was blown. A hole was an 'ON' with a puff and a sound, and no hole was an 'OFF' and no sound.

GENERATIONS OF COMPUTERS

There is a general agreement that the first generation of computers was in the era of hardware built using electromechanical devices, and/or vacuum tubes for the switching. These computers consisted of machines such as ENIAC (Electronic Numerical Integrator and Calculator) and EDVAC (Electronic Discrete Variable Automatic Computer). They were revolutionary, slow, but useful. For instance, this generation contributed to the war effort in the 1940s by cracking secret enemy codes.

The second generation of machinery used semiconductors – transistors – to reduce size and power consumption and increase speed. The first of these machines appeared in 1959.

By the 1960s and 1970s, the third generation was born with the advent of the 'integrated circuit' (IC) which is a small piece of semiconducting material (usually a silicon 'chip') with many transistors and other devices formed on its surface. This reduced interconnection problems considerably, again reduced power and size, and increased speed.

At the same time, memory devices, so crucial to the development of the computer, were becoming more efficient and of greater capacity. For many applications of computers, the capacity and speed of memory is as important as the processing power of the machine. Memory was also, at this time, becoming confined to ICs, as opposed to early magnetic 'core' memory which consisted of millions of minute magnetic rings, or cores, threaded onto conducting wires.

In the 1980s, a further, fourth, generation has been loosely identified by the greater density of integration of devices onto the chip. Such devices are called VLSI (Very Large Scale Integration) chips, and hold many hundreds of thousands of devices on the surface of a single IC.

Finally, a fifth generation of computer has been researched for many years. The step forward involves computer intelligence, rather than any specific hardware evolution. However, it has so far proven elusive. Perhaps this also requires an attendant hardware revolution for its realization.

LEVELS OF COMPUTER

▶ Levels: mainframe, mini, micro.

There are three main levels of computer hardware: mainframe computers, minicomputers and microcomputers. Mainframes are easy to distinguish from microcomputers, but minicomputers are not easy to distinguish from the other two – the defining line has become hazy.

Mainframes
A mainframe is a large multi-cabinet electronic installation, usually held in a specially controlled room which is expensive, fast and capable of handling the very largest volumes of data which are used in industry and commerce. It is an irony that the larger and apparently more cumbersome the machine, the faster it is.

Minicomputers
A minicomputer is smaller than a mainframe, and usually does not require particularly special conditions, though some care is required. It is still fast and capable of handling large amounts of data but not, in general, quite as fast or high in capacity as a mainframe.

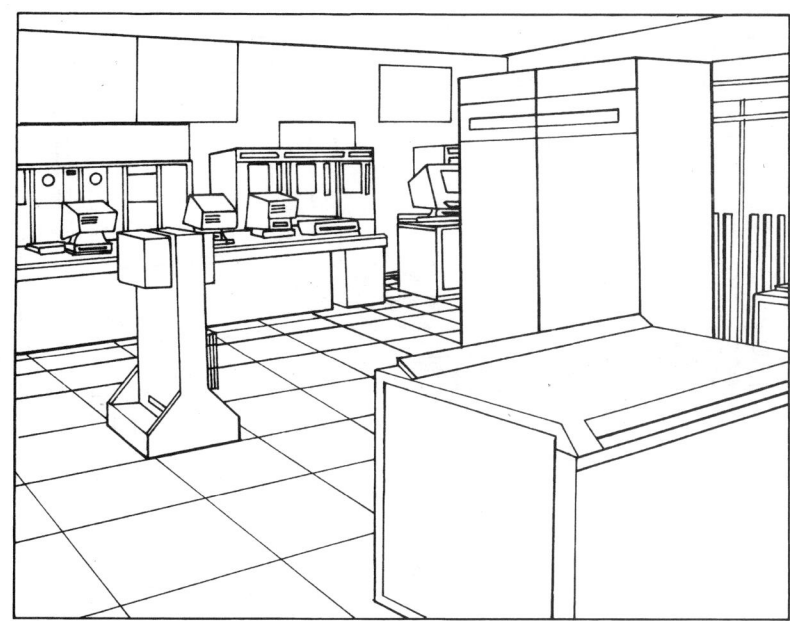

Figure 2.4 A mainframe

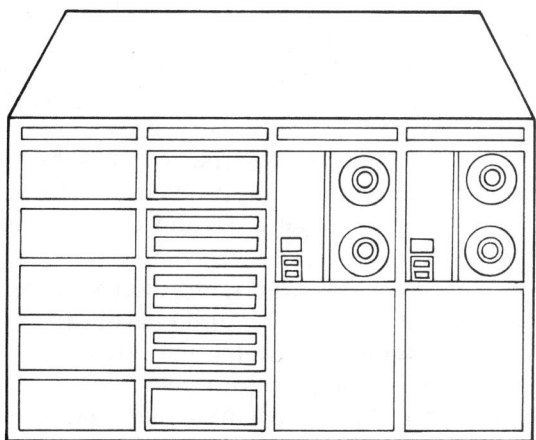

Figure 2.5 A minicomputer

Microcomputers

A microcomputer fits on a desk, is not generally as fast as a mini, and has lower memory capacity. However, the line between minis and micros is becoming very blurred as technology crams more and more into a small box. There are differences in the actual internal construction of micros, minis and mainframes which cause the speed differences. However, you should know that fast micros are challenging the realm of the mini. Indeed, throughout the world, companies are 'downsizing' from minis to micros, and even from mainframes to multiple micro installations.

Figure 2.6 A desk-top microcomputer

WHY ARE COMPUTERS IMPORTANT?

As you can see from the short history above, computers as we know them today are relatively recent. This has been shown to be largely a consequence of the recent nature of the enabling technologies required. However, the need for computing machines has always been there. If we look into ancient history, the earliest civilizations tried to keep records, account for commerce, count their people and solve mathematical and engineering problems, and even dreamed of producing automatons for the tasks and drudgery of everyday life.

Imagine trying to run a large organization such as a national driver and vehicle register. There are millions of drivers and many more millions of vehicles in the country. Each driver has to be registered with his or her unique information, and similarly each vehicle. Apart from the slowness of a manual system, consider the appalling drudgery of the task of updating that amount of data all day, every day.

 As a simple exercise, look at a registration document for a car, and a driving licence. Find the approximate number of individual characters (letters, numbers, symbols) on the two documents. Multiply this by, say, thirty million to represent the number of cars and drivers in a country. Then look at a thick modern paperback book, containing several hundred pages. Count the number of characters in this book – you will have to think of a quick way of estimating this! Now work out how many such paperbacks you would need to store the driver and car registration details above. This gives you some idea of the sort of data storage problems a modern computer can handle.

The introduction of computers has two main goals. The first is to increase the speed and accuracy of information manipulation and calculation. The second is to take over low level tasks which are degrading, boring and as such often not performed accurately or efficiently.

A surfeit of information

► See Chapters 5 and 12.

From time to time you will hear computers being blamed for being inefficient and impersonal. The latter is true, but the former is a myth. A computer is an efficient machine, it is its application which sometimes goes awry. The degree of efficiency which a computer, when properly applied, can bring is truly momentous. Imagine, again, trying to update a country-wide vehicle and driver register manually. Every week many thousands of vehicles change hands, many thousands are bought from new, thousands are scrapped, thousands are stolen and must be tracked within the system by the police, thousands of people pass their test, change their names, apply for their first licence, run out of time on their provisional licences, leave the country, change addresses, die, and so on.

Now consider the many thousands of other registers of all kinds, across a highly controlled and advanced Western nation such as the UK. Think about the USA, then start to consider the other countries of the world. You can quickly see how employing people to process that amount of data is likely to require rather more than the complete working population of the world!

This gives you some idea of the problems of 'data processing' as it is called. It does not even mention the many millions of computers throughout the world engaged on scientific, personal and technological tasks. For instance, the weather forecast is performed by computer. Computers are needed to collect and process the data to and from the communications satellites used to collect weather data. No set of humans could physically work quickly enough to phone the data through, and then process it to produce modern weather data. Of course, it used to be performed manually, but the degree of availability of weather data to the aviation and shipping industries is many times more efficient than it could ever have been using a manual system.

There are many more examples, and as our civilization expands technologically, the computer becomes more and more welded to human needs. Just as the pencil and notebook were intimately tied up with the birth of the scientific method, so the computer has become an internal element to every part of technology, and most other fields.

 Try to find another example of a very large computer-based system and try to estimate, broadly, how much data it must hold.

Computers in everything

You should not think of a computer as just a keyboard and screen. Complete computers, of various levels of sophistication, are embedded in the electronic things which we have around us. Remember that a computer is a general machine. It is not just a video game, or a wordprocessor, or a machine for keeping the accounts of a business. It can store a set of instructions to perform any task for which it has suitable inputs and outputs. For instance, if it is connected to a robot arm, it could be programmed to pick up a glass of wine and hand it to you without spilling a drop – in general, it is the mechanics and power sources which limit this area of technology.

In the machinery around you, there are computers which have been programmed to look like a vast variety of objects. For instance, in your video recorder there is a complete computer system running the many switches, buttons and indicators which you can touch and see. It also runs the mechanics of recording and playing back colour images and sound. This is no mean task, and the program to control all this machinery is complex and subtle. Washing machines can contain computers, similarly food mixers, fuel injection systems in modern cars, the watch on your wrist, an electric typewriter or printer, and so on. They are everywhere. Perhaps science fiction is right when it suggests that one day we will forget where they all are, and lose control to the machine!

As you can see, there are two main classes of computer machinery. These are the screen and keyboard variety (micros to mainframes), and the embedded computer. The first allows us to perform human tasks such as processing large amounts of data, typing letters, preparing business plans, playing games, writing our own programs for general needs, etc. The second is more a class of controllers which can appear within many different devices from washing machines to printers. Despite the large physical differences between these two classes, they are actually very similar in nature.

In the next chapter, we will look further into the components of a computer system, both hardware and software.

Chapter review
- Mechanical calculators were the first numerical machines.
- The concept of a computer includes the notion of the 'stored program'.
- Computers started as mechanical machines.
- Hardware is the machinery of computers, currently realized using fast electronic components.
- Software is the programming which commands the machinery to process problems.
- A variable is an object which can take any value.
- A binary number, or variable, can only take one of two values : 1 and 0.

- Digital computers store information as binary numbers, using ON/OFF switches as memory elements.
- ASCII is a binary code for general characters.
- We are currently using the fourth generation of computers.
- There are three main levels of machinery – mainframes, minis and microcomputers.
- Microcomputers can be small enough to be embedded in running any other kind of machinery.

▶ Now that you have completed this chapter, look back to the objectives at the beginning and check that you have accomplished each of them.

(3) The main components of a computer system

Chapter objectives

By the time you have read this chapter, you will understand:

▌ various components of a computer system

▌ how computers store information

▌ how memory and disks operate

▌ how to communicate with computers

▌ the way in which computers output information

▌ the meaning and structure of programming and algorithms

▌ how computers start up and run

▌ real-time, batch, on- and off-line systems

▌ how to apply computer systems

▌ the following key terms: central processor, memory, input/output, bus, VDU, laptop, palmtop, LCD, terminal, disk, drive, floppy, hard disk, magnetic, internal memory, peripheral memory, backup, giga, printer, dot matrix, PCB, CPU, clock, fetch, execute, front panel, reset, IC, MPU, motherboard, network, flow diagram, algorithm, address, register, microprogram, loop, machine code, compiler, interpreter, high level, low level, applications program, operating system, memory map, RAM, volatile, ROM, BIOS, firmware, bootstrap, non-volatile, control, single chip, database, file, analysis, network, real time, batch, on line, off line, stock control, wordprocessing, spreadsheet.

► This chapter is about the way in which a computer system works, from the lowest level of electronics upwards. This includes a description of the main components of any computer system – hardware and software. The last part of the chapter is concerned with the applications of computers and with the types of information which flow around a system.

WHY LEARN ABOUT THE INSIDES OF THE MACHINE?

A common question which is asked is 'Why bother to understand how computers work?'. After all, most people simply use a computer rather like a ball-point pen – few bother to look at the mechanics of a rolling-ball ink-delivery system.

The answer is that it is perfectly possible, with current highly accessible software products, simply to use a system and never know how it does its job. However, to become involved with the application of computer machinery, or even to be able to make intelligent guesses when something goes wrong, an understanding of the internal workings is of considerable help. Also, a general understanding of the way in which computers function will:

- make it easier to use a given system from scratch
- make your understanding of computer manuals more efficient
- help you to find new applications for computers
- allow you to understand the latest hardware products
- assist in deciding the best product for a given application.

There are many jobs which involve the use of computers. Some of them do not need an understanding of the system in any way. The operator is trained to press the buttons on a keyboard in the right order, and nothing more may be required. Jobs which do require at least some understanding include (among many others):

- system troubleshooting
- specification and purchase of new computer equipment
- training new operators
- installing systems
- electronic control applications
- analysis of problems and systems
- system design.

The important point to bear in mind is that in the high technology world you have an immediate advantage over uninformed users if you know something of how computers work, rather than just how to type. You never know when a given piece of deep knowledge may come in useful. For instance, understanding the basis of the systems themselves is of great help in determining whether a current system is capable of expansion to new and forthcoming applications.

 From your everyday knowledge of the world, make two lists of jobs which use computers, or computer-controlled systems. The first list should contain jobs which do not require any technical knowledge of how computers work, and the second should contain jobs where at least some background knowledge might be useful. For instance, supermarket checkout operators use quite sophisticated computer equipment these days – which list would this job be on?

MAIN COMPONENTS OF A COMPUTER SYSTEM

► See Chapters 4, 6 and 7.

Every computer system, of both classes mentioned above, no matter how large or small, has at least one 'central processor'. This is the element which 'understands' program instructions. 'Understand' in

▶ The most important hardware components are:
• central processor (microprocessor in microcomputers)
• memory
• input/output (I/O) system.

this context means 'is able to execute' instructions, often using stored data, and storing the result as more data. Every computer system also requires one or more types of memory – even if it is only a very small amount of 'scratchpad' memory to store intermediate results during a calculation. All computers have an 'input/output' section, to allow them to communicate with the outside world – whether to a human sitting in front of a screen, or a bunch of clothing in the drum of a washing machine.

These three (central processor, memory and input/output) are the major hardware elements of a computer system. Others include the interconnection medium between devices (called 'busses'), the power supply to run the electronics, and so on. The other major component of any system is the software.

In looking into the components of a computer, we are viewing the way in which software and electronics (hardware) interface. For instance, software is basically composed of BITs – 1s and 0s. These are not some abstract, theoretical language components, they are the electronic voltage levels, usually +5 volts (for a '1'), and 0 volts (for '0'), which the electronic components of the system shuffle around and, via special amplifying interfaces, present to the outside world.

Figure 3.1 The external characteristics of a desk-top computer: microcomputer

Figure 3.1 shows the familiar external characteristics of a typical desk-top computer system – a microcomputer. As you can see, the main computer components are housed within a processor box, or cabinet. This connects through cables to power supply, keyboard, a visual display unit or VDU (sometimes called a 'screen') and a printer. On the front of the cabinet is a set of indicator lights, some buttons, and two 'peripheral memory' devices – 'floppy' and 'hard' disks. These store data magnetically in large quantities. There are other types of peripheral memory, but the disk units indicated here are the most common.

▶ Laptops.

Another common type of computer is the smaller portable 'laptop' or 'notebook' computer (see Figure 3.2). Essentially, these combine all the above units into a single cabinet, usually with an 'LCD' (liquid crystal display) screen which uses very little power.

The display hinges down over the keyboard to turn the machine into an easily carried unit, and hinges back to allow the machine to be used normally. Other levels of portable computer are also being produced, such as the 'palmtop' computer which tries to combine the whole system into a cabinet small enough to be carried in the palm of the hand. The practical limit on size is decided by the size of the human finger, if this is the operator's main method of communication with the machine. A practical keyboard must be large enough to be able to be used.

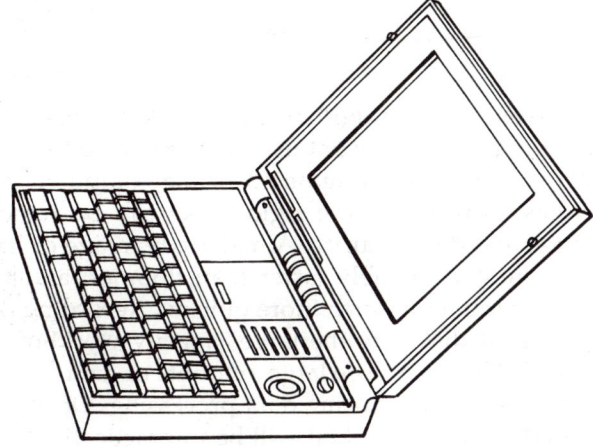

Figure 3.2 A laptop computer

As a comparison with larger computing installations, if we were looking at a mainframe, we would see many cabinets, with the parts distributed over a much larger volume, and running many VDUs and keyboards. However, the basic principles are similar.

For future reference, a VDU and keyboard combination is sometimes called a 'terminal'. This normally means one of several stations from which a user can interact with a computer. The word 'terminal' is not confined to VDUs and keyboards – almost any point of entry into a computer system can be regarded as a type of terminal. Sometimes a terminal is a complete computer system, and sometimes just the input/output device itself. You will see how the word is used as we progress. It follows, for instance, that desktops, laptops, and so on, can all be terminals. A mainframe, however, is not a terminal – it may have many terminals with which the users can interact.

► Terminal: point of entry into a computer; often a VDU and keyboard.

Floppy and hard disks

► See Chapter 7.

Floppy-disk drives accept flat (floppy) disks protected by stiff outer covers. Floppy disks are so named as they are circular pieces of flexible plastic with a magnetic surface sprayed thinly onto both surfaces (see Figure 3.3). Data is 'written' onto the disks using similar technology to the recording heads of magnetic tape machines. The disk drive spins the disk, and as it spins the magnetic record/play-back head moves across the surface – you will see more clearly how this works later. Floppy disks are inserted into the drive by hand, and may be removed and stored in a library to keep and protect valuable data.

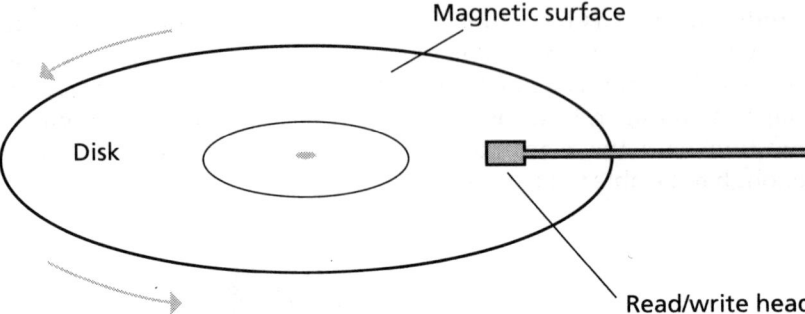

Figure 3.3 A magnetic disk system

► Hard disks.

Hard-disk drives contain a rigid magnetic disk. In most small computer systems, such disks are not usually removable from the drive – they form a permanent component of the computer system. In larger systems, however, these rigid disks can be removed, for library storage and data security. A major advantage of hard disks is that they spin considerably faster than floppies, and thus gain access to the information much more quickly. Recording density is also greater. Hard disks are the large-capacity workhorses of the memory world. They can store large amounts of data, which is easily and quickly accessible during data processing. Of course, if too much is stored on a hard disk, it will be impractical to back up all the data onto floppies, which have such a smaller capacity. This back-up problem is one which a well-run computer installation must be able to handle.

► Floppy disks.

Floppies are slower and hold less data than hard disks, but are always able to be removed from the machine. They are much more compact and robust than hard disks. This means, for instance, that they are ideal for the permanent library storage of important data as a backup to the normal internal memory of the machine. If the data is stored on a floppy, and is sitting on a shelf, it cannot be harmed if the computer has a brainstorm and decides to write gibberish over everything in sight – such failures are not totally unknown.

Software and data can also be purchased on floppy disk, and in that way transported into your machine. A floppy-disk drive is a window into the computer from the external world for the input and output of data and programs. You could, for instance, write a report on your computer, copy the text onto a floppy disk, and send the floppy disk through the post to a colleague who would be able to insert it into the floppy-disk drive in his or her machine and view the report on a screen. Note the distinction between 'disk' and 'disk drive'.

Disk capacity
For your information, current floppy disks have a range of data capacities between around 360,000 BYTEs (approximately 360K BYTEs) and a few million BYTEs (mega BYTEs, or MB). Remember that each BYTE represents, typically, a single character (letter, numerical digit, or special symbol) via the ASCII code.

Current hard disks start at around 20 MB, and range to several billion BYTEs (1,000 MB is also called 1 'giga' BYTE). Bear in mind that a normal-sized paperback with around 200 pages will probably hold, say, 60,000 words at around 6 characters (including a space) per word, making 360,000 characters. Thus, the smallest floppy mentioned above will be able to hold roughly a complete paperback book.

 Before reading on, estimate how much information, in books, the very largest hard disk mentioned above might hold.

In this context, 'large' means high in memory capacity, not physically large. Hard-disk units in microcomputers are often around five inches across, six inches long and a couple of inches thick. However, hard disks of around three inches in width are becoming common. In these small volumes, it is possible to hold over 1,000 million BYTEs, or characters. This is more than 170 million words. As a typical paperback has 60,000 words, you should have worked out that this can hold nearly 3,000 paperbacks – a fair-sized book shop! Furthermore, memory is shrinking in physical size at a prodigious rate – even these capacities may soon seem quaint.

► In Chapter 7 you will meet other kinds of magnetic memory including data tape and CD-ROMs.

VDU and keyboard

► See Chapter 4.

As you know, in order to allow a human to communicate with the machine, there is normally a terminal – a typewriter-like keyboard, with a few extra keys for special commands, and a TV-like display unit. The computer takes in information from the keyboard, and presents its output to the operator on the VDU.

Keyboards are becoming standardized, but VDUs vary considerably. There are simple monochromatic screens, high-resolution screens for fine detail, low- and high-resolution colour screens, large screens for technical-drawing applications and so on.

Many people are used to using a keyboard of some kind, and the standard computer keyboards appeal to this familiarity. However, as we shall see, there are many other input devices such as 'mouse', 'scanner' and video camera. Similarly, the VDU output device appeals to your familiarity with a TV, and the computer printer is similar in some ways to a typewriter. A printer is said to give 'hard copy', that is copy which does not disappear when the machine is switched off, as happens to VDU information.

Printers

► See Chapter 4.

There are many kinds of printer on the market, and this area of technology is evolving as fast as computers. Originally, printers were modelled on manual typewriters. They had metal type-characters fixed to the ends of swinging arms which came up and hit the paper through a ribbon. Such a mechanical arrangement is inherently too slow and cumbersome for fast computer work. Soon after that, the

IBM golf ball, and the daisy-wheel printers became popular, again with individual type-characters hitting a ribbon.

 Can you think of a major disadvantage common to all these machines, given the increasing need for flexibility of output? Think about this before reading the next paragraph.

The greatest revolution in printer technology came with the availability of the dot-matrix printer. In this type of printer, a pattern of dots is chosen from a standard matrix and printed onto the paper. These dots can be controlled to form patterns looking like letters and numbers, or graphical patterns which fit together to form pictures. It provides the most general type of hard-copy output, and the accuracy of printing depends upon how many dots are crammed into the matrix, i.e. how small the dots are, and how close together they can be printed. We will look at this and other types of modern printer later in the book. Note how previous types of printer were confined to a given set of type-characters, while the dot matrix can form any text or graphical output.

COMPUTER STRUCTURE

Figure 3.4 shows a block diagram of the inside of the processor box of a microcomputer. Electronic switches shuffle voltages around the system performing fast data communications using just two voltage levels. These voltage levels are carried along electrical wires, or copper tracks on the surface, and within layers, in pieces of rigid material called printed-circuit boards (PCBs).

The complexity of modern computers means that the interconnection of electronic devices must be performed in a highly organized or 'structured' manner. There are certain agreed standards for the interconnection of electronic devices, and one of these standards is that of the 'bus system'. Essentially, many different devices are plugged into the same set of electronic tracks, the 'busses', but only certain of the devices are switched on at any given instant. Otherwise, the various devices plugged in would electrically clash. As you can see, the busses thread their way from one end of the system to the other, connecting everything together.

▶ Busses are the tracks down which electronic signals travel to transfer information from one part of the system to another.

Various blocks are plugged into the bus system. There is internal memory, peripheral memory (including disks), an electrical power supply, interfacing to input/output devices (including keyboard and screen), and a 'central processing unit' (CPU).

The job of turning on the correct 'plugged-in' device at exactly the right time is performed by this one single unit – the CPU. All digital computer systems have at least one CPU somewhere, and its tasks do not stop at bus control. It is also responsible for fetching the instructions and data, one by one, from memory, and executing those instructions. It contains internal memory of its own, called 'registers', and each time it fetches an instruction, or a piece of data, it stores it in a register before processing it.

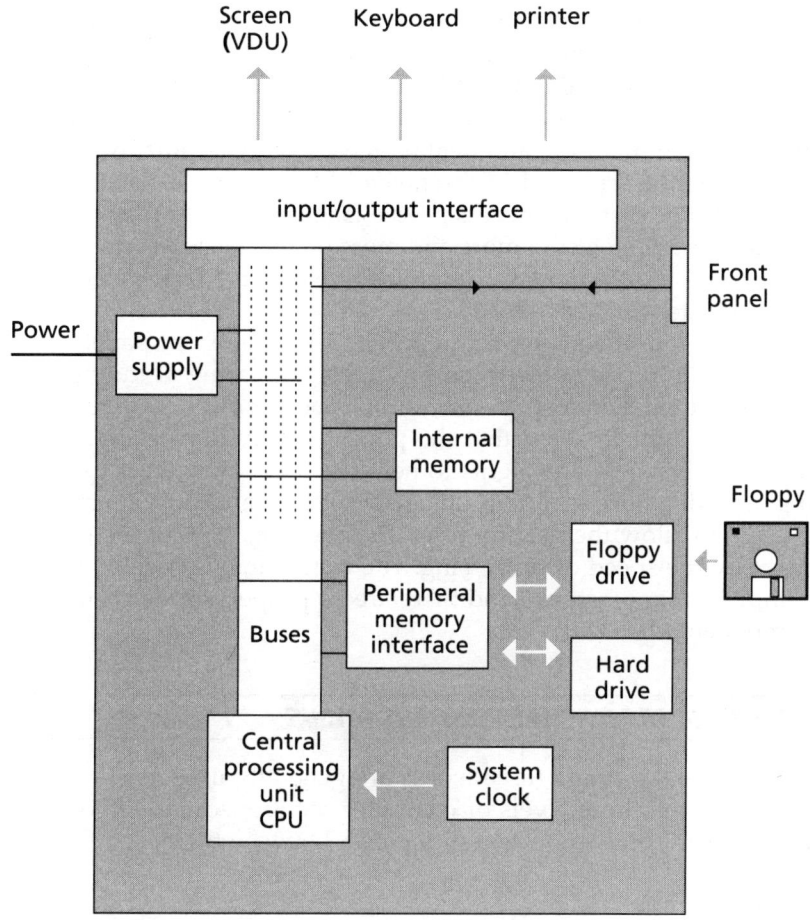

Screen (VDU)   Keyboard   printer

input/output interface

Front panel

Power

Power supply

Internal memory

Floppy

Floppy drive

Peripheral memory interface

Buses

Hard drive

Central processing unit CPU

System clock

Figure 3.4 Inside the processor box of a microcomputer

▶ Clock.

Furthermore, to exert time control on the whole process, the CPU is fed with pulses from a 'system clock'. As the clock 'ticks', the CPU fetches and executes. It is said to be performing 'fetch and execute' cycles. It may take many ticks of the clock to perform a complete fetch and execute cycle, but that is a matter which is decided by the complexity of the instruction being processed, and the designer of the CPU. It should always be borne in mind that different CPUs use different numbers of clock cycles to fetch and execute the same type of instruction. It is, therefore, not always possible to compare different computers purely by clock speed. Of course, if the same type of CPU is used for each of two different computer systems, and their clock speeds do differ, then this difference forms a fair basis for the comparison of their relative processing speeds.

In general, the CPU derives its instructions, and data, from the block labelled 'internal memory'. It is there that the stored program resides for immediate execution. Those instructions might themselves have been moved in from a disk unit one by one by the CPU, via the peripheral memory interface, at some earlier time. This is a time-consuming business, and when you load a program from disk you will find yourself waiting for the program to be transferred from the disk to the internal memory before it can be acted upon by the CPU.

▶ Internal memory within the CPU or MPU contains the program for immediate execution stored in registers.

As you can see from Figure 3.4, the CPU is a sort of bottleneck. It must control the whole system electronically, it must transfer each piece of program and data BYTE by BYTE from peripheral memory into internal memory, it must fetch and execute each instruction from internal memory, and deal with each piece of data in and out of the program separately. For a given CPU, it is the clock which determines how fast this process proceeds. Little wonder that you will see machines being sold more and more on the speed at which their clock runs. As technology improves, faster and faster electronic components will be produced.

► Front panel.

A final component shown in Figure 3.4 is the 'front panel'. This refers to the range of switches and lights appearing at the front of the computer. For instance, there may be a power switch and a power-on light to show that the power supply is working. There may be other indicator lights to help the user see what is happening, and diagnose simple problems. Switches and buttons may be present to allow the user to 'reset' the machine, and/or increase or decrease the speed of processing. The front panel is decided by the computer manufacturer, and there are no proper standards for this component.

MICROS, MAINFRAMES AND MINIS

As you can see, these three words are generally used as shortened forms for the three levels of computer mentioned earlier. We can now look at some important differences between them.

Micros

Micros generally have CPUs which are built onto single ICs. These are usually contained within a square or rectangular piece of plastic or ceramic, and have many electrical pins sticking out, which plug into a main printed circuit board (PCB).

For future reference, the CPU of a microcomputer is called a 'microprocessing unit' or MPU.

Very often, this main PCB is called a 'motherboard' and it forms the central part of a system normally confined, as we have seen, to a single cabinet that can be placed on a desk. On the motherboard are formed the busses, and other electrical connections, along with some or all of the interfaces mentioned above. Often, too, there are sockets on the motherboard which allow other boards to be plugged into the system. On these extra boards (daughterboards) may be held interfaces to the disk drives, the VDU, more internal memory, or whatever. The exact architecture chosen depends upon the way in which the original electronic engineer was thinking when producing the design. However, there are certain standards which exist – and one of the most common is that of the IBM personal computer, or IBM PC.

Within the same cabinet, as we have seen, there is usually at least one hard-disk drive, usually containing a permanent hard disk, and a floppy-disk drive.

Mainframes

The mainframe differs by distributing the system over a much larger volume. For instance, a mainframe CPU is not a single chip. It does not use an MPU. It may have many PCBs or modules which when taken together do the job of one or more CPUs. Its internal memory, similarly, will often be very high in capacity, and be distributed over a number of systems and subsystems. Its disk units will be separate floorstanding units containing removable multi-hard disk packs. There will be a lot of heavy cabling distributed around, and several different types of I/O interface. The machine will probably be running many users apparently simultaneously, and require separate interface subsystems in hardware to allow for it. Also, the main part of the machine will probably be contained in a temperature- and humidity-controlled room.

Why is all this necessary? The answer, unfortunately, is rather technical, and it has to do with the physics of fast electronic devices, and how they are formed, as well as the methods by which the parts of the system are tied together. The emphasis is on speed and capacity, and certainly not on compactness!

Minis

Minis fall somewhere between these two. They may have distributed CPUs, similar memory devices to mainframes, but rarely require a fully controlled environment.

A large company having thousands of employees and a number of sites will probably have a mainframe. A smaller but still sizeable company, with a hundred employees and a couple of sites, could well have one or more minis; while a small company with dozens of employees and a single main site, and perhaps other companies which do not need large amounts of instant communication, will probably be able to run with several micros, connected together in a 'network'.

A network is a set of separate computers which are able to share facilities and data around the site. Each computing station, or terminal, can be a separate computer for a separate function, but they can all have access to the company's main business data when necessary.

These examples of computer installations are not definitive. Different situations, other than simply the size of the company, are important in determining the level of hardware purchased, but the scenarios described above will be familiar to most people.

SOFTWARE – PROGRAMMING LOGIC

So far, we have concentrated on the electronic and physical components of a computer system. We will now look at the software or programming of the system. In order to gain a basic view of the way in which software is processed by the system, we will concentrate on the microcomputer, and its microprocessing unit or MPU. These

► See Chapter 10.

basic principles, with a few additions, apply right up the scale to mainframes.

In general, for digital computers, programs consist of lists of instructions or tasks which are executed in sequence, starting at the top. Within the program, the flow of execution can be turned around into a closed loop, and various parts of the program can be executed in or out of strict numerical order – this is up to the programmer. In general, it is up to the programmer to split a given problem into separate logical steps from start to finish, each step of which is comprehensible to the computer as a statement in its language. The logical sequence of tasks required to achieve a result is called an 'algorithm'.

The method of splitting a problem into a logical sequence of small comprehensible tasks is very natural to us. For instance, in order to tell someone how to tie a shoe lace, the first task is to gauge the level at which the explanation should be given – in other words, the language type which can be used. For instance, the language chosen would differ between an adult and a child. The next step is to split the task into its component steps (see Figure 3.5). The first one might be to grasp the ends of the laces, one in each hand. The next step to cross the laces over, and so on. This process can be helped by the use of special 'flow' diagrams, as we shall see, because most people pick things up visually more easily than by a set of words. This is the complete opposite of the computer's view of a program – you do not generally feed diagrams into a computer, the

▶ Algorithm – set of instructions in logical order. Named after the ninth-century Arab mathematician al-Khwarizmi, from whose major work's title 'algebra' is also derived.

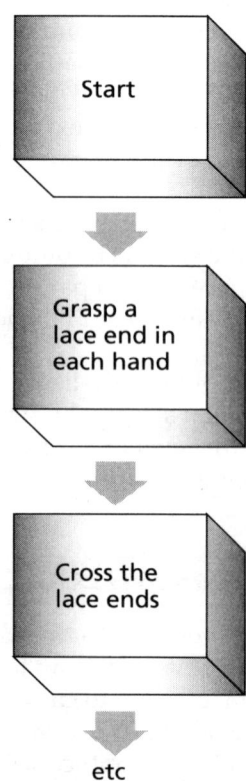

Figure 3.5 Splitting a task into small steps arranged in a logical order

whole program is presented as program words and statements which command the computer to do something, step by step.

Machines which work in this manner are sometimes called 'von Neumann' machines – they execute lists of instructions, step by step, from a memory-stored program. Von Neumann (with others) set out the theoretical framework for the stored-program digital computer in 1946.

▶ Von Neumann laid down the theory for machines following sets of instructions – hence computers were once referred to as von Neumann machines.

 Write an algorithm to tell an adult how to catch a particular bus to work in the morning. The emphasis here should be on splitting the activity into logical steps from getting up in the morning to arriving at work. Do not worry about trivial detail. Write each statement (instruction) on a separate line, and try to limit yourself to a maximum of, say, a dozen statements.

PROGRAMMING THE MPU

The above view of software is straightforward, and in many ways rather natural to us – we are used to explaining things to people in a logical fashion all the time – but how does this apply to integrated circuits such as MPUs?

▶ See Chapter 9.

The MPU is only interested in looking at internal memory, and fetching groups of 1s and 0s, interpreting them as instructions or data, and executing them. In order to do this, a list of instructions must be stored in memory and coded into 1s and 0s. The MPU then fetches the BITs from the correct place in memory, which means that each memory location must have a unique electronic address.

In fact, the electronics are arranged, broadly speaking, so that when the MPU wishes to fetch a group of BITs it puts out an electronic address on the appropriate bus lines, with a special electronic request signal, and the appropriate memory location simply recognizes its own unique address, and sends the data back along a group of bus lines. The MPU is ready and waiting. It collects and puts the BITs into a suitable internal MPU register. It may recognize this group of BITs as an instruction to fetch a couple more pieces of data to work on. The fetch process then has to occur a couple more times before the MPU is satisfied. It then executes the instruction with its data, and may then repeat the fetch process in reverse to store the result in a particular memory location in internal memory. (See Figure 3.6.)

The group of BITs making up an instruction is in a form which the MPU understands directly. It is said to be in 'machine code'. The MPU can only understand machine code, and each type of MPU understands a different machine-code language. The designer of the MPU gives the chip an internal program, called a 'microprogram', which does the work of interpreting instructions, and controlling the fetch and execute process.

The microprogram is switched on all the time that the MPU has a power supply – it never stops, even if the computer seems to be doing

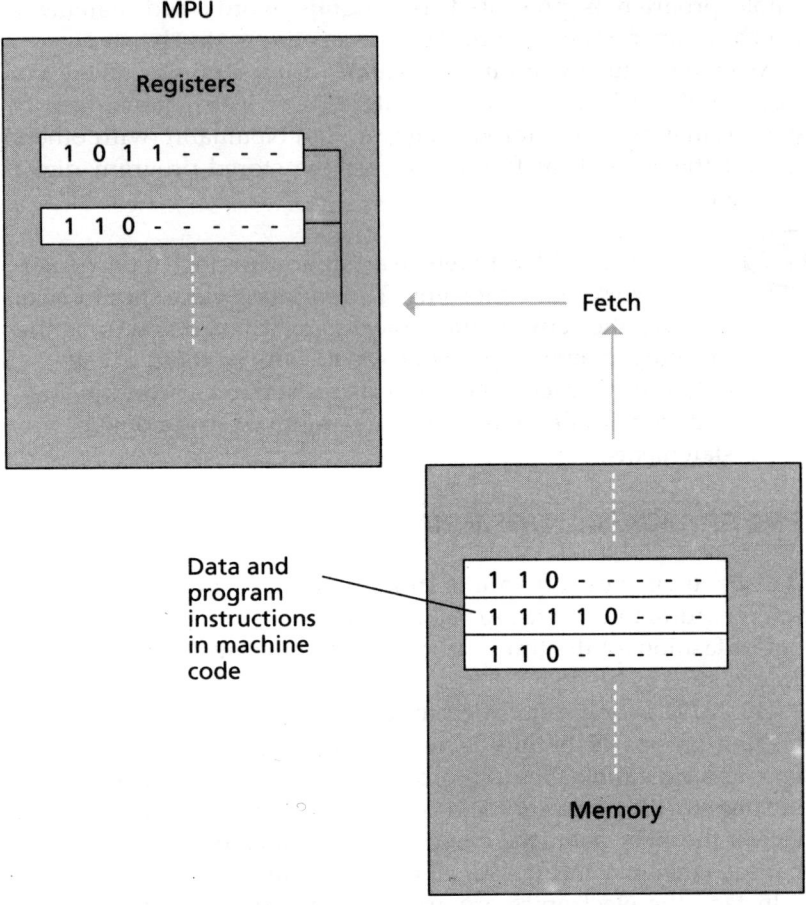

MPU

Registers

1 0 1 1 - - - -

1 1 0 - - - - -

Fetch

Data and
program
instructions
in machine
code

1 1 0 - - - - -
1 1 1 1 0 - - -
1 1 0 - - - - -

Memory

Figure 3.6 The fetch and execute routine in a microprocessor

► See Chapter 8.

nothing. For instance, while the system is awaiting further input, say from a human user, it will be executing a circular section of program which just makes it go round in circles checking the keyboard with each circuit, for the required input. This is often termed a 'wait loop'. As computers are very fast indeed compared to humans, they can spend a large proportion of their time in such loops. This is a wasteful aspect of computing, and there are several ways of constructing software systems to take advantage of this wasted time, but these depend heavily on the particular application being processed.

Conventionally, languages are classed by their level – the lower the level, the 'nearer' to the CPU itself.

In order to use a computer for a specific task, it is necessary to make it run an 'application' or an 'applications program'. It would be most wasteful if the user of a computer system had to be bothered with the machine-code translation each time, or with the 'housekeeping' tasks of the system such as preparing programs to run the keyboard and VDU. It is essential for general computer users that these tasks are taken out of their hands. This is achieved by the use of an 'operating system', and all computer systems for general use come with such a program as standard. (See Figure 3.7.)

Compilers and interpreters

Machine code is a difficult and slow language for humans to write and understand, so computers themselves are used to help the programmer produce the code. This is done using special translation programs called 'compilers' and 'interpreters'. We will look at this in more detail in Chapter 8. For now, you should appreciate that humans generally write programs using 'high-level' languages which are nearer to human languages, and computer programs take the program and translate it into 'low-level' machine code for the CPU.

► High-level languages are easier for humans to understand, and difficult for machines. Low-level languages are easy for machines to understand and difficult for humans.

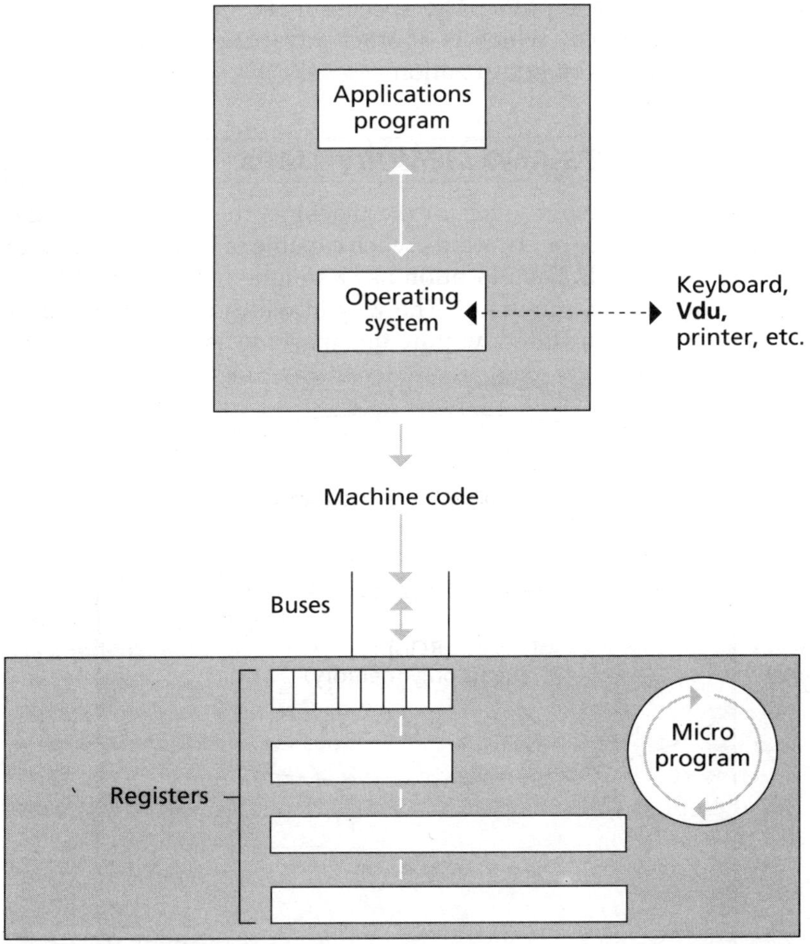

Figure 3.7 Levels of software

OPERATING SYSTEMS

The operating system is basically a set of housekeeping routines. It ensures that the keyboard and screen are properly configured, and ready to input and output data to and from a given program. It ensures that the internal and peripheral memory is used correctly, and it controls other peripherals such as printers.

► See Chapter 8.

► The operating system looks after the housekeeping routines of the computer.

Operating systems are produced by major software manufacturers, or 'software houses'. The IBM-PC style of computer, for instance, generally runs, and comes with, an operating system called 'MSDOS'. The operating system is constructed so that applications program writers know how to 'hook' into it and use the housekeeping procedures which it contains. This means that they can concentrate on the application in hand, and not worry about the actual BIT by BIT control of the screen, keyboard, printer, and so on – the operating system is there to supply all those tasks.

We say that the applications program runs 'under' a given operating system. If you have that operating system on a machine, the program may be 'loaded', perhaps via the floppy-disk drive, and will run on the computer. The specific make of computer is not generally important, which is another advantage of an operating system: it imposes standardization.

MEMORY TYPES AND MEMORY MAPS

▶ See Chapters 6 and 7.

To return to the lower levels of the machine, the memory is organized as a sequence of 'locations', each capable of storing a group of BITs, often a BYTE. Each location has a unique numerical address, starting at location number 0. The way in which the various kinds of memory are included within the machine is defined by the 'memory map'.

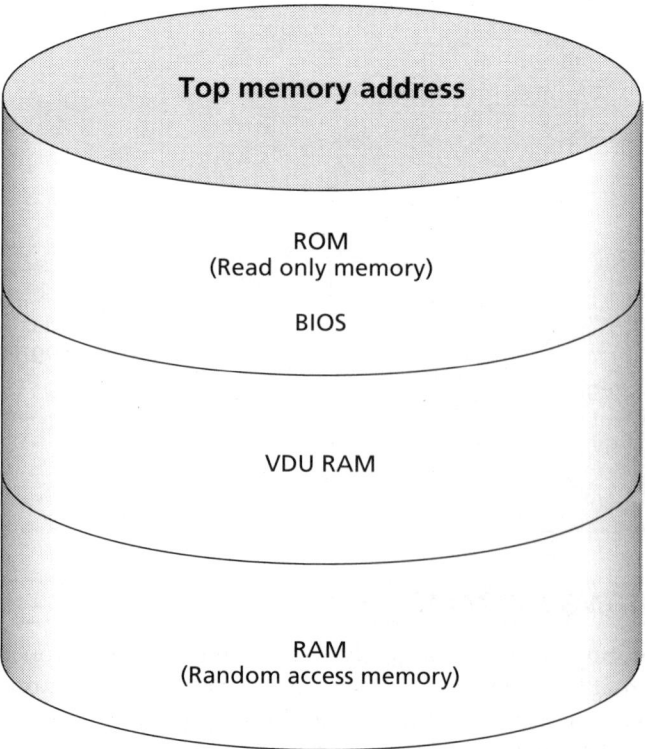

Figure 3.8 The memory map of a microcomputer

As you can see from Figure 3.8, there are various regions, or ranges of addresses, within the memory map devoted to different memory types. You should not assume that every machine will have exactly this pattern of memory usage, but it is fairly widespread. Also, notice that there are regions between the three memory types shown where no memory resides. Even though all the addresses are available for use from bottom to top, these are not always fully used, it depends upon the particular configuration which is required for a given computer.

At the bottom of memory is a region called RAM – which stands for random access memory. This is the type of memory which has replaced core memory in modern computers, and it is where the programs and data which you load into the machine reside. This type of memory can be changed at will, but disappears when the machine is switched off. It is said to be 'volatile' for this reason.

▶ RAM – random access memory – you can alter this when you use the computer.

Further up the memory map is a region which has been labelled VDU RAM. In many machines the screen shows the contents of a region of RAM into which data has been loaded for presentation to the user. The electronics associated with the VDU interface are able to interpret the data stored in that RAM as graphics, text, etc., to ensure that the correct picture is presented to the human operator.

Finally, in this machine, there is a region of memory at the top called ROM – read only memory. It is also labelled BIOS – basic input/output system. The memory in this region is of an electronic type which is not changeable. It is fixed or 'firm', and sometimes called 'firmware'. It is there when the power is switched on, and its contents are not destroyed when power is switched off.

▶ ROM – read only memory – the fixed memory of the computer.

The ROM contains the basic program routines for operating the electronics of the machine, and also includes a special program which will bring in an operating system from a disk memory. This program is called a 'bootstrap'. It is a loop which contacts the disk interface electronics, and loads in part of the operating system from disk into the RAM at the bottom of memory. It then causes the computer to fetch and execute from the start of that program, and from then onwards the operating system itself is in charge – it loads in any further program routines it requires, and takes over the working of the machine. The ROM is a region of 'non-volatile' memory which is always there to start the process, the rest comes from disk.

▶ Bootstrap – instructions for loading part of the operating system from a disk memory.

RESET

When power is applied to a computer's electronics, all the RAM in the system is indeterminate – it could contain anything. The same is true of the registers within the MPU. Remember that the microprogram in the MPU is always fetching and executing as long as power is present. At the very start, it looks at the registers, sees BITs stored there in a random pattern, and tries to make sense of the word which the BITs make up. If it finds a pattern which it recognizes, which is very likely by the law of averages, it will execute that instruction. It could be anything, and the whole machine careers off into an indeterminate loop of random processes which might never stop, and will probably never result in anything sensible occurring, such as execution of the bootstrap in the ROM BIOS!

A process has to be included within the electronic design of the machine which will 'grab' the MPU, and force it to fetch and execute exactly the right part of the ROM BIOS to start the process of running a controlled program, such as the operating system. This is achieved, in fact, within the electronic design of the MPU itself. It will have an electronic pin called the 'reset' pin. The electronics will have been designed so that very soon after the power comes up, an electronic pulse, called the 'reset pulse', is generated, and sent to the reset pin of the MPU.

Different MPUs react in slightly different ways to a reset pulse, but generally they will stop everything, and begin a special reset routine, which is illustrated in Figure 3.9.

▶ Reset points the CPU or MPU in the right direction to start the system running on the right lines.

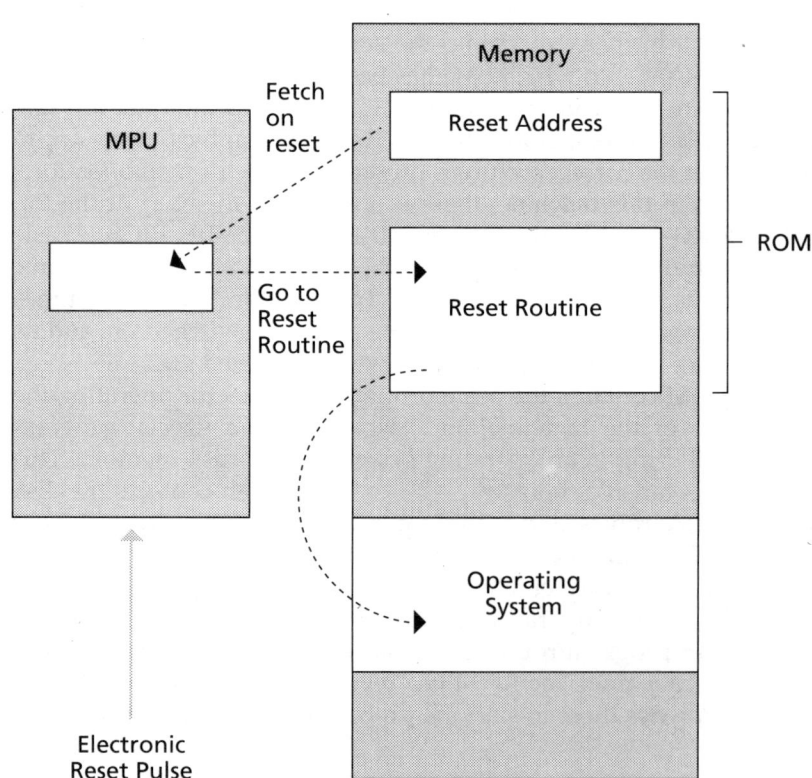

Figure 3.9 The reset routine on a microcomputer

This routine forces the MPU to fetch an address stored in a special place in memory. In order to ensure that this information is always waiting in those places for the MPU after a reset, this information has to be stored in ROM. It is up to the computer's designer to place ROM at just the right place in the memory map.

Once this special information has been fetched, the MPU interprets it as the start address of a program which it must immediately begin to process – the microprogram then proceeds to fetch and execute from that address. In this way, the machine has been grabbed and controlled to run a program in a predictable manner after a reset. The next step would be to enter the operating system.

In fact, a reset pulse may be applied at any time while the machine is switched on. Often, there is a special button on the front panel of the computer which allows the operator to force a reset at any time. This is obviously dangerous if the user is in the middle of something, but it is also a useful way of exiting from a state where the computer appears to be 'locked up' or is acting irrationally.

Once the computer has been reset and has loaded the operating system, the user has the opportunity to command the computer to load and run an applications program. This is where an interaction is required via the keyboard and screen. It is normally necessary for a computer user to learn the basic commands which can be typed in at this point, unless some special software has been provided to make the commands obvious in some manner.

DEDICATED MACHINES

So far, we have looked at complete computers, with screens, keyboards, printers, etc. However, the introduction of the MPU has also changed the face of 'control' electronics. In the past, if a machine had to perform a set of tasks, a mechanical system, driven by a motor, might sequentially switch on and off a set of functions. A common example is that of the washing machine. An MPU, with some ROM to hold a basic sequential program and some RAM for scratchpad storage, will perform the same function, via an electronic input/output (I/O) interface. This computer system is small, compact, uses little power, and is not capable of being reprogrammed by the user. It is a dedicated controller, and can even be formed onto a single chip, with ROM manufactured into it to store the control program.

When the power is applied, reset simply causes the ROM-based program to start, and off it goes! The program running the controller is written on a normal computer system, stored onto special programmable memory, tested, and then manufactured into ROM by the silicon-chip manufacturer, or even manufactured directly onto the MPU chip. Such chips are generally called 'single-chip micro controllers' or something similar.

The single-chip micro controller will even have electrical I/O pins which are switched on and off by the program, and via amplifiers directly switch the various functions of, say, a washing machine, a video recorder or a vehicle's fuel injection system.

HOW COMPUTERS ARE USED IN INDUSTRY AND COMMERCE

As you can see, there are many applications for the basic machinery of computers, from simple electronic control to the handling of large amounts of data.

► See Chapters 5 and 12.

The commercial applications of desk-top or other screen-based computers are broadly split into a number of areas.

Computers are used to store and retrieve data in 'databases' for commercial purposes (see Figure 3.10). This might include, for instance, a file of customers, the goods they have currently on order, their credit details, credit limits and credit history. This information might be used to link into a stock-control system which checks that the goods on order are in stock, or alternatively reorders if necessary. This general customer information might also be used by a sales and marketing system to target the right customers for a new product, or to sell other existing products more efficiently. Also, a list of customer addresses is a saleable item, as long as the legal aspects of such a sale are adhered to.

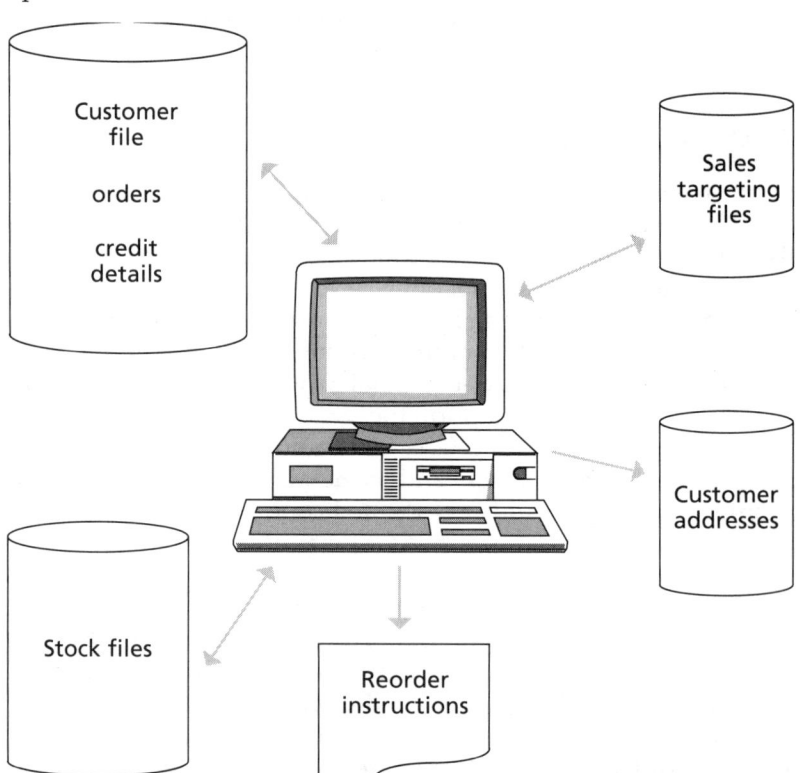

Figure 3.10 A computerized customer control system

The computer is useful for financial accounting systems. This includes the basic functions of keeping daily and yearly business accounts, VAT analysis, payroll and PAYE tax data, and so on. Again, this may link into other systems, and allow for an overall control of the day-to-day business of the company.

A computer is good at helping in analysis. This might include special programs written for mathematical design by engineers, it might be the analysis of the trading position of the company, or the construction of cash-flow tables or business plans for future expansion. Analysis cuts across every part of business and commerce and uses the computer's ability to perform calculations fast and accurately.

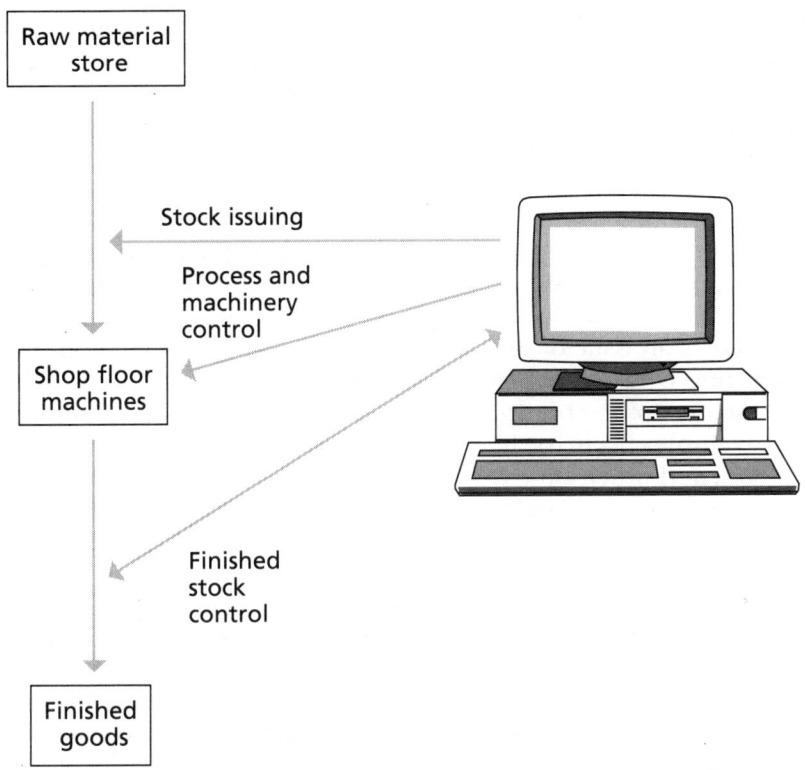

Figure 3.11 A manufacturing
control system

Also, overall control of the running of a company's operation can be aided considerably by a computer system. Such an example would be the control of a manufacturing process (see Figure 3.11). This would include the 'production control' of how raw material is withdrawn from stores, issued to a shop floor, processed through a factory, and finally added to the 'finished goods' store. It also might include the actual control of machinery on the shop floor. For instance, a modern car-production plant will be run by an overall production controller, which ensures that the various stages within the production floor are progressing at a suitable speed, and performing any automated activities correctly.

There are many uses for computer systems but, from a business point of view, these are some of the main applications.

 Look in one or two computer magazines and find a couple of proprietary programs for each of the first three computer application areas mentioned above. You might find it a little harder to find an example of the fourth one mentioned – that of overall production control. However, if you can find a specialist magazine dealing with manufacturing systems, you should see some examples of that application too.

The communication of information

We have talked about how information has to be stored and re-   ► See Chapter 11.

trieved, and passed around a company's operation, but how is this done?

There are many ways to move data around. Information might simply be printed from a computer onto paper, and end up on a manager's desk for personal approval and comment. Data can also be moved around electronically. For instance, if many computer systems are tied together into a 'network', they all potentially have access to each other's data, and a manager could simply type questions into a desk-top computer; the answers would be found somewhere around the network, and transported to the terminal.

▶ Networks.

There is an issue of security here, of course. Everyone, from the Managing Director downwards, would not wish everyone else in the factory to be able to access their own personal pay details, for example. Security is a very important part of a computer system, and much time is spent on solving this type of problem. However, as everyone's pay is on the machine, someone has to know the Managing Director's details – who do you think that should be?

Computers which are very distant from each other can be made to communicate information via a telephone link, which might include a path to and from a satellite, or underground cables. The actual medium of transport is irrelevant, and simply left to the telephone company – it is the data which is important to the computers at each end of the line.

A central computer which has to control a shop floor will be sending and receiving data electronically to other computers at the shop-floor end. These might be directly interfaced to automated machinery, which will thus respond to the control of the central computer as instructions are issued. The central computer will be implementing a production plan which a human production planner will have constructed, perhaps with the aid of the machine itself. The company's computer system knows how many of a given product is required and who has ordered them, and can supply this basic data to the production planner who then has to work out a timetable for that production – this is the production plan. It is then up to the central computer to issue the instructions, and watch the plan being implemented.

Real-time and batch systems

The production-control example above is said to be a 'real-time' system. That is, its program is devoted to processing inputs and outputs which are available to control the process immediately. When you are sitting in front of a computer screen, using the keyboard, you are working in real time. If, on the other hand, you give program and data to a computer operator to be run on the computer whenever convenient, you are said to be using a 'batch' system. A computer operator will take all the requests for computer time, work out a timetable for running the programs, and batch them all together to be run according to that schedule. The output will then be handed back in a batch to the users.

A batch system may seem rather old-fashioned and cumbersome for the modern user, but such systems are necessary in certain specialized computer systems. For instance, the fastest so-called 'supercomputers' which are constructed to run at many times the speed of normal installations are rare and expensive, as is processing time on them. The demand on a given installation can be quite heavy, and such a computer might be engaged in processing one specific application most of the time anyway. However, the owners of the machine might be able to schedule in other users' needs at certain times without interrupting their own use, and in this case computer processing must be carefully planned, as must the cost which is charged to the user. A given computer problem may actually be solved faster by using a supercomputer in a batch setting, than by trying to run the same project on a normal desk-top machine. Very complex graphical problems or involved mathematical calculations are typical examples where booking a batch run on an ultra-fast machine may yield dividends.

On line and off line

The production-control case on page 39 is also an example of an 'on-line' system. That is, it is continually connected to the application, and processes inputs and outputs as they occur. An 'off-line' system, as far as the shop floor is concerned, would be, for instance, an accounting system for the workers' pay.

These definitions are a little hazy, and you can see that 'on line' has a lot in common with 'real time', for instance. However, while a desk-top computer could be said to be 'real time' as far as the operator is concerned, it could be off line to the shop floor, even if it is performing analysis on whatever the shop floor is doing. A production planner might want to run some general analysis software, and so could request an operator of the production control computer to off-load some specific data onto a floppy disk for this purpose. He or she might then plug the floppy into a desk-top computer, and work in real time on this machine, but off line to the shop floor.

To some extent, the expressions on- line and off- line depend upon the viewpoint. An accounting system in continuous use while customer orders are accepted and processed could be said to be real time and on line. However, as far as the shop floor is concerned, that system is off line. Data from systems associated with order taking are filtered down through the production planning stage to the on-line shop-floor system in an indirect manner, and perhaps in batches.

CHOOSING A SYSTEM

Many criteria are considered when choosing a system for a given situation. The science of fitting software and hardware to an application is called 'systems analysis'. This is often as much a matter of taking instruction from a client as analysing the nuts and bolts of the business.

▶ See Chapters 5 and 8.

▶ Systems analysis: the science of fitting a computer system to an application, or vice versa.

For instance, a given company may have a number of employees, a certain number of financial transactions per day, and a certain amount of stock, so the analyst can work out how a standard system might be designed to fit the situation. The owner of the company may well then give a figure for a computerization budget which is far less than the analyst would consider adequate in the circumstances. The analyst then has the job of scaling the computer system down towards the client's financial constraints, while allowing for at least most of the needs to be satisfied. In general, it is always important to allow for expansion, and in this case it becomes paramount. If the computer system is installed properly, it is very likely that the company will appreciate its initial shortcomings, and wish to expand it, probably to the level that the analyst considered necessary from the start.

Other criteria to be considered include speed of throughput of information in different parts of the company, how many people need access, and how distributed in distance these users are, how many terminals are required, what type of personnel will be operating different terminals, and so on. Only then can an overall system be considered, and a full analysis of the existing system be undertaken. The object of this is to recast the whole working system into a form which will be easily computerized, but without changing too much, or the system will come as a shock to the workforce.

►See Chapter 5.

It is always important to explain to a potential user that certain things will have to be done differently, but at the same time to make the system as naturally familiar as possible.

An example for a computer application

Fred, the owner of a small company, Fred's Car Repairs, has ten employees. He has a stockroom of around 2,000 separate car parts, but orders rarely-used parts from various motor suppliers in his town. He has roughly a hundred active customers, and perhaps two thousand others who have used his services more than once, and whom he wishes to keep on file. His partner Jane acts as a full-time secretary, receptionist and accounts clerk. A full-time stock-controller is also employed, who also acts as a buyer of parts as they are needed. The rest of the workforce consists of mechanics. Fred employs a bookkeeper twice a week to write up manual books and do the VAT returns.

Fred needs a computer system, initially, to do two simple things: keep the finances straight, and control stock. He will need a terminal and printer in the stockroom, a terminal and printer for Jane, and perhaps a terminal for himself to perform various types of analysis such as cash flows and keeping control of the way in which the business is proceeding. These terminals are probably more than simply VDU–keyboard combinations, they will probably be fully-fledged computers, held together in a network so that data can be shared all around the system (see Figure 3.12).

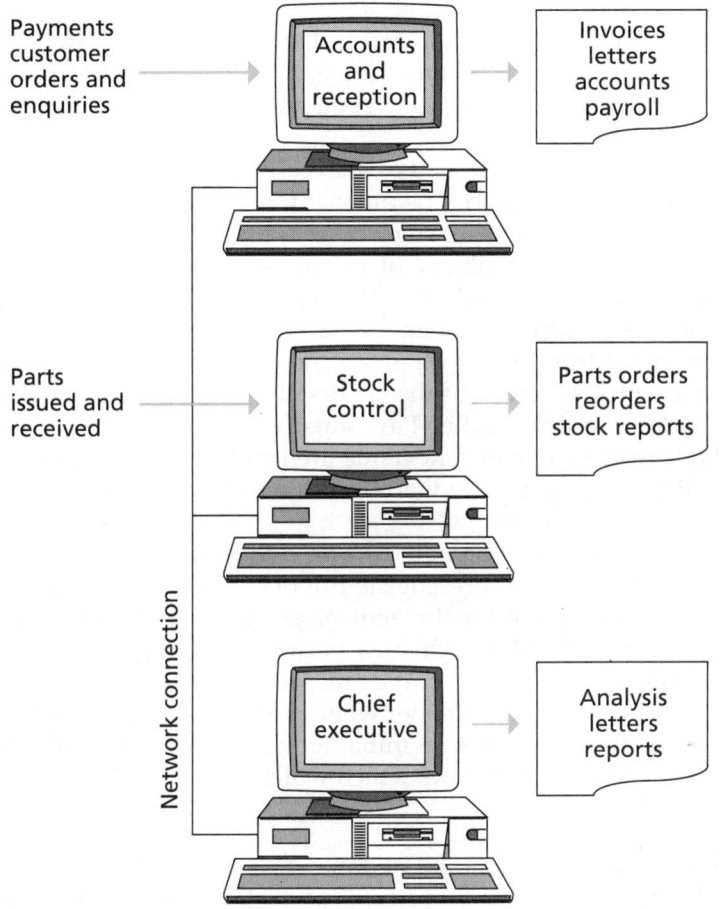

Payments customer orders and enquiries → Accounts and reception → Invoices letters accounts payroll

Parts issued and received → Stock control → Parts orders reorders stock reports

Chief executive → Analysis letters reports

Network connection

Figure 3.12 A small business network

We will look at types of actual program packages in Chapter 5, but you will see that if Fred buys a system having three terminals, a printer on each, disks, a standard financial package and a stock-control system, he will be able to streamline several parts of his business. Added to this should be a word-processing system to replace manual typing of letters, etc.

Jane can immediately stop using a typewriter for producing invoices. She will be able to input the information of goods and services which have been supplied to a customer, and the computer will print an invoice automatically. The financial information will be fed automatically to the financial package in order to keep a tally of the VAT position, write up the books, and supply that information in exactly the right form to the accountant for auditing at the end of the year. This dispenses with the part-time book-keeper, and keeps auditing costs down.

Each time the stockroom issues anything to a mechanic, its part code is typed into the stockroom's computer, and the machine automatically deletes that part from its record of stock. Each time goods are received into the stockroom, they are entered into the system, and this 'replenishes' the computer's view of the stock. If a part is withdrawn from stores, and stock of this part is low, the computer notices, alerts the buyer to the low level, and indicates the need to re-order.

Stocktaking at the end of the year becomes easy, and at that time any mistakes can be put right. It is also easier to keep an efficiently low level of stock by keeping careful control.

The eternal problem of calculating pay and tax for the employees is solved at a stroke by a well-constructed and properly supported financial package. The tax information is updated from time to time by the company which produces the software, and thus the tax details are always accurate, and printed automatically. Pay slips, end-of-year analyses and returns to the Inland Revenue are produced as required, and all the expensive drudgery of administering employees' pay simply disappears.

Fred will also be able to buy additional packages which will allow him to present the full details of the financial state of the company on the screen, assess how the business is progressing and 'watch' how various assumptions will make it perform in the future. We will see how this can be achieved in a very powerful manner when we look at spreadsheets.

Figure 3.12 shows an initial look at the system, with some of the information flows which will occur.

 Estimate the amount of data which will be needed in files for customer names, addresses and telephone numbers, and the master file which keeps details of the stock. If you know something of the way in which a small business operates, copy out Figure 3.12 and add further details of information flows which you can think of. Consider the type of day-by-day information which a business needs in order to keep it running.

Properly implemented, the computer system can save money, take over certain repetitive and boring tasks with accuracy and speed, streamline parts of the organization which are not fully efficient, and allow for proper planning for the future.

Of course, if the system is analysed wrongly, implemented badly, or the software does not work properly, or is poorly interfaced with the workforce, the computer can quickly become a hated monster, and will be rarely switched on. Unfortunately, particularly in smaller companies, this has been all too common in the past. The only solution to this problem is to spread awareness of the shortcomings and potential advantages of computers across a wide spectrum of users. Of course, they do not need to know about the 1s and 0s which thread their way around the system they are using, but they should understand the users' view of the application of computers.

You, on the other hand, as an IT specialist, must understand as much about computers and how they work as possible. This will give you the deep background from which to assess available computer systems, and fit them carefully to a given application.

 Take the example of Fred's Car Repairs again. Draw two columns on a sheet of paper and in one column write down the kinds of people who are going to be affected by the introduction of computers into the firm. In the other column write down how their jobs are likely to change, and how they might feel about it.

Chapter review

- Desk-top computers have a computer box, a keyboard and a VDU screen.
- Laptop computers integrate the whole machine into a small unit.
- Magnetic disks exist in two main forms – floppy and hard.
- Magnetic-disk memory is called 'external' or 'peripheral memory'.
- Internal memory is fast electronic memory from which the current program is being fetched and executed by the processor.
- Printers are used to make hard copy, on paper for instance
- A program is a sequence of software tasks, each of which is capable of being executed by the processor.
- A binary code, called 'machine code' is used to program the processor itself.
- Internal memory is located using electronic addresses, expressed in binary notation.
- The 'memory map' is the complete map of addresses available in a system.
- 'Reset' is a special hardware signal which starts the processor fetching and executing from scratch.
- A 'real-time' activity is one where the computer is taking in information, and presenting results immediately.
- A 'batch', or 'off-line' activity is one where a task is prepared away from the computer, and run when convenient.
- A computer system should only be chosen following an analysis of the needs of the users.

► **Now that you have completed this chapter, look back to the objectives at the beginning and check that you have accomplished each of them.**

4 Input/output

Chapter objectives

By the time you have read this chapter, you will understand:

▌ the range of input and output (I/O) devices available for computers

▌ how I/O devices interface to computers

▌ how keyboard, mouse and associated input devices work and are used

▌ how output devices such as printers and VDUs work and are used

▌ how a computer is interfaced to real world situations

▌ the meaning of WIMP and GUI

▌ typical graphical screen presentations

▌ the following key words: I/O, keyboard, mouse, trackerball, light pen, graphics tablet, touch screen, digitizer, scanner, OCR, Teletext, fax, neural network, SQUID, sensor, A/D–C, D/A–C, feedback, VDU, printer, screen, pixel, graphics, raster, vector, display, compression, fractal, hard copy, inkjet, laser, NLQ, plotter, roller drum, flat bed, GUI, WIMP, window, icon, pointer, tile, pull down, menu bar.

This chapter is about those devices through which humans communicate with computers. These are becoming more varied with every passing year, but there are still some 'old favourites' with which you need to be familiar.

INPUT DEVICES

Keyboards

Keyboard applications
- Any application where 'alphanumeric' data is to be input to the computer, i.e. letters, numbers, etc., for instance:
  - Wordprocessors (WP)
  - Spreadsheets
  - Databases

► In order to gain the maximum information from this, and other chapters in this book, you should start to buy one or more of the popular computer magazines. Just choose a couple of thick magazines from the shelves of a large newsagent. Try to choose ones which are general, and do nor refer to a specific series of machines. Make sure they have plenty of adverts as well as a large amount of editorial. The magazines regularly review new machines, regularly repeat general information about computers, and are the only way to keep up to date with this very fast-moving field.

- Desk-top publishing (DTP) programs
- Dedicated commercial programs in industrial applications such as production planning and control.
- Accounts programs.
- Interaction with the computer's operating system.
- Computer programming.

Keyboard interface
- Usually via a coiled 'telephone' wire to a round plug which pushes into a socket on the outside of the computer case.
- For a small computer, this may be integral to the case itself.

The keyboard of a computer is still one of the most important I/O devices included. It allows a human to command and interact with the computer in a complex and subtle manner, though a certain amount of training, or at least experience, is required to use the interface at speed – particularly for typing long letters or reports.

▶ To gain the maximum benefit from this section it would be a good idea to read it with a real keyboard nearby.

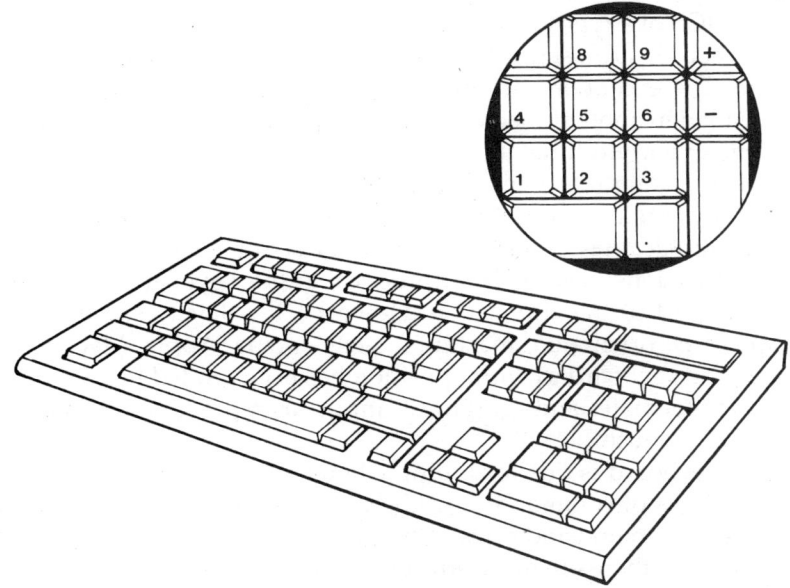

Figure 4.1 The keyboard layout of a typical IBM desk-top computer

A typical keyboard is arranged in a QWERTY typewriter style, for purely historical reasons. However, there are quite a few extra keys used by the operating system for special functions. Not all computer systems have exactly the same keyboard, but most conform to the majority of keys shown in Figure 4.1, and all IBM PC AT types of machine have a standardized keyboard.

There are usually several function keys (F1, F2, etc.) which are used for dedicated operations, determined by the particular applications program being run.

There are also usually three keyboard 'modifiers'. The most important, and universal, is the one which modifies the keyboard to upper case characters. This is called the **SHIFT** key. When pressed,

▶ Function keys (F1, F2, etc.) – more on these in Chapter 5.

▶ Modifier keys: **SHIFT**, **CONTROL**, **ALT**.

► Lock keys.

► The keyboard is controlled by the BIOS part of the operating system.

the upper layer of key symbols is available, and upper case letters. **CONTROL** and **ALT** keys are also common, and are used by programs and operating systems in various ways to produce modifications to the normal meanings of the keys.

There are usually several lock keys – for instance, the keyboard can be locked in upper case mode by **SHIFT LOCK**. Also, the keyboard shown has a **NUM LOCK**. This locks the numerical keypad on the right into number-mode. The keys shown have the numerical meanings on their key-tops. Incidentally, not every machine has a numeric keypad – keyboards differ from machine to machine.

The keyboard usually simply plugs via a cable into the back of the computer box, and requires no other special interface. It is simply a matrix of switches, as described on page 47, and the keyboard electronics are controlled by the operating system. In a lap-top computer, the keyboard is formed as part of the computer box itself, as is the display.

The part of the operating system which handles the keyboard is contained in the BIOS – basic I/O system – which is also used to handle the reading and writing of data to and from various other I/O devices. Later we will look at the types of command available in the BIOS of a typical operating system.

Keyboards are used in most applications where computers are found. The exceptions are in simple control computers which are embedded in another machine – such as a vehicle-fuel management system, or a multi-tune door bell.

When a computer is first switched on, you will usually have to press keys on a keyboard unless the computer automatically goes into a graphical-user interface, as we shall see on page 67. Certainly, for applications such as wordprocessing, the keyboard forms an integral part of the application. However, it is fair to say that for graphically orientated machines such as the Apple Macintosh series, the keyboard's central position has been eroded in favour of more immediate and graphical input using a pointer device (usually a mouse).

The keyboard is fine for typing a letter, or communicating complex streams of commands, but there are limitations caused by the time needed to find and physically press the keys. For some types of information, there are more efficient devices.

For instance, if the screen is showing a flat surface on which a graphical pattern is situated, or even a grid of data, it is quicker for a human to point at different positions on the screen using a 'pointer' device. There are several types available – mouse, light pen, graphics tablet, ordinary fingers, digitizer/scanner, and so on. We will look at these now.

Mouse and trackerball

> ### Mouse and trackerball applications
> - In graphical user interfaces, where the mouse is used to point at a given command, and a button pressed to select it, without using the keyboard.

- In many modern programs, in company with a keyboard, to select commands quickly from a menu on the screen.
- For controlling general drawing programs.
- Games or other applications where decisions and commands are needed.

Mouse and trackerball interface

- Usually via a thin wire plugged into a socket on the computer.
- One of the serial ports is normally used, though not always.
- Wireless link – no cable – using infra red, etc.
- The trackerball may be integral to the computer case – next to or on the keyboard – this saves an extra computer cable.

A mouse is a small plastic housing which can be pushed around a desk or a special pad (see Figure 4.2). The computer detects the mouse's movement, and not its absolute position. As the movement occurs, software moves a pointer, or 'cursor' around the screen 'following' the mouse. Buttons on the mouse allow the operator to pick a command when the pointer reaches an appropriate place.

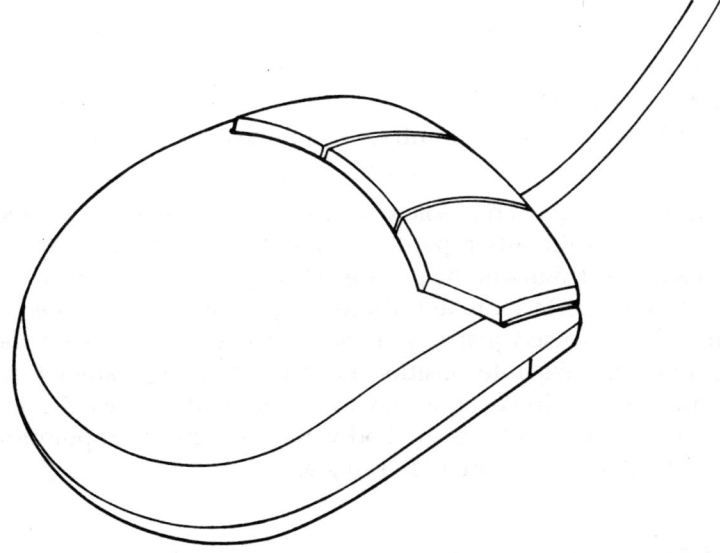

Figure 4.2 A mouse with three buttons

Graphics packages, which allow the user to produce drawings, use a mouse as a sophisticated pen and pointer. Most modern packages are produced to allow the user to pick commands and generally communicate using a mouse. One of the most important advantages of a general pointing device is that you do not have to look at it – you simply follow its progress across the screen, and adjust hand movements accordingly.

A trackerball is rather like a mouse which is mounted upside down. The underneath of a mouse often has a ball which is rotated as the mouse is pushed around the table – the computer is actually

▶ A joy-stick is a trackerball on a stick.

tracking movements of the ball. A trackerball simply presents this ball for the user to move directly. A trackerball can be incorporated into a keyboard, connected by yet another cable, for the user to move around by the side of the keyboard, which saves having an extra device. The interface for a trackerball is the same as for a mouse, and most systems do not distinguish between them.

The applications for a mouse, or trackerball, include games, drawing packages, many standard business packages, and any software where the user has to control a pointer, or choose options from a screen.

 More and more software is being written to include support for a mouse. Look at any magazine, and see if you can tell from the adverts how many packages are obviously suitable for use with a mouse.

Light pen

> ### Light-pen applications
> Not used much, but might be seen in special industrial applications where a screen shows a menu of alternatives, and one has to be picked by the operator.

> ### Light-pen interface
> Normally by dedicated circuitry, via a thin cable and socket.

The light pen is largely an obsolete device, but has some specialized applications. It is literally a pen-like stick which is held up to the VDU screen. Electronics in the pen detect the light coming from the screen, and the interface can tell where it is pointing on the screen at any time. This is used just like a mouse to select things on the screen, and here absolute position is being detected, rather than simply movement. However, it is awkward to hold up the light pen to the VDU surface, and this method is not as accurate at pointing owing to the thickness of VDU screen glass.

Graphics tablet

> ### Graphics-tablet applications
> • Draughting programs.
> • Special industrial applications to supplant a complete keyboard.

> ### Graphics-tablet interface
> • Via a thin cable to plug and socket.

- Usually uses a serial port, but may have dedicated
  circuitry and a special interface board, or may use a
  parallel interface.

In principle a graphics tablet is very similar to a mouse (see Figure 4.3). A 'puck' is moved around the surface of the tablet, and its absolute position is detected by a matrix below its surface, and communicated to the computer.

In many ways, the tablet is a true representation of the screen surface. This is useful in accurate drawing packages where the tablet can be the equivalent of a computerized draughting board. Also, accurate measurements of a given drawing can be made by placing the drawing over the tablet, and using the puck to follow the drawing's lines. This is also a good method of accurately loading, or 'digitizing' a given drawing into the machine. The word 'tablet' usually implies a small desk-top unit, about A4 size. However, graphics-input devices of this type also come in full drawing-board size for digitizing large technical drawings.

▶ Digitizing: see page 52.

*Figure 4.3 A graphics tablet
with regions designated on
surface*

Also, a given graphics package could include an overlay for the tablet containing special command squares. When the puck is moved over to a command square, and its button pressed, this can communicate the appropriate command to the program.

Touch screens

Touch-screen applications
- Dedicated computer systems with a menu of options to
  choose from on the screen – often seen in financial dealing
  rooms.

- Non-keyboard applications – no cables needed to any input devices.

> **Touch-screen interface**
> Just included within the hardware of the VDU, and the software.

For a touch screen, special detectors can be included in the VDU screen's surround which can detect the presence and position of fingers pressed to the screen surface. These are much used by financial dealing systems, and by sales systems which allow members of the public to choose options from a screen, without having to interact with a separate mouse or keyboard. The screen itself is all that needs be presented.

The screen displays an array of button-like areas, and touching a button area is equivalent to pressing a key on a keyboard. The advantage is that the software is in full control of the button matrix, and can change it at will to allow the user to communicate to different parts of the program as it changes the button matrix. Effectively, it allows the software to provide a completely customized keyboard.

Digitizer/scanner

> **Digitizer applications**
> - To bring in graphics to a drawing or DTP package for use in a given document or drawing.
> - To bring in text from hard copy, using optical character recognition (OCR).
> - To assist in bringing in sample material for general storage or aid with presentations.

> **Digitizer interface**
> - Dedicated electronic interface with cable plug and socket.
> - Serial port with cable.
> - Parallel port with cable.

Imagine that you have several pages of notes, or a number of pictures which you wish to input into the computer. You could use a keyboard and type in the text data, and then put the drawings onto a graphics tablet and trace around the lines to input to a drawing package. However, all this can be done almost instantly using a scanner which takes the sheets one by one and digitizes the information straight into the machine.

Such digitizers exist in two main forms (see Figure 4.4). The hand-held scanner, which is stroked across the sheet surface, and the flat-bed scanner, onto which the sheet is laid face down – the whole sheet is scanned at the same time.

▶ Hand-held and flat-bed scanners.

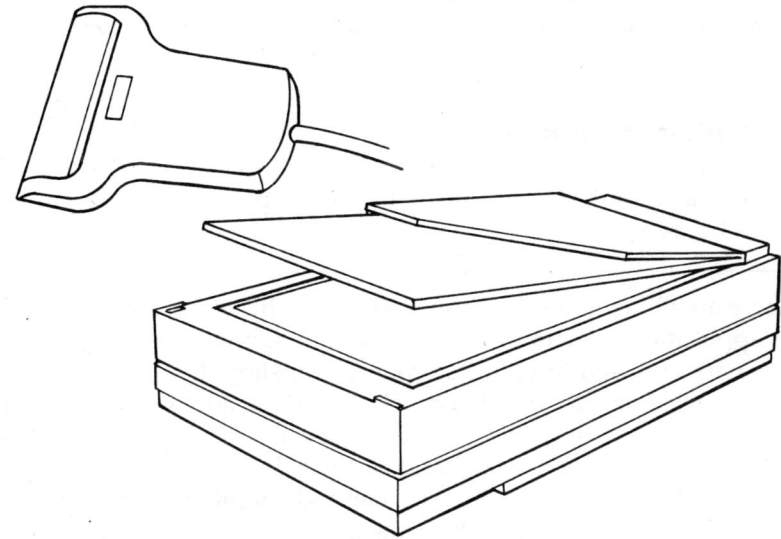

Figure 4.4 The two types of scanner

Either way, the problem then arises as to how to treat the data thus captured. Pictures are comparatively easy. The patterns of light and dark are simply transferred onto the computer screen, and can be stored in a file as a complete picture for you to use and modify with a drawing program. The essence is that the computer is not treating the data intelligently – it is just storing it as a pattern of dots, rather like a newspaper picture. Scanners can also digitize in full colour, so the amount of data which has to be stored can be quite large, but there is not usually any processing to be done – it is just stored as it is.

Text is another matter. You will not usually be interested in the patterns of the letters and words, but the content. This is where some clever software is required, and most scanners come with letter- and word-recognition systems. That is, they can scan the text and decode it as text which you can take into a text-processing package and use and modify as you would any other piece of writing. This type of software is called OCR (optical character recognition). In general, unless you are very lucky, you will have to go through the text carefully looking for processing errors, but this process is still much quicker than typing the whole thing in from scratch.

Of course, if the object of scanning is just to hold a copy of the document, you may not be interested in converting into text – a straight microfiche-type storage, without interpretation, may be sufficient. In this case, scanning is quite efficient – it could always be interpreted later as and when it is needed.

► Intelligent scanning involves letter and word recognition – optical character recognition (OCR).

Dedicated input devices

Dedicated input applications
- Tills at checkouts.
- Input of photographs.

- To read numerical information on cheques, etc.
- Information communication – such as fax and Teletext, etc.

Dedicated input interface
Too varied to list here, but would include serial, parallel and dedicated interface circuitry with cables, plugs and sockets of all kinds.

▶ Bar-code readers – supermarkets will not now accept any packaged product which does not have a bar code. The whole stock-control system is run automatically by bar-code identification.

▶ Machine-readable characters on cheques: OCR characters.

▶ Teletext: digital information transmitted alongside television programmes.

There are many input devices which are dedicated to a specific type of application or data type. For instance, special wands and laser scanners are used to read bar codes. You should be familiar with these devices at supermarket checkouts. The reader detects the pattern of thick and thin light and dark bars on a product's packaging, and can recognize it using a large file stored in memory. There is, in fact, an international standard for bar-code numbers which ensures that no two products have the same code.

At the bottom of bank cheques, there is another type of dedicated input method. The standard printed code numbers, which are formed using a special typeface, are machine-readable characters, called OCR (optical character recognition) characters. These are printed to ensure that they can be recognized with as near to 100 per cent accuracy as possible. They help in the process of clearing cheques and keeping account of transactions.

Video cameras are also sometimes used for 'intelligent' computer input, but the software for recognizing information in the field of view is quite complex, and restricted to a few specialized applications. For instance, experimentation is continually in progress to use a video-camera system with intelligent recognition software to notice when manufactured items are defective – broken biscuits, for instance.

Video cameras are also used to capture photographic images, in a similar way to the digital scanner.

There are also many transmitted-information acquisition systems available for computers. For instance, along with the TV picture, digital information is broadcast continuously by the TV companies in the UK – this is called Teletext. A suitable tuner and decoder can be purchased for a computer, which interfaces with a plug-in board for an IBM PC, or to external sockets for other computers. The computer can be set to be used just like a TV Teletext display, but in addition data can be acquired automatically by the machine, and stored in files for later processing. A typical example would be the financial-market data available during the day, which could be used to trigger alarms for selling or buying. Also, the computer could accumulate historical data to aid buying and selling strategies.

Other general stores of information are available via the telephone. There are many services available, and there are even computer clubs which communicate through telephone communications.

Facsimile (fax) machines are becoming an essential part of even the smallest business. Essentially, they are a way of digitizing and sending complete patterns from a sheet of paper. No intelligent or analytic processing of the actual information sent is required. Computers can have fax interfaces added to them which will take a stored document, digitize it to the fax specification, ring up another fax automatically, and transmit the fax. The machines can also receive and store or print faxes. With the addition of a scanner, such interfaces can also take in general sheets just like a standard fax machine.

► Fax.

Future input devices

An ultimate goal of computing is direct communication with a human using the normal, natural communication channels of speech. Speech recognition has been worked on continuously for many decades, and many claims have been made that it has finally been cracked. Unfortunately, despite some attempts at commercial systems, the problem is not solved yet for a general human voice. Certainly, there are systems which can recognize a specific human's voice over a restricted vocabulary, but still not 100 per cent of the time. In general, such systems require a period of training where the machine learns a given voice.

► Voice recognition.

There have been some advances recently which may yield better results using 'neural networks' which mimic the learning methods of the brain. However, these are still some way off.

► Neural networks: attempts to build computer systems which mimic the activity of the human brain.

Other input devices include detection of eye movement to give a restricted set of commands to the computer, and movements of various other parts of the body such as toes and wrists, and so on. These have applications particularly for disabled people, and this field is expanding considerably at present.

Another, rather futuristic approach, has been to try to detect the weak magnetic fields produced by electrical impulses in the brain. A new form of magnetic detector (the SQUID – Superconducting Quantum Interference Device) has been used to capture this type of input, but this is at a very early stage indeed.

► In microsurgery, a headband worn by the surgeon allows a tiny television camera inside the patient to be moved and zoomed, as the surgeon's head moves.

Input from the real world

Real-world input applications
* Collection of data from a shop floor or other industrial process.
* General sensing of the outside world.

Computers are also used to gather scientific information from the environment, or from engineering and industrial processes. Sensors are used to convert measurements, or events, into digital input for processing by machine.

For instance, an automated weather station would need to sense parameters such as temperature, air pressure, wind direction, humidity, light level, rain density, perhaps cloud density, and so on. Each of these measures a quantity which is continuously variable, and the levels sensed need to be turned into binary numbers which reflect the value of the parameter being measured. For instance, if it is dark, then the light level would be 0 – the same in binary, and any other system. If on the other hand it is a dull afternoon, a binary number must be generated which reflects the numerical value of the light level.

▶ Analogue to digital conversion (A/D–C), or vice versa (D/A–C), transforms variables with continuous values into digital on/off forms or vice versa.

The conversion from continuously variable, or analogue, parameters into digital form for use by a computer is called analogue-to-digital, or A/D conversion. It is achieved with special electronic circuits, usually confined to a chip. The A/D converter (A/D–C) will take in a voltage level proportional to the parameter being sensed, and convert this into a binary number which can be read directly by a computer, and then, perhaps, transmitted to another computer over a remote link for analysis.

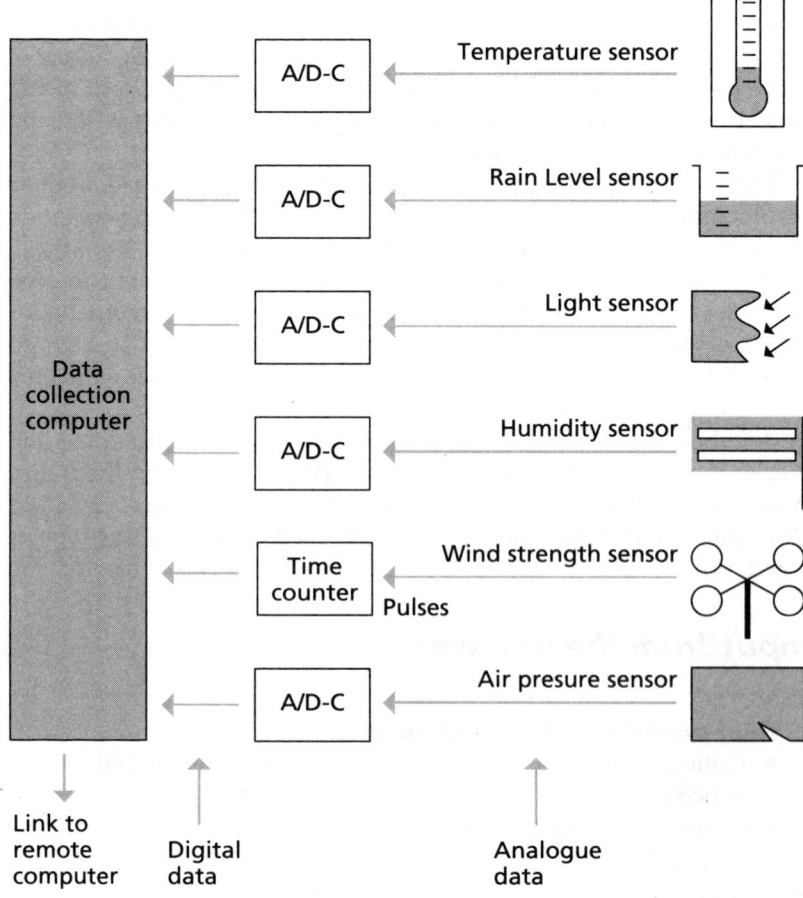

Figure 4.5 The conversion of analogue data to digital data for meteorlogical recording and transmission

Figure 4.5 shows a block sketch of such a system. Here, sensed quantities are converted from their natural form to be read by the computer. The naturally occurring parameters may be in continuously variable form, such as temperature, or in the form of pulses at varying speeds, such as from the wind-speed sensor. These pulses need to be counted for a set time, and this converted into a measure of speed.

In general, an on-site data collection computer will take in this information, convert it to a package of intelligible information, and then communicate the data to a remote computer which might collect information from many weather stations.

I/O and control

The final stage of this process of data collection and analysis is to 'close the loop', and use the information to control the thing from which data is originating. Of course, this is still rather difficult with the weather! However, a large industrial process will proceed by the process controllers looking at the product, and adjusting the process as it proceeds in order to produce the right amounts and quality of product (see Figure 4.6).

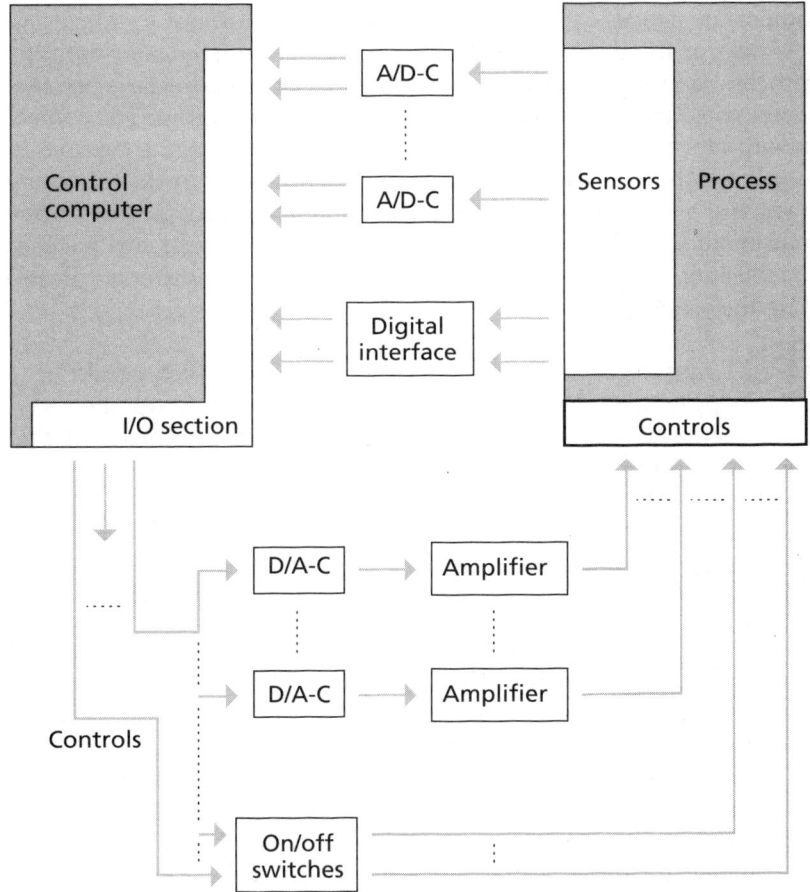

Figure 4.6 A system for controlling an industrial process

A computer is excellent at this type of application. It is accurate, flexible, incapable of boredom and very fast. In Figure 4.6, data is collected via sensors from the process, using A/D–Cs to convert analogue data into digital form, and some data is collected by on/off switches, and probably many other types of sensor. This data is used by a program running in the control computer to calculate the correct control signals to continuously adjust the process for the best effect.

Adjusting the process must be done using digital signals which are converted, in many cases, back into analogue signals. For instance, the amount of gas being fed to a set of burners is a continuously variable control. To do this, the computer will send out a binary number proportional to the amount of gas to be fed to the burners, and this will be converted to a proportionate voltage level using a digital-to-analogue converter (D/A–C). This voltage then usually needs to be amplified to turn the motor which controls the gas. In addition, some actions can be controlled by on/off switches, and these will be controlled by setting single BITs to on or off.

▶ Feedback or control loops.

This illustrates the concept of computer control, and is called a 'feedback' loop. Data is gathered from the process, adjustments are made, which change the data, and the new data is again used to adjust the process. The program has to be careful not to adjust too quickly, or the data will be changing back and forth faster than the process can react; a certain amount of care and steadiness is needed, and this is the skill of control design and programming. The control has to be capable of reacting at high speed, but also be capable of applying the control orders with care. Humans can do this quite well, but a well-designed control computer can react to many more parameters, and much faster when needed. Humans are good at overseeing, and adjusting the way in which the computer is controlling the whole process.

 Draw a diagram, similar to the Figure 4.6, which would apply to a household central heating system. Show the sensors, and the types of interface which would be used, and also show the controls and their interfaces.

OUTPUT DEVICES

The most common output devices for a computer are VDU and printer. VDUs range from single-colour, or mono screens, through to high-resolution colour screens, and come in a range of sizes. Large screens, mono or colour, are used to provide high-resolution output surfaces for draughting and large-format typesetting applications. Normal-sized screens can also be used for these applications, and are quite adequate for word-processing, and all the usual business applications such as cash flows, business accounts, and so on.

Printers range from simple low-resolution devices which are usually cheap and robust, to large, fast high-resolution graphics printers which look rather like photocopiers. There are several types of printer on the market at present, and we will look at the various methods they use on pages 63–7.

Again, low-resolution cheap printers are fine for everyday-business applications such as accounts, but better printed material is usually necessary for business letters, and drawing output.

Visual display units (VDUs)

VDU applications
- To allow the user to see what the computer is doing in general.
- Any application where 'alphanumeric' or graphical data is to be displayed to the user:
  - wordprocessors
  - spreadsheets
  - databases
  - desk-top publishing programs.
- Dedicated commercial programs in industrial applications such as production planning and control.
- Accounts programs.
- Interaction with the computer's operating system.
- Computer programming.

VDU interface
- Via a fairly thick cable, plug and socket, designed to minimize electrical interference.
- For small computers, the display may be integral to the computer case.

Computers normally come with a VDU and, when choosing a computer, it is important to specify the VDU level which should be included. Desk-top machines come with a TV-like VDU, i.e. a large heavy box with a TV tube whose surface is shown at the front. Laptop machines come with a smaller, thin, flat liquid-crystal display (LCD), which may be backlit to ensure that the characters shown are easily visible. The aim is to keep size, weight and power consumption to a minimum. In the future, as LCDs improve, they may be able to supersede the large, cumbersome VDU, and desk-top machines will merge with laptops to some extent.

The display on a VDU can take, basically, two forms. These are text-only and graphical displays. The usual format for text-only displays is around eighty characters across the screen, with twenty-five lines, or rows. There are other formats, and graphical packages use variable formats, but 80×25 is a basic standard minimum which you should expect. This allows the screen to display enough text for an operator to write letters, reports, or even whole books. The display on the screen is just a window into a larger document. The screen will also generally contain command and data concerning the particular package being used.

► Text-only and graphic display.

The text characters, and indeed all displays, are made up from dots in a matrix. The number of dots per inch (dpi) determines the resolution of the display – the more the better.

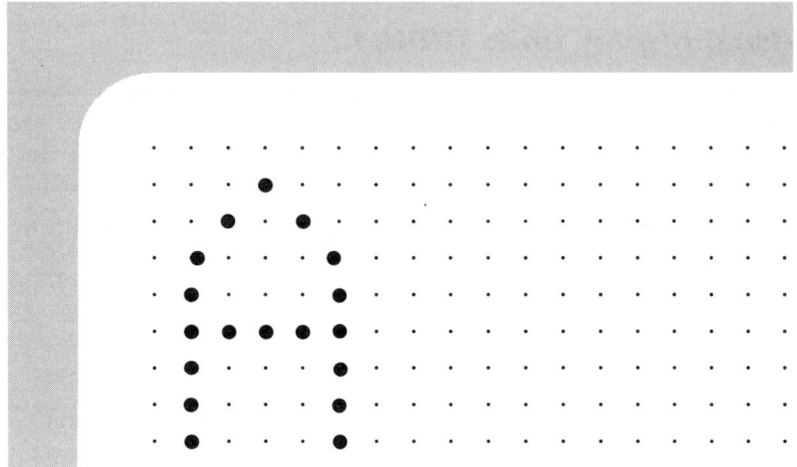

Figure 4.7 How a character is formed on a VDU screen

► Each character is made up from pixels.

Each character is made up from an array of dot positions – shown by the small dots in the diagram. The letter A, for example, might be displayed in the top left corner of a screen by just lighting up the dot positions shown (see Figure 4.7). The smaller dots are not displayed – they just illustrate all possible positions. The dots are called 'picture elements', or 'pixels' for short. Different machines and software use different actual pixel arrays for characters, etc., but this is a possible example. Ideally, the individual dots should not be visible, they should weld together to form a continuous character, as you might write it on a piece of paper. This can only occur if lots of small dots are crammed together into a high-resolution character array.

Graphical images are formed using the same principle, with the whole screen being split into separate dot positions, each dot being addressable by the computer software. This takes a fair amount of memory storage. Add to this the fact that each dot could also be displayed in any one of hundreds of colour shades, and you can see that high-resolution colour screens can use a very large amount of memory. A typical 'VGA' IBM-PC-style interface board to run a high-resolution colour VDU screen might itself contain 1 MB of RAM. Not all of this will appear within the memory map of the computer, but will be split into pages of, say, 16K in size. To fill the complete array, the software must switch from page to page, storing pieces of the display data into each page so that the whole image comes together correctly on the screen.

Dot resolution is variable on most VDUs, but is typically 800×600 dots using VGA, giving a total screen array of nearly half a million dots – each capable of being one of 256 colours.

► On cheap hand-held computer games with LCD displays, dot resolution is usually very poor and the pictures very fuzzy.

It is important to match the VDU resolution with the particular software being run. There are certain standards for display type, and a given piece of software should specify the minimum VDU screen type which is required to display the program's output successfully. Most programs also allow the user to set them up for the particular display which is contained in the computer.

More and more, programs which you will buy come with colour, graphics and mouse use. It is a good idea to ensure that these basic elements are available on any machine purchased.

VDUs are not always used to display material directly to a user in front of a machine. For instance, a thin, translucent, coloured LCD VDU is manufactured to be placed in a projector in place of a slide. Light is projected through it onto a screen to allow a lecturer or presenter to display his computer work directly to an audience. Indeed presentation techniques are advancing continually, and this will be an important field in the future. Computers are useful for allowing sophisticated visual aids to be produced from libraries of images in a short time.

Raster and vector displays

The images on the surface of a mono TV tube are formed by a thin beam of electrons hitting a special phosphor just behind the front surface of the glass sheet you look at. This produces a very small spot of light on the surface, and it is normally being scanned back and forth across the screen, from top left to bottom right, in a series of horizontal lines. As the spot moves across these lines, it is switched on and off very fast to build up the light and dark dots of a complete screen of display. The human eye is too slow to see the actual movement, which blurs the fast movements of this 'flying spot' into one surface picture.

A coloured screen uses three such beams, or flying spots, each forming a different coloured image. These are blended together by the eye into a full-colour display. The set of horizontal lines on the screen is called a 'raster', and this is said to be a 'raster display'. However, a raster display is not the only way in which the electron beams can be moved around.

By controlling the electronics of the TV tube, the spots can be made to move around the screen in any way which is convenient. For instance, suppose an engineering drawing is being constructed, and so far it consists only of a single circle in the centre of the screen. This circle, in the raster method, would be formed from hundreds of lines which are mostly dark, but lit up just at the points where they intersect with the circle's position. This could just as well be displayed by controlling the electron beam to follow only the circle's line, and forget the rest of the screen. If another figure were to be added to the circle, the flying spot could fly around this as well. The result is a spot which is just confined to running around the lines of the drawing, and nowhere else. This produces remarkably sharp images for technical drawings, and is called a 'vector display'.

Vector displays are good at showing line drawings, but poor at presenting coloured photo-like graphics. They require much less memory storage for line drawings than the many thousands of separate dots stored within a raster display. High-resolution architectural drawings, printed circuit layouts and engineering drawings may be displayed on vector VDUs. However, the versatility of raster displays have made them the main type of VDU for general applications.

Graphics (and other) compression

One of the expanding areas of graphical display is that of the near-photographic resolution achievable by typical high-resolution VDUs. The problem is that the higher the resolution of a given image, which may have been captured from a colour TV camera, or a video-tape machine, the greater the memory required for its storage, which can turn out to be immense. It is true, of course, that memory devices are becoming cheaper and higher in capacity with every passing month, but it is still a problem to store good quality photographic images. Another aspect is the transmission of them over telephone lines, and other media, once digitized. The vast amount of data involved makes the process slow and expensive.

The solution is to perform a form of compression of the data, which does not significantly degrade the picture. Incidentally, this is exactly the same type of problem which is encountered in sending digitized voice or any other general data over a communication line.

Compression effectively removes unnecessary data, and abbreviates others, according to a set algorithm. The compression is performed before storage, or communication, and then reassembled according to the inverse algorithm, when the picture or other data is retrieved, or received at the end of a communication line. Such compression cuts the amount of actual data which needs to be sent over a telephone so significantly that complete video pictures can be sent in real time, thus linking people together in both sound and picture. Without compression, the communication speed would limit the video information to a few still pictures at well-separated intervals.

One method of compression of photographic images is called 'fractal compression'. It uses powerful mathematical algorithms to compress the data of full-colour digitized photographic images by a ratio of up to 200:1. This would enable, for instance, a hundred full-colour photographic images to be stored on a 1.44 MB floppy disk. As you can see, without such compression the disk storage of photographic images would be too memory intensive to be practical. The decompression of the images is much faster than the compression, which is normally performed using fast hardware to speed up the process. Thus, the computer user can gain access to the images fast and easily just using decompression software.

► Compression means reducing the data-storage requirements for an image according to a set of precise rules, transmitting the image, and then reconstructing it using the same rules in reverse.

Many computer programs are distributed in compressed form to cut down on the number of floppy disks which have to be supplied. Decompression is performed on the compressed files before storage on the main system so that the programs are available for immediate use.

Printers

Printer applications
- Typing up letters, reports, text documents of all kinds from:
  - wordprocessors
  - spreadsheets
  - databases
  - desk-top publishing programs.
- Dedicated commercial programs in industrial applications such as production planning and control.
- Accounts programs.
- Interaction with the computer's operating system.
- Listing programs during computer programming.
- To produce mono and colour images from graphics and drawing programs.

Printer interface
- Thick parallel cable to plug and socket – this is the most common interface – called 'Centronics' parallel interface. Cable is sometimes thick and rather rigid, containing many wires, or a flat multi-wire ribbon.
- Serial port, cable plug and socket.
- Special electronic interfaces may sometimes be needed for specialist applications such as tally-roll printers in industrial settings.

A paper print of the output of a program is called 'hard copy'. In many ways, it is the safest form of backup for computer information, and has the automatic security associated with paper files of information in every part of business life. There are several ways to produce this hard copy, not only on paper. The image can be produced on the side of cardboard packages in a production process, the bottoms of cans of food for the sell-by date, the surface of plastic film for projectors, and so on.

As we saw in Chapter 3, the printed image, most often presented on paper, is normally made up from an array of dots, just as is the VDU image. The most common sizes of printer will print 80 or 132 columns of characters on each line, and print on either single sheets, or a continuous roll of paper, depending upon the printer itself.

There are three popular printer technologies currently on the market: the impact dot-matrix, the inkjet and the laser printer. All use a dot-matrix method of building up the image.

▶ Three main types of printer: impact dot-matrix, inkjet/bubblejet, laser printer.

Impact dot-matrix printer

Impact dot-matrix applications
- All types of printing and graphics in mono – colour versions produce an unsatisfactory image, though useful for draft.
- Useful for bulk printing due to robustness, and low cost.
- Will print multi-part stationery.
- Can be adapted to print labels of any kind.
- Simple mechanism useful for specialist industrial applications.
- Very noisy in confined spaces.

Impact dot-matrix interface
As for all printers.

The impact dot-matrix printer (see Figure 4.8) uses a vertical line of pins which are pushed out of a head by electromagnets onto an inked ribbon in front of the paper. An image is thus formed on the paper. As the head is moved across the paper surface, several complete rows of dots are printed across the page with each pass. There are two main standards of resolution: nine-pin and twenty-four-pin heads. The latter forms a higher-resolution image than the former. The software is able to 'contact' each pin separately, and hence can build up a graphical array of dots to form any pattern or image. This technology has the advantage that multi-part stationery can be used for various business purposes.

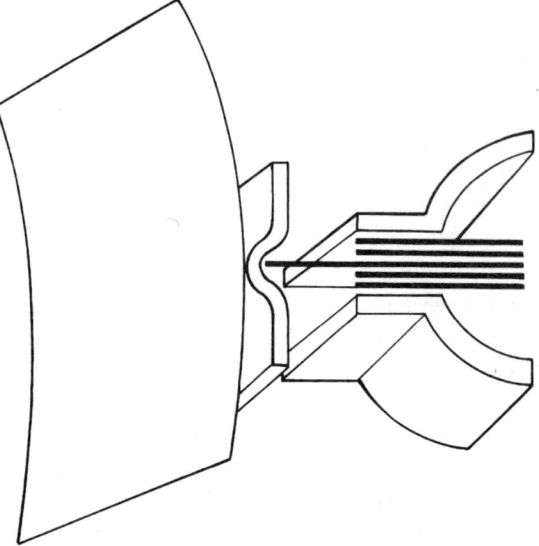

Figure 4.8 An impact dot matrix head, ribbon, paper

Impact dot-matrix printers can normally print in one of two main modes: draft quality and near-letter quality (NLQ). For the latter, two passes are made over the work, with a slight change in position each time. NLQ is quite slow, but gives good results – particularly on printers with twenty-four pins. Impact dot-matrix printers tend to be cheaper and more robust than most other printers available. Draft is a low-resolution, fast-printing mode for quick reports. It might print several hundred characters per second, while NLQ will normally print well under a hundred per second.

The smaller impact dot-matrix printers will print 80 characters, or columns, in normal width printing, and 132 columns if the print is compressed. This mode may be switched on and off from the software, or often by pressing a button on the printer's front panel. Larger printers can take wider paper and print 132 columns in normal width characters, even more if compressed. Single sheets can usually be fed through, or a continuous roll of paper used to save having to feed sheets in one by one. There are also automatic sheet feeders available to allow the user to have continuous single-sheet printing if required.

▶ On an impact printer NLQ might take well over a minute to print a single full A4 page of text, while draft could take twelve to fifteen seconds.

Inkjet printer

Inkjet applications
- Suitable for all printer applications.
- Produces excellent print quality at high speed.
- Will supplant impact dot matrix for most applications.
- Can be used for non-contact printing – such as spraying labelling information on the side of packages.
- Excellent for graphical and drawing output.
- Can give excellent colour images.
- Does not impact paper, and so is no use for multi-part stationery.
- Quiet in operation.

Inkjet interface
As for all printers.

Inkjet printers work by ejecting small bubbles of ink straight onto the paper surface. The resolution is quite high with such printers, and dots tend to weld into each other more completely than an impact dot-matrix image, thus giving a better illusion of continuous graphical images. The speed tends to be nearer to dot-matrix draft mode, with considerably higher resolution.

Printers built on this principle usually use separate sheets, rather than continuous stationery, though there are continuous-feed versions. The ink is supplied in a disposable cartridge, which sometimes contains the print head itself so that, each time the ink runs out, the whole cartridge and head is replaced, though kits exist to refill the cartridge a few times.

Laser printers

> #### Laser applications
> - Used for highest-resolution printing of text and graphics.
> - Typesetting.
> - Fast lasers used for high-volume bulk printing.
> - Lasers are also used for all the normal printer applications mentioned above, but not multi-part stationery.
> - Quiet in operation.

> #### Laser interface
> As for all printers.

The best printing resolution is produced by a laser printer, though cheap lasers and good inkjets are very similar.

Laser printers work rather like photocopiers. Lasers are used to form an image on the paper electrostatically, which attracts fine 'toner' powder to it. Heat is then used to fuse the image into the paper. Since a laser is used to form the image, it can be composed faster and contain many more minute dots than any other method – the resolution is higher, and printing faster.

The speed of a laser printer, as with a photocopier, is independent of the amount of text or graphics on a page. Typical lasers will print around five to ten pages per minute. They are more expensive to buy and maintain than the other printers above, but are more reliable, faster, and produce a near perfect image, which does not suffer from improperly inked ribbons or poor ink flow, for instance. Many documents which used to be typeset on professional photo-typesetting equipment are now produced using a laser printer. Often, even an inkjet printer is sufficiently high in quality for outputting camera-ready copy.

Lasers generally print on single sheets, and can be loaded with a stack of paper sheets. The toner used to form the image is usually held in a cartridge, which must be refilled or replaced from time to time.

Other printers

▶ Line printers.

For fast, high-volume printing, line printers are still to be found. These printers are designed to print a complete line of characters simultaneously. They have always been used by large organizations with very large volumes of printing to perform, such as mail order firms, public utilities, and so on. They print fast, and are often impact devices so a second paper copy can be kept if required. However, these are now being superseded by very fast laser printers, and the need for paper copy is being replaced with ever more reliance on peripheral memory backup, such as high-capacity tape. For some time, this was regarded a little suspiciously compared to paper, but the volume of backup needed in the modern world simply makes paper an uneconomical option.

Plotters

> ### *Plotter applications*
> - Output where lines are drawn, rather than text or block graphics.
> - Architectural and general industrial draughting and technical drawing – large plans and drawings.

> ### *Plotter interface*
> As for all printers.

Printing continuous lines, such as for architect's drawings, is often performed using a pen plotter. Here, a single pen, or a set of coloured pens, is held on the machine, and when an image is to be drawn, a specially designed holder comes over, picks up a pen, and takes it over to the start position. The pen is pushed down onto the paper surface, and dragged over the surface to produce a straight or curved line. The pen is then replaced. If the product is to be in colour, a new pen is picked up, and the process continues until the image is complete.

Two main formats of plotter are used in draughting – the flat-bed plotter and the roller-drum plotter. In the former, the paper is placed on a flat bed, and the pens move horizontally and vertically over the whole two-dimensional surface. The roller plotter rolls the paper in and out, while the pens are confined to move side to side only. By this combination of movement, the whole piece of paper is scanned. The roller plotter can make very large drawings for architectural use, for instance.

▶ Flat-bed plotters and roller-drum plotters.

However, the pen plotter produces the same type of image that a draughtsman would produce, by a similar method. It is akin to the vector display VDU introduced above. Instead of building up an image from a surface of fixed-position dots, the pens just follow the lines of the image to be displayed. Again, this method is good for line drawings, but poor for general graphical images, which could require blocks of colour, or a photo-like realism. An inkjet or laser printer would be more appropriate for such applications.

▶ Pen plotters.

BRINGING INPUT AND OUTPUT TOGETHER – THE GRAPHICAL USER INTERFACE

The ultimate fusion of input and output occurs with a modern graphical user interface, or 'GUI'. Here, keyboard and mouse are used to input instructions and commands, and a high resolution, usually colour, screen is used for output. The idea is to make the interface with the user both highly visual (graphic) and 'user friendly', i.e. simple to use. In many ways, this is the way in which computers are moving, and many machines now either have a GUI as a standard part of their operating system, or have a GUI package included with the machine.

▶ Graphical user interface (GUI).

The Apple Macintosh series of computers was designed for this type of I/O from the start, and as such gained a lead on the IBM PC standard, as far as ease of use was concerned. The Macintosh is designed to present simple graphical information to the user, who can select functions and programs using the pointer device, rather than having to remember the form of commands to be typed into a command line from the keyboard. This represented a major step forward in computing, and you will come up against this method of I/O continuously in all commercial and home-computer settings.

The IBM PC standard has copied the GUI system in order to provide computers which have the same characteristics as the Macintosh, and to this end a program called 'Windows' was produced for IBM-type machines. However, due to the very graphical nature of the Macintosh, it has a firm foothold in graphical industries such as typesetting and presentation design.

The GUI system is said to use 'WIMPs'. Unfortunately, the exact definition of this acronym is a little confused in the literature. You will see it defined variously as:

> Windows Icons Mouse Pointer
>
> Windows Icons Mouse Program
>
> Windows Icons Menus Pointers.

The exact definition is not crucial, as these all refer to the same ideas. Here, we will take the last definition because it is the widest of the three. This is explained further in the boxes.

Windows

A GUI screen is often divided into separate areas called windows, and more windows can be brought up onto the screen, for further information, or to access further software levels, usually using a pointing device. For instance, the opening window of an encyclopedia will allow the user to choose an area to access. Accessing a given subject area might bring up a window of further choices, each of which could open further windows of data, rather like leaves of a book. These leaves are often referred to as 'tiles'. The previous tiles are still available, but overlapped by the new information. Previous tiles can be picked up and laid on top of the pile at will, just as in a sheaf of papers.

Icons

The GUI system often displays small suggestive graphical labels, called icons, on the screen for the commands and programs which are available.

To run a given program, or issue a command, the pointing device is used to move the screen pointer onto its icon, and a press of the pointer's button causes the program to run, or a command to be performed – very little keyboard entry is needed, and few commands have to be specially memorized.

Menus

One of the main points about using a GUI is that you can find your way around a program just from the visual screen information being presented. The ultimate goal is to dispense with paper manuals for programs. In other words, anyone should be able to buy even a complex program, and then load, run and operate it from scratch, just using the screen information presented. This is not easy given the great sophistication of modern programs, but it is possible in principle. Certainly the main uses of a given program can be treated in this way, if the software writer is good at communication (not always the case!). The more abstruse parts of a given package can always be made available via the manual, or special 'help' software.

A successful approach to helping the user is to present a set, or hierarchy, of 'menus' on the screen, which label actions or options available in the current program. Sometimes the menus are presented along the top, or down the side, of the screen, in areas referred to as 'menu bars'. Sometimes the menus overlap each other thus tiling the screen surface as with the window areas mentioned above.

The user reads through the menu of possible actions, and simply chooses one. This may in turn lead to another more refined set of options, and so on. This is not by any means restricted to the GUI presentation – it is a universal approach to presenting programs to users, and has been used since VDUs and keyboards were first offered as input/output media.

In a GUI, the mouse is used to point to a menu item, and clicked to choose it. Alternatively, in a complex program, the mouse clicks on an icon, and an appropriate menu is unfurled on the screen to allow the user to choose alternatives. Such active menus are called 'pull-down' menus. When a menu icon is selected, the menu is effectively pulled down from it like a window blind. This is the 'menu' part of WIMP.

Figure 4.9 shows the use of a pull-down menu. At the top

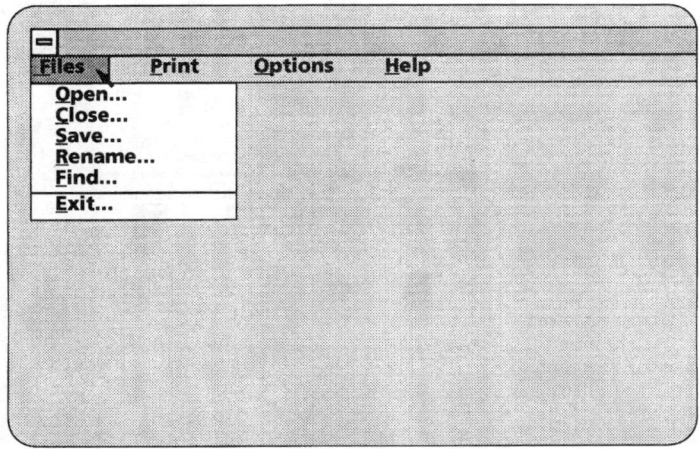

Figure 4.9 A pull-down menu

of the screen there is a menu bar, and each label refers to a pull-down menu of options. As you can see, the pointer has been 'clicked' on the one headed **FILES**. This has pulled down the list of options under this menu, any of which the user can choose by clicking on it. Further pull-down menus may be encountered beneath these options, and so on until the user reaches the required command. You should be able to appreciate how much easier it is to choose from a complex set of commands using pull-down menus, mouse and button, instead of having to type in the commands, perhaps correcting typing errors as you go.

Pointers

As you can see, the pointer device is implicit in everything introduced above. It is not just a piece of hardware with one or more buttons on it, it is also a piece of software which converts movement and button pressing into actions on the screen. In general, there will be a counterpart pointer on the screen which moves with the mouse or whatever. The screen pointer itself indicates where the operator is on the screen at any time. In addition, the screen pointer may be changed from a simple arrow to a cursor, or a highlighted area, or anything else that the program needs in order to transmit information to the user. For instance, in some programs, after an icon or menu item has been selected, the computer may take some time to process the command – during that time, the pointer is often changed into an egg timer, which actually shows sand falling through from top to bottom to indicate that the user must wait.

Typical screen presentation

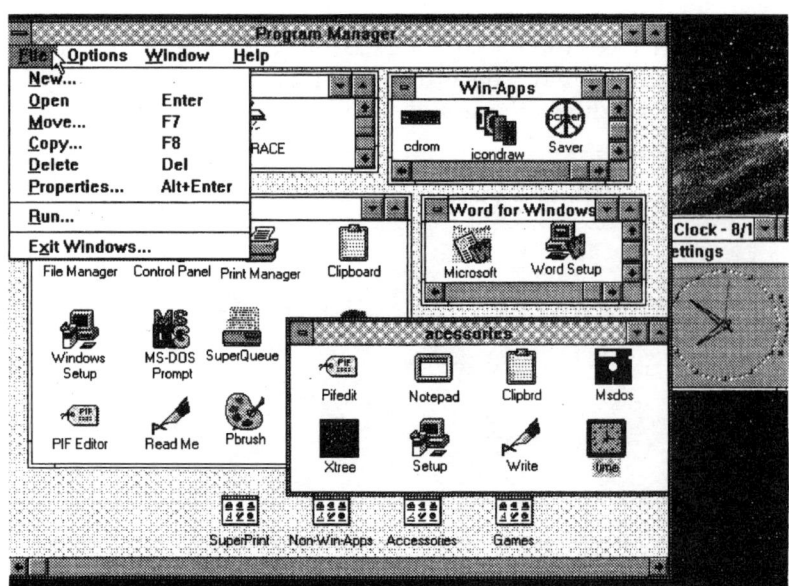

Figure 4.10 A typical screen

Figure 4.10 gives an example of a typical GUI screen presented by Microsoft Windows. Here, several windows are shown open, and in fact the appearance in this case is a little cluttered. It shows how information can be overlaid, tiling the complete screen, in a flexible manner as required. There is even a clock appearing at the far right-hand side, in the background. All the windows shown contain graphical icons which refer to programs. The pointer simply has to be moved over to one of them, and clicked to start the process of entering any of the programs shown. This might run in its own window, or take up the whole screen – the user usually has control over this. The tiles or windows are easily varied in size, and moved around at will.

The four headings **FILE**, **OPTIONS**, **WINDOW** and **HELP** are pull-down menu headings in a typical menu bar. In fact, you can see that the cursor, or pointer, is in the **FILE** heading, and the mouse clicked to pull it down. There are eight options, some of which will enter other menus of options, depending upon the task involved.

In many ways, as far as the user is concerned, this GUI is an example of a type of operating system (OS). It allows all the operations which we will see associated with typical OSs, when we look at them in Chapter 8.

However, GUIs are not just used as operating systems, or for controlling the way in which you run other programs and processes. Many modern programs are written in the GUI form, either to run in a windows environment of some kind, or to run in a stand-alone mode. The GUI is becoming the preferred method of VDU 'look' for user communication across the spectrum. A mouse and keyboard, if properly controlled by the software, can provide much faster communication than the traditional keyboard alone.

 The only way to learn to use a WIMP system is to sit in front of one and pick it up from the screen itself. You are strongly recommended to find one and have a go – this is the direction in which computing is heading, and much modern software development is involved with rewriting common applications to use a GUI presentation.

Chapter review
- Human input to a computer is most often by a keyboard.
- Mouse and other similar devices are used to point to and select specific regions on a VDU screen.
- Light pens are pointers which point directly to the screen surface.
- Graphics tablets and digitizers allow a menu of commands to be selected from a table surface, and allow drawings to be digitized.
- Touch screens allow the finger to be used as a pointer device.

► **Now that you have completed this chapter, look back to the objectives at the beginning and check that you have accomplished each of them.**

- Dedicated interfaces allow data to be input from and output to the real world.
- Continuously varying values can be controlled via A/D and D/A converters.
- VDUs display computer output on a screen surface.
- VDU characters and graphic patterns are normally made up from pixels – small dots, or picture elements.
- Printers can also make up output from a matrix of dots.
- Impact dot matrix printers print the dots by impact against a ribbon.
- Inkjet printers spray dots of ink onto the paper.
- Laser printers have the highest resolution.
- Plotters produce draughted material using pens.
- GUI – graphical user interface – is a graphical method of presenting human–computer communications.
- WIMP – Windows, Icons, Menus, Pointers – describes a particular type of GUI for selecting commands and controlling software.

Computer applications packages

Chapter objectives

By the time you have read this chapter, you will understand:

■ how the 'front end', or human interface, of modern packages looks

■ wordprocessing (WP) systems, and how they are used

■ how text is input, edited, filed and printed

■ the way in which numerical information is presented in a spreadsheet

■ how mathematical modelling is performed

■ the meaning of 'business graphics'

■ desk-top publishing (DTP) programs, and how they are used

■ the meaning of a database, and how database programs are used

■ the storage of data on a database – its structure

■ how a database is manipulated and queried

■ flat-file and relational databases

■ sorting and indexing data

■ how drawing packages work, and how to present graphical data

■ the meaning of computer-aided design (CAD)

■ how business accounts can be performed on computer

■ techniques for backing up data

■ the following key words: WP, DTP, business graphics, clip art, WYSIWYG, integrated, front end, command line, GUI, help, word-wrap, justified, ragged, proportional spacing, portrait, landscape, spreadsheet, cell, SUM, modelling, cash flow, procedural, database, file, record, field, flat file, relational database, sort, index, SQL, CAD, wire frame, preview, autodimensioning, CADCAM, finite element analysis, NC machine, BIT image, vector, accounts, ledger, data backup.

POPULAR APPLICATIONS

It is crucial that you understand the main applications for which personal computers are used. However, you should also know that

► This chapter covers wordprocessing, desk-top publishing, spreadsheets, databases, drawing and design programs and computer-aided manufacturing and accounts packages. As you look at the applications below, you should be aware all the time that the computer is being used to acquire, store, manipulate and present information.

the only way in which you will be able to pick up these applications is by using them for yourself. This chapter will give you a flavour of the different applications, and perhaps show you what to look for, but you must try the programs out for yourself, preferably with your own personal applications.

FRONT-END PROCESSING

▶ Front-end presentation: the interface between user and machine. The two main types are:
• command-line processing
• graphical user interface (GUI).

In Chapter 4 we looked at the concept of 'front-end' presentation – the term used to describe how the screen, keyboard, mouse, etc. – are used and laid out. You will know that there are broadly two types of interaction method available on personal computers. The original method uses basic commands remembered and typed in by hand at a command line with a cursor. This is called 'command-line processing'. The more modern method is called a GUI and uses a WIMP presentation.

All of the types of package we will look at here can be purchased in either form at present – older programs will normally be in command-line processing form. However, most packages are moving quickly over to a WIMP-orientated form. In some cases this is an advantage, and in others it is of minimal use.

 Before reading on, look at a typical computer magazine, and list the different common types of software package you find there. For instance, 'wordprocessor' will be one of the first entries. You should be able to sort out the very common applications from other more specialized products by how widely each application is advertised by different software publishers.

Then make up a table with three columns headed:

Application	Information type	
	Main	Secondary

In the first column write down a vertical list of the applications you identified from your search of magazines, leaving plenty of space between each one. Then as you read through the remainder of the chapter use the second column to write down the main type of information with which the application is concerned (e.g. 'text', 'graphics', etc.). In the last column write down the secondary information types. You should keep this table by you during your studies, and add to it as you find more applications, and more information about the ones mentioned above. As time goes on, try to define the information types more and more closely. For instance, as you find out more about CAD programs, rather than simply writing 'graphics' next to them, define the types of graphics more closely.

WORDPROCESSING

Given that the word 'computer' to most people means a screen and a typewriter keyboard, it is fair to say that wordprocessing is probably the most natural application possible for the machine. The operator sits at the screen, typing in letters and words, and they appear, as if on an ordinary piece of paper, on the VDU. Also, almost every on-line application of a computer system has an element of wordprocessing in it. For instance, when typing commands into the operating system, the system is processing the characters you are typing in at the command line. It even allows you a measure of the flexibility which a wordprocessor (WP) will allow. For instance, having typed in a command, you have the opportunity to go back and correct it using common wordprocessing techniques.

Before using a WP program, it is necessary for the operator to know a number of important commands. For instance, how to start the program, how to interpret the command information which appears on the average WP screen, how to start and end a session, how to store, retrieve, edit and print the text. If a GUI is being used, starting the program is simply a matter of clicking on the WP's icon, or in some way choosing the program from a menu. Otherwise, the name of the program will need to be typed in at the command line, and this will act as a command to start the program running.

Once the program is running, a non-GUI screen might look something like Figure 5.1.

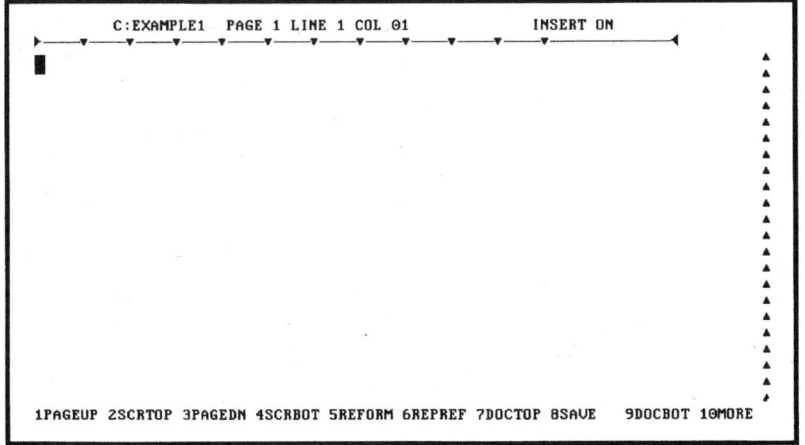

Figure 5.1 Screen layout for command-line wordprocessing

Most WP screens have information around the text area which reminds the user of available commands, and also provides some of the parameters of the text area itself. All WP screens are different, but Figure 5.1 shows some common basic elements.

In this example the text area is a large blank area, bounded top and bottom with lines of information. The top line contains the

► Text area surrounded by margins containing information.

▶ Ruler for setting **TAB** positions.

▶ Function keys: **F1**, **F2**, etc.

▶ Screen size.

▶ Some wordprocessing programs give a display which is WYSIWYG – what you see is what you get – meaning that what appears on the screen is laid out as it will be when printed. Few wordprocessing programs are entirely WYSIWYG, and this is a major difference between them and desk-top publishing programs.

name of the document being wordprocessed (EXAMPLE1), preceded by the label of the disk drive on which that document resides (C). Next comes the current page number (1), then the position of the cursor, and hence where the next letter typed at the keyboard will appear – here, the cursor is sitting at the top (LINE 1) of a blank document, and is in the extreme left-hand column (COL 1). Finally, on the top line of the screen, there is an indication that the processor is in **INSERT** mode. That is, if the cursor were sitting on a given character (letter, number, punctuation mark, etc.), typing will insert characters, and push existing text away to the right, without over-writing it. The mode can be changed to over-write if necessary.

The next line shows the 'ruler' giving positions of the 'tabs'. When the **TAB** key is pressed on the keyboard, the cursor moves over to the next tab position, just like a typewriter. These positions can be selected and moved. Below the ruler is the cursor, shown here as a black rectangle. As characters are typed in, the cursor moves to indicate where the user is in the document, and hence where the next key pressing will appear. The user has control over the cursor position using 'arrow' keys on the keyboard, and perhaps a mouse. The cursor can be moved anywhere, and hence text can be added to any part of the document.

The bottom line of the screen, here, shows some commands – many more may be shown in reality, but this is an example of some basics. It suggests that pressing function key number 1 (called **F1**), will move the whole display up one page – assuming there is a page above the one shown (not the case here). **F2** will move the cursor to the top of the screen, **F3** will move down a page and **F4** moves the cursor to the screen bottom, and so on. In fact these commands are already available as standard labelled keys on most keyboards (**PG DN**, **PG UP**, etc.) and thus the function keys shown (**F1**, **F2**, etc.) might well be devoted to a more useful set of commands in reality. Again, this choice is often given to the user when setting up the WP program.

As you can see, three of the (usually) twenty-five lines on the screen are taken up with command information, and in general this is a minimum amount of data on a typical WP screen. Often, many more lines than this are devoted to command information, and in fact it can intrude considerably into the available screen space in some WP programs. Usually, you have the option to choose how much information is available on the actual screen. At the start, when you are learning the program, it is useful to have up to a third of the screen devoted to reminding you of the many commands which you will need as you use the program. When the commands have become familiar, and automatic, you can dispense with this 'help' information, and free up more of the screen to display more of your text.

Typical characteristics of WP programs

The most important thing to remember when using a WP is that you simply type the words of the text in a continuous line, and let the program arrange the text on the line in the best way possible. Each time you press the **RETURN** (or **ENTER**) key on the keyboard, the cursor terminates the current line of typing, and moves to the next line. However, if you simply type continuously, the program adds spaces, and arranges as many words as possible on the line, without cutting words off at the end – unless you specifically ask for hyphenation. Either way, it is important to give the program the job of arranging the layout of the text as you type. This has two functions, and provides the most important difference between a WP and a typewriter.

First, you can go back and edit and correct the text before printing, and the lines of words rearrange themselves as you edit. Second, you are not bound by fixed word-positions on the page. As you edit the text, the WP rearranges in an active manner, always producing the neatest and most compact form for the text.

This active arrangement of the text is called 'word-wrap', and is a major feature of any WP program.

▶ Word-wrap.

In general, when you enter a new WP program, and are faced with a blank sheet of 'paper', you can usually simply type in a continuous line, and the program will automatically word-wrap. Often, the problem is what to do next. Not all WP programs are very forthcoming about the exact form of the commands which are available. It may even not be immediately possible to see how to exit the program! In general, you should become familiar with the program before entering it, either by looking at the manual, or finding out how to call up 'help' information before going ahead.

Paragraphs are treated in various ways by WP programs. Naturally, you will not want the text of one paragraph to wrap into that of the ones nearby. It is important for the program to separate blocks of paragraph text from each other.

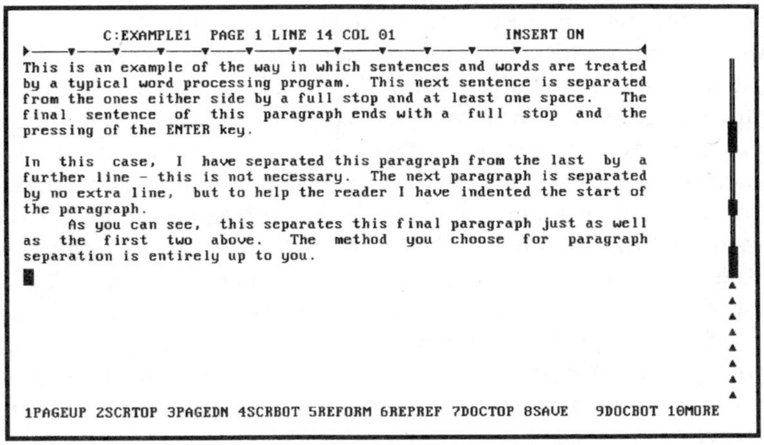

▶ Paragraphs.

```
        C:EXAMPLE1  PAGE 1 LINE 14 COL 01              INSERT ON
▶──────▼────────▼────────▼────────▼────────▼────────▼────────▼──────◀
This is an example of the way in which sentences and words are treated
by a typical word processing program.  This next sentence is separated
from the ones either side by a full stop and at least one space.    The
final  sentence  of  this  paragraph ends with a  full  stop  and  the
pressing of the ENTER key.

In  this  case,  I  have separated this paragraph from the last  by   a
further line - this is not necessary.  The next paragraph is separated
by no extra line, but to help the reader I have indented the start of
the paragraph.
     As you can see,  this separates this final paragraph just as well
as  the  first  two  above.   The  method  you  choose  for  paragraph
separation is entirely up to you.
■




1PAGEUP 2SCRTOP 3PAGEDN 4SCRBOT 5REFORM 6REPREF 7DOCTOP 8SAVE   9DOCBOT 10MORE
```

Figure 5.2 Screen layout for command-line word-processing with text typed in

▶ Paragraphing: by **RETURN**, or by **INDENT**.

In Figure 5.2 some text has been added to the last example, showing two methods of separating paragraphs. The first two are separated by a blank line. This is achieved by pressing the **ENTER** key twice. The second and third paragraphs are not separated by a blank line, but by indenting instead.

Spaces and lines are the main separators in a wordprocessor. Full stops are not usually regarded as special in any way – they are just part of the words. It is important that you do not leave a space between a word and its punctuation mark, or the program may word-wrap the punctuation mark as if it were a separate word.

▶ Justifying: left, right, full and centre.

There are many different formats for text on a page. For instance, some people prefer to type fully 'justified' text, while others prefer 'ragged right'. Justified text is aligned to both left and right margins – like the text on this page. Ragged text has a ragged right-hand side, where not all words end at exactly the same column – like the marginal notes on this page. This latter is more akin to typewritten text. Either convention can be selected on most WP programs.

Editing the text is a crucial concept in wordprocessing. You have the facility to delete, alter and insert new text anywhere in the document. Normally, a document will be typed in fairly fast, and then re-read to make corrections. This is quite the opposite of typewriting, where accuracy during writing is important – even with correction mechanisms. It is not usually possible to move text aside on a typewritten page in order to insert or delete words or letters.

▶ A major difference between typewriting and wordprocessing is that in wordprocessing the actual production of the hard copy – the printed version – is the final act after fully preparing the document. It is almost an automatic afterthought.

Printing and filing

Two important functions of wordprocessing are storing of documents and printing. Storing is an integral part of the WP concept. After a document has been prepared, it should immediately be given a name and stored. Some WPs do not even allow printing until this storage function has been completed. This ensures that the document is not lost if there is a power or other computer failure. It is prudent, with important documents, to store a backup of the document on a separate floppy disk, as well as the internal hard disk of the machine. This further protects against hard-disk failure within the machine.

▶ Templates/form documents.

Storage is not just restricted to final completed documents. Partial documents can be stored, at any stage, to ensure that the work so far cannot be lost. Partial documents containing commonly repeated structures can also be stored – these are known as templates or form documents. For instance, if you always head your letters in a particular way, a part-complete document can be stored with this structure in it. This can be called up into the current document to form the basis of a new letter, without altering the part-complete version, which remains available for next time. Other applications of the same concept might include files of standard clauses used in legal documents, standard invoice patterns, standard paragraphs for technical manuals, frequently used introductions to reports, and so on. A given WP program may have special sophisticated ways of handling these standardized structures, but the concept is the same however it is handled.

Printing is a complex subject, and the one area where most people have trouble from time to time. There are so many different standards of printer in existence that setting up for general hard-copy production can be very involved. Most WPs have a long list of printer drivers which allow the user to personalize the output for a given printer. However, many new printers emulate other more popular models, and may well not appear in the WP's list of possible printers. This is a difficult area, and much experimentation is usually needed. However, it is fair to say that printers are gradually becoming more and more standardized. Most standard text printing can now be performed correctly, but graphic printing can be more problematic.

► Printer set-ups.

Before printing a document, attributes such as the correct size of top, bottom and side margins must be set up, page numbers have to be set, and so on. If the text is to be printed fully justified, it may use a system called 'proportional spacing'. This allows a finely adjustable and balanced variable spacing between words on a line to ensure that the complete line takes up just the width of the page. Less sophisticated programs insert whole numbers of ordinary spaces to achieve the end width, and the result is less attractive.

► Proportional spacing.

Even properly set up documents may not print properly on some printers which cut off print too close to a given margin, or add their own marginal spacing on top of the WP command. It is important to experiment and ensure that the printer set-up commands of the WP do what they are supposed to do.

Modern WP programs also allow the text to be printed in two formats, called 'portrait' and 'landscape'. The normal method of printing a letter, for instance, is in portrait form, that is, a rectangular piece of paper is arranged with the long sides vertically down the page, and the shorter sides across the top and bottom, as in a typical portrait painting. Text is typed across the sheet, from left to right, and down the page in lines, parallel to the shorter top and bottom sides.

► Printing in portrait and landscape.

Landscape form turns the sheet of paper through ninety degrees, that is, it arranges the paper with the longer side at top and bottom, as in most landscape paintings. Text is formed across the (now wider) sheet, and in lines down the (shorter) sheet. This gives horizontal lines of text which are much longer, but there are fewer lines. This format is useful for some types of information sheet which are to be folded in the middle, and thus turned, effectively, into four sides of smaller paper in a folded-over brochure form. Landscape is also very useful indeed for spreadsheets where long horizontal lines of data can be presented on normal-sized paper. A cash flow, for instance, might be able to present enough columns to show monthly figures for two years when printed in landscape format, but less than a year in portrait.

The choice of portrait or landscape might also be able to be made by the printer itself. Some printers allow the pressing of a few buttons on their front panel to cause the text to be printed in landscape, instead of the more usual portrait format.

► Footers and headers.

► Embedded commands.

► Block, cut and paste, change font.

► Spell checks.

► Optical character recognition (OCR) allows handwriting to be transformed into wordprocessor text.

Most WPs allow for a repeated heading on each page – such as the title of a book or report – and a 'footer', which is repeated at the foot of the page, perhaps incorporating an incrementing page number. There is usually a considerable amount of flexibility in these functions. For instance, headers can alternate from left to right for even and odd pages, and so on.

In GUI-type WP programs, there is usually a pull-down menu which allows you to choose all the parameters of the print. Non-GUI programs often rely on special command characters stored within the text itself to command the printer during the printing process.

Block and overall functions

Most WPs allow for the whole document to be searched for a given text occurrence, and even for automatic, or manual, change to each occurrence if desired. Also, a block of text can be selected, usually indicated by highlighting it in some way by perhaps reversing black and white, or by colouring. The selected block can then be acted upon by block functions. For instance, it could be deleted, moved or copied to another part of the text, or it could be italicized, emboldened or underlined, and so on. In a GUI-based WP, the mouse would be used to drag the screen pointer over the block in order to highlight it. This is a quick and visual use of a mouse in a WP. The mouse would then be used to select the appropriate action from a menu.

Other overall functions include searching for spelling and even, in some WPs, grammatical errors. These can be corrected automatically, but usually it is prudent to watch very carefully what the machine is doing to your text. These functions are by no means foolproof, and may add many more errors than they try to correct. They can be useful to indicate where special care is required within the text, but the user should perform the actual change.

Often a complete document can be changed in some way by an overall function. For instance, the typeface might need changing, or the size of the type, the means of separating paragraphs, the line spacing, and so on.

The future for wordprocessing

You may be forgiven for considering that this well-established program is incapable of much further evolution. This is not true. Apart from the obvious moves towards more DTP-type functions, and more GUI functions, there are moves to make wordprocessing intelligent.

Machines have been produced which allow the user to write in words using a pen-like stylus directly onto a screen. This is not normally a VDU screen and light-pen, but rather a notepad-sized sensitive LCD screen. The machine puts up a pattern of icons which can be chosen by pressing the pen onto them, but also leaves a large area of blank screen where anything can be drawn or written. The drawings and general notes can be stored as they are, without intelligent processing, just like leaves of a paper pad. Alternatively, the text part can be converted from freehand characters to an actual document of characters in ASCII, or whatever. The document can then be wordprocessed, or stored and printed. It should also be able to be modified by pen.

The concept involved here is that of character recognition, and is the same as the concept used for optical character recognition introduced when we looked at scanners in a previous chapter. However, this is more sophisticated as it acts on general handwriting – a considerably more difficult problem. Most people have trouble reading other people's handwriting, and the problem is not fully solved yet. However, these new machines can make a reasonable job of the recognition, and with a little correction can increase the efficiency of the human–machine interface.

The Macintosh machines have always been able to integrate many applications together, which means that output from one type of application can be incorporated into another. For instance, a spreadsheet can be used to put together a complex grid of numerical information, and this table might be needed in a piece of text for a report, for instance. Non-Macintosh WPs are becoming more able to take data from other applications to allow mixes of data types, just as we do naturally ourselves as we are writing certain types of document.

▶ Integrating wordprocessing with other facilities.

As WPs become more and more sophisticated, it is hoped that the interface to the user will improve. This can be quite daunting for a new user. The commands are not always natural, and even using a GUI can be confusing, especially as there has been little standardization in GUI presentations, other than, perhaps, within Microsoft's Windows program.

Points to look for in a wordprocessor
- Ease of use of the commands – is there plenty of help information?
- Lots of space on the screen – is it possible to clear the screen of command information once you are used to the package?
- What is the largest document which can be written – would you have to split your definitive novel into bits?
- How far is the display WYSIWYG? Is it only WYSIWYG for one size of type, or does it show all types of all sizes correctly laid out on the screen?
- Are there DTP facilities, including clip art (if you need these in your applications)?
- Can it import text from other wordprocessors?
- Can it fully integrate with a spreadsheet, or other package.
- How comprehensive are the printer drivers?
- Does it use colour and WIMPs? – not essential in a WP, but you should be aware of this point.

- Can it run stand-alone, or do you need to run it under another front-end processor such as Windows?

These are the basics, but there are many more facilities offered by modern programs, as you will see when you start looking.

 Using computer magazines or catalogues, make a provisional selection of two wordprocessing packages. Then divide a piece of paper into two columns, one for each package. List the given attributes for each package in the columns. Use the list of points in the inset to decide which is the superior package.

SPREADSHEETS

► Spreadsheets:
• present numerical information visually
• provide answers to 'what if' questions.

There are two crucial concepts which make spreadsheets important. The first is the simplification which they bring to the job of dealing with numerical information by treating numbers visually. The second is the concept of 'what if?' which allows the user to use trial-and-error techniques to solve a problem. These two concepts will become clear to you as we look at how spreadsheets work. We will not be looking at a specific product, but rather common generic facilities which are offered.

► Spreadsheets are either command-line or GUI presentations.

As always, there are two modes for screen presentation – GUI and purely keyboard command. In many ways, a mouse is less useful in a spreadsheet – it is irritating to be taking your fingers from the keyboard all the time to move pointers around. In using a spreadsheet, you will normally be entering text, numbers and formulae, through the keyboard, and moving around the sheet to change and view various parts as you go. This is efficiently achieved using a few simple keyboard commands.

The main part of a spreadsheet's screen is a large blank area which is split into rows and columns. At each row and column meeting, there is a 'cell'. These are not usually boxed as such on the screen, but each is labelled by the row and column grid, in the same way as we saw in Chapter 3 for memory locations. There will be a cursor on the screen, very much as with a WP program, and using the keyboard arrow keys, or perhaps the mouse, you can move the cursor to any cell, and type in information.

► Cells.

These cells are regarded simply as memory locations containing a number, formula or a piece of text. The text is used in the sheet for comments and headings – only the most rudimentary wordprocessing facilities are usually provided for text input as the spreadsheet is much more concerned with numbers and numerical values.

The power of the spreadsheet comes from the ability to store and evaluate formulae within each cell, whose variables depend upon the values stored in other cells. You can think of the cells as numeric-valued formulae. For instance, if you have a set of numbers to add up, simply type them into a set of cells, vertically or horizontally, and then put the **SUM** formula for that program at the end – the spreadsheet will automatically add these numbers up, and present the total to you in the 'sum' cell. For a column, this would look something like the following:

	A	B	C	D
1				
2		23.98		
3		128		
4		15		
5		16.88		
6		11.768		
7		2		
8				
9	sum equals: 197.628			
10				
11				
12				

Here, the columns are labelled with letters, starting at 'A', and the rows are labelled with numbers starting at '1'. Thus the cell labelled B2 contains the number 23.98, and so on. The cell labelled A9 contains text which is used to make the sheet understandable to the viewer – it is a comment. In cell B9 we have stored the formula 'the sum of cells B2 to B7'. There will be a simple convention for writing this considerably more simply into B9 – it might be, for instance:

SUM(B2:B7)

In formal terms, this particular SUM function is used to add a set of numbers, and in this package must have a pair of round brackets containing two cell labels separated by a colon.

It is important when communicating with a computer to be quite accurate about the characters used. This is true in all commands and programming statements in general. The use of the **SUM** function here is, effectively, a programming statement. It takes in a set of data, performs an instruction and produces some output. This is a useful rough-and-ready definition of programming.

In the spreadsheet example above, the **SUM** formula is not seen – only the result. However, it is usually possible to display all the formulae on the sheet by issuing the appropriate command at the keyboard – this is a common facility for spreadsheets.

► Using formulae in a spreadsheet.

The above example illustrates the ease with which numbers can be displayed and manipulated by a spreadsheet – which was the first concept mentioned. The second (i.e. What if?) is illustrated simply by realizing that if you now move the cursor to one of the number-occupied cells and change its contents, the **SUM** will also change to accommodate the new set of numbers. The **SUM** in B9 is a continuously updated addition, which will change automatically if numbers are added, deleted or changed. If you want to know something like: 'What if I add the number 66.882 to the list?' – this spreadsheet will provide an instant answer.

► 'What if' questions.

But how can numbers be added? Surely this will increase the length of the column of six numbers, and the **SUM** will then be

► Unless you decide otherwise, the spreadsheet recalculates every time you alter the data.

dealing with more numbers than can be found between the cells mentioned in its round brackets?

It is always possible to add new rows to a spreadsheet, anywhere, and that is how spaces are formed to contain new numbers. For instance, to add a seventh number to the column, between the numbers 128 and 15 (i.e. between B3 and B4), first a command must be issued to insert a new row between 128 and 15. This gives the following:

	A	B
1		
2		23.98
3		128
4		
5		15
6		16.88
7		11.768
8		2
9		
10	sum equals:	197.628

Notice that the **SUM** in B10 has remained the same, despite now ranging over seven cells from B2 to B8 instead of B2 to B7. This is because the cells referred to in the **SUM** function have been automatically adjusted for the new space – if you look at cell B10, it will now contain the formula:

SUM(B2:B8)

This is an example of the intelligent assistance which a spreadsheet should give you continuously. The better the spreadsheet, the more help it gives – though the above example is the minimum you should expect. Now 66.882, or any other number, can be typed into the new B4 cell, and the **SUM** will update as you do it, so the new total in B10 will be 264.51.

It is possible to turn off the automatic calculation update on most spreadsheets. Sometimes, in a very large sheet, it takes a long time to perform the total recalculation which is needed. The full recalculation can be performed at any time chosen by the user when all the amendments have been made. However, we will assume here that our spreadsheet is set for automatic recalculation.

There are many more facilities available than are shown above. Many more functions than **SUM** can be used – there are usually all the scientific functions such as trigonometrical, statistical and financial formulae, and so on. It is also possible to erase, copy and move whole blocks of the sheet, and **SUM**, for instance, can add numbers in a block of rows and columns, rather than just a simple line of values.

Many spreadsheets will allow you to specify a range of cells containing numbers and formulae and present these values on a graph of various kinds, including line graphs, histograms, pie charts, and

► Graphs.

so on. This is usually available in full colour too to help further in the visualization of the numerical information.

You can usually move the cursor around the spreadsheet from cell to cell, or page to page, and move to the start or end of the sheet by a single command. Also, a lot of information is usually presented around the edge of the screen to help you while using the sheet. For instance, the current cell label is displayed, along with the contents of that cell as a formula. The amount of memory available is often shown, as well as a large amount of other status and help information, depending upon the particular spreadsheet product you are using.

Sometimes, you do need to use a spreadsheet simply to add sets of numbers together, but this is a rather simple exercise, and a calculator might be more appropriate in many instances. The main use of a spreadsheet is in 'modelling'. That is, putting together a network of numerical information as an analogy, or model, of a given situation.

For instance, if you wish to start a business, and borrow money from a bank to start up, the bank will normally ask you for a model of the first couple of years of the running of the business – they call it a 'business plan' or a 'cash-flow forecast'. The main idea is to model in a visual form the evolution of the financial side of the business as closely as possible. The format must be chosen to be clear and explanatory, so that the viewer can understand enough to be able to assess the accuracy of the assumptions which go into it, as well as the outcomes. Much of the expertise in using a modelling package such as a spreadsheet is in learning how to set up sheets clearly to resemble a given situation and system. This is also part of the skill of 'systems analysis'.

Another example of mathematical modelling would be, for instance, in mechanical engineering, where stresses and strains must be calculated for a variety of different situations. The stress-and-strain formulae can be stored in cells of the spreadsheet, depending upon input data stored in other cells. As that data is changed, you will be able to see the output numbers changing, and use it to make a decision as to the design of a mechanical system.

The list of applications for a spreadsheet is enormous, and spans right across industry, science, commerce, and so on. We will now look at perhaps the most common application – the cash flow forecast. There are no set rules for constructing such spreadsheets, but anyone who has had to set one up by hand will appreciate the ease with which it can be done using the machine. The following has many things in common with most cash flows which you will meet.

An example of numerical modelling with a spreadsheet

Here, we will consider six months in the running of a manufacturing business which has been in existence for long enough to know the basic parameters, and wishes to predict how cash flow will look over the next half year. The spreadsheet in Figure 5.3 is simplified to ensure that the main points survive, but would be more complex in a real-world situation.

	A	B	C	D	E	F	G
1	CASH FLOW OF A. N. OTHER AND SONS – 13TH JANUARY						
2		FEB	MAR	APR	MAY	JUN	JLY
3	INCOME (IN £K):						
4	INVOICES OUT	10.00	15.00	25.00	15.00		
5	WORK IN PROGRESS		15.00	35.00	50.00	25.00	5.00
6	ANTICIPATED WORK					10.00	30.00
7							
8	EXPENSES (IN £K):						
9	SALES COSTS	4.00	5.00	4.00	3.00	3.00	3.00
10	RAW MATERIALS	15.00	20.00	15.00	25.00	20.00	10.00
11	LABOUR COST	5.00	5.00	5.00	5.00	5.00	5.00
12	LOAN PAYMENTS	2.00	2.00	2.00	2.00	2.00	2.00
13	RENT	2.30	2.30	2.30	2.30	2.30	2.30
14	HEAT/LIGHT		2.40			3.00	
15	RATES & SUNDRIES	3.80	3.80	3.80	3.80	3.80	3.80
16	TELEPHONES		1.20			1.20	
17	SUNDRIES	2.80	2.80	2.80	2.80	2.80	2.80
18							
19	MONTHLY TOTAL	-24.90	-14.50	25.10	21.10	-8.10	6.10
20	ACCUMULATIVE TOTAL	-24.90	-39.40	-14.30	6.80	-1.30	4.80

Figure 5.3 Cash flow for A.N. Other & Sons

This cash flow might be designed by the owner of the business to present to a bank manager in order to show its short-term financing requirements.

 Before reading on, examine this spreadsheet, and try to answer the following questions about this six-month period:

1. What is the maximum overdraft required?

2. What is the total income from 'work in progress'?

3. Row 19's cells contain the difference between two **SUM**s – what is the definition of the two **SUM**s involved in C19?

4. What is the formula in D20?

5. Could a bank manager be expected to understand this spreadsheet without much more explanation?

This spreadsheet has been constructed from the knowledge and experience of the business. At the top there is some text to label the sheet and explain its purpose to all those who will use it. Then comes a row of shortened month headings, and the word 'income' followed by the financial units being used. This shows, as for 'expenses' further down, that all figures refer to thousands of pounds, to two decimal places.

Row 4 refers to invoices for work which has been completed, which have been sent out to the customers involved. The pay-back shown in that row would result from the business's knowledge of the time that their customers usually take to pay. The next row is for invoices which will be sent out as work is finished, and the following row is a prediction of the income from work which is expected, but has not yet been won. Naturally this latter is completely fictitious, but depends upon the business experience to date. A bank manager would consider this in the light of previous experience with this company.

Expenses are fairly straightforward, and vary according to the plans the business has, and these figures should be backed up with documentary evidence if needed. For instance, sales costs vary according to the planned marketing effort, and telephone and energy costs are levied quarterly.

The formulae employed in this spreadsheet are confined to the last two rows. All other numeric entries are 'numeric constants', input to reflect either known quantities, or historically estimated values.

The 'monthly total' row contains the sum of the income, less the sum of the expenses. The income in the column B would be defined by:

SUM(B4:B6)

In fact, this could also be written as B4+B5+B6. Spreadsheets allow mathematical formulae to be constructed with these usual arithmetic operators: +, −, * and /. The last two here are multiplication and division. Throughout computing, the multiply operation is usually designated by '*' to distinguish it from the letter 'x' which may be more familiar to you for multiplication.

▶ In computing: * means multiply; / means divide.

The expenses in column B would be calculated as:

SUM(B9:B17)

The final month's total of income less expenses would thus be:

SUM(B4:B6) – SUM(B9:B17)

This is the formula which would be typed into cell B19.

In general, the formula in a given cell can be almost any type of mathematical formula, depending upon the actual functions which are available with the package, and including any other cells whose value have been fixed before they are used. This means that if the sheet's calculation is performed row by row, from left to right, and down the sheet, it is important that no cell depends upon a formula using cells which are further along its row, or on rows further down, as they will not have had their values calculated yet. You can change the order of sheet's calculation to column by column instead of row by row if this helps in a given situation.

This point highlights the 'procedural' nature of a spreadsheet – it is running a program of numerical instructions all the time, and you should be aware of this while you use it.

The next cell along from B19, which is C19, has the formula:

SUM(C4:C6) – SUM(C9:C17)

This is simply adjusted to apply to the C column instead of the B column. In general, you do not have to type in every one of the formulae in row 19 – the sheet helps by allowing replication of the formula across the row, adjusting automatically. This is a very powerful command, and of great convenience in constructing even quite large spreadsheets at speed.

The final row of the sheet is the one which the bank manager would be most interested in – it is the infamous 'bottom line'. This line is constructed to show how much surplus or overdraft there is accumulating from month to month in an imaginary bank account. For instance, in February, there is a deficit of £24.9K. This deficit transfers to March, and adds to the £14.5K which is generated there. This makes a total accumulated debt of £39.4K – as you can see. This is then partly offset by a surplus of £25.1K in April, taking the debt down to only £14.3K in that month, and so on. The formula used in this bottom line simply reflects this common-sense view of the numbers. The first formula in B20 is simply a repeat of B19 – and this is the formula used. The next cell, C20 takes the value of B20, and adds in the March figure. Its formula is:

B20 + C19

The next cell, D20, just adjusts for the next columns, and is:

C20 + D19

and so on. Again, these do not have to be typed in repeatedly, a special replication command does it for you – though you have the option to prevent it from adjusting any or all the parts of any formula which is being copied to ensure that it does not hamper any special requirements you may have. The importance of all the commands is that they are flexible, but as helpful as possible.

The conclusion of the exercise would be that the business is healthy, but has a negative cash requirement of up to £40K – which would have to be covered by a short-term overdraft, or some other injection of temporary funds.

The business manager can change the spreadsheet around, play with the figures, try 'what if' questions on any of the figures, or even add lots more rows and columns at will. The automatic calculation will keep the sheet up to date throughout.

At the end of the procedure, the figures in any part of the sheet can be presented in a graphical manner, to make them stand out more easily, and then, in an integrated package, the data could be stored in a database for later use. However, storing them in the spreadsheet form is adequate for any further analysis which may be required.

As an example of a graphical form of presentation, Figure 5.4 shows a graphical presentation of the bottom line.

▶ Graphical presentation of output from spreadsheets.

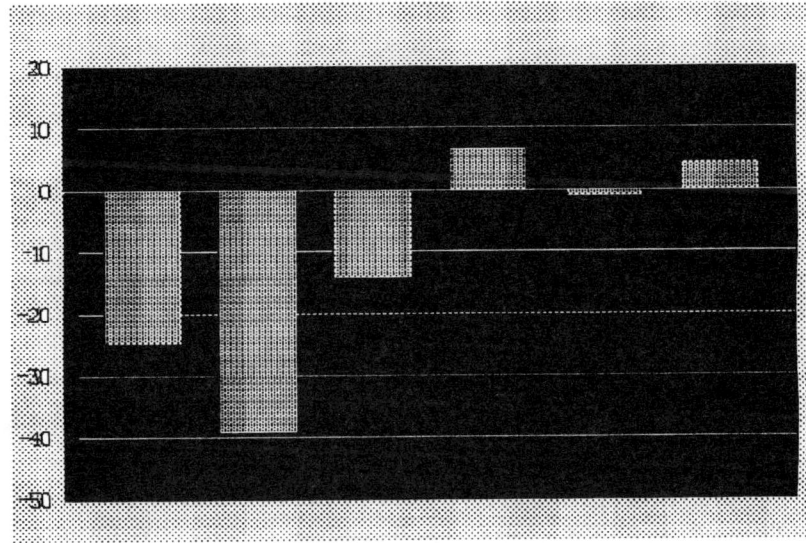

Figure 5.4 Graphical presentation of cash flow for A.N. Other & Sons – month-by-month deficit or surplus

Each of the six values in the bottom line is represented by a vertical bar, with negative quantities shown below, and positive above the 0 line. This shows clearly how the six months start off in heavy deficit, and then recover strongly.

More than one set of data can be shown on the same graph. Figure 5.5 shows block graphs of three sets of data, made up from rows 9 to 11 of the A.N. Other example. This compares costs of sales, raw materials and labour costs. It needs some further labelling to make it clearer, and the user would spend some time customizing this raw image.

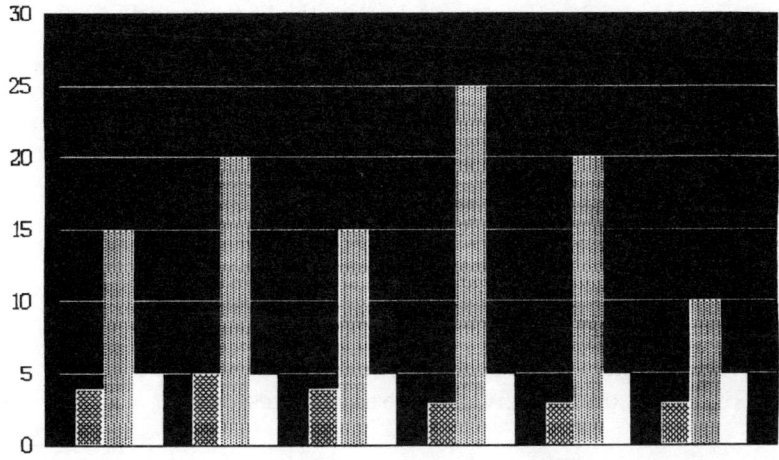

Figure 5.5 Graph displaying multiple data sets

There are various other graphical forms for data, such as pie charts, line graphs, scatter diagrams, and so on. It is possible to purchase separate graphics-presentation programs to perform this work, but a good spreadsheet, or integrated package, should supply this to a standard which will fit most needs.

The future for spreadsheets

In some ways the spreadsheet has reached a sort of zenith. Sophisticated packages can show 3-D graphical images of the data, and they can have high-level languages which allow the user to build complete programs of commands using the basic spreadsheet to supply all the numerical manipulation functions. Such programs are generally called 'macros'. In their basic form they are just lists of keystrokes which can be written down and executed later within the spreadsheet, as if the user were typing them in again.

The future for spreadsheets is probably to be found more in their application to different levels of machines. Historically, the programmable calculator allowed, say, scientists to have personalized basic calculation routines to be stored for their own use, displaying the output on the calculator screen. It is more and more likely that such an application will now be stored on an electronic personal organizer having its own simple spreadsheet program. This gives a much more visual effect, and is more easily programmed than the early programmable calculators, which used a complex and abstruse programming method only capable of display on a very simple screen.

Points to look for in a spreadsheet
- What is the largest sheet you can have, with the amount of memory available in your machine?
- Is all the status and help information useful and clear?
- Does it use colour? This can be very helpful, though not essential in a spreadsheet.
- Does it have a full range of scientific and business functions and commands?
- Does it have a good macro facility to allow you to write programs using the spreadsheet as the background?
- Are the graphics-presentation facilities good, and easy to use?
- Can you have more than one window into the spreadsheet open at once? This allows you to view two or more parts of a large sheet at the same time, and watch the effect in one area of making changes somewhere else.
- How easily and naturally does it handle text, including tabular information? Spreadsheets can be very useful for constructing tables – and not just of numerical information.
- As with the wordprocessor, you should check whether it only runs under a given front-end processor.

Using computer magazines or catalogues, make a provisional choice of two spreadsheet packages. Draw up a list of points in two columns, one for each package, and then use the list of points in the box above to decide which is the better package.

DESK-TOP PUBLISHING (DTP)

There are many types of DTP program on the market, and the cost of these packages varies considerably, though the facilities available are becoming more and more standard. The essence of DTP is the freedom to choose to display, and print, text in many different character fonts and sizes, mix in graphical images, and arrange the text on the paper in any way you like. A typical newspaper sheet is illustrative of the many different types of image which must be capable of being produced by the package. There will be many different types of character, many different sizes, boxes containing photographs, other boxes containing adverts, and so on. It should be possible to take a headline, play around with the size and type, and in this manner arrive at just the look you require.

▶ DTP gives the freedom to display and print text in many different character fonts and sizes, mix in graphical images and arrange the text on the paper in any way you like.

Another important attribute is to be able to take straight text from a WP program, and import it into the DTP package for manipulation into the form required. This type of integration is usually possible via the ASCII code. The WP text is converted to a simple list of ASCII codes, upon which all packages agree, and this is taken into the DTP package for its use.

▶ From WP to DTP via ASCII.

Given the very visual nature of DTP, a GUI presentation is almost mandatory. Picking up a graphical object, and dropping it in the appropriate place would be considerably more difficult using, say, arrow keys and keyboard commands. It is much quicker to move the pointer over to the object, 'click' on it, move the pointer over to the new place with the object following it, and then 'click' it in place. This operation is called 'dragging'. There are many different options for manipulating and originating text and graphics, and selecting these is straightforward with pull-down menus, etc.

▶ Older DTP packages used command-line processing and were not easy to use.

Figure 5.6 (on the next page), although rather contrived, is an example of the varied way in which text and graphics can be mixed on a DTP sheet. It shows how text can be placed anywhere, in any style and size, and mixed with any available graphics. Much more than is shown here can be achieved with DTP; and any newspaper, magazine or presentation graphics would prove a good example of what can be achieved. To illustrate the link between WP and DTP further, this particular example was constructed using a program which calls itself a wordprocessor, but clearly has many, if not all, of the facilities of a full DTP package, including a library of clip art.

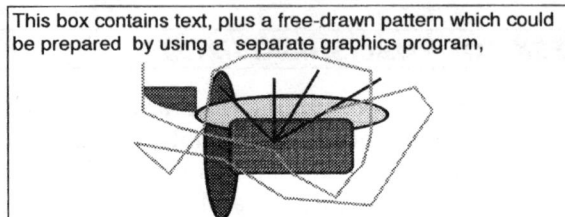

Volume 1 No. 1

Text can be confined to any size of box, with or without a border, and then moved around the paper surface using a pointer device. Objects can be added anywhere, either free-drawn, or taken from a library of clip art.

This box contains text, plus a free-drawn pattern which could be prepared by using a separate graphics program,

or the drawing facilities of the package. It is included in this box, to illustrate the mixing of text and graphics.

Figure 5.6 Hard copy from desktop publishing

This van is a piece of clip art which has been imported into the sheet - it could have been scanned from a photograph.

The point is that *text and graphics* can be mixed in any way, *and moved around* to produce any effect required. *There are usually many different type faces available,* and any size of text is allowed.

Points to look for in a DTP program

- It must be easy to start up and begin producing text and graphics.
- It should have a natural easy-to-use GUI interface.
- There should be plenty of type fonts, and clip-art pictures.
- Importing text and graphics must be easy and comprehensive.
- Free-drawing should be included, for your own special effects.
- The package should use the mouse and pull-down menus to the full.
- It should allow fairly normal wordprocessing in its basic form, and then allow this text to be treated in a full DTP manner.
- A large range of printers should be supported, as well as general output to disk for conversion by a bureau to film for professional printing.

Using computer magazines or catalogues, select two DTP packages, with a view to using them in a particular way: for example, printing pamphlets for a small association, or producing high quality camera-ready copy for a large company brochure. Draw up a list of attributes in two columns, one for each package. Then use the points listed in the box above to decide which is the better package for your purpose.

DATABASE PROGRAMS

A database is simply a collection of data. A telephone directory is a database of subscribers to the telephone network, a dictionary is a database of words and their meanings, and so on. In computing, the words 'database' (DB) sometimes refer to the actual store of data itself, as in these examples, and sometimes to the program which manipulates them – you will have to rely on the context to sort this out in general. However, we will be precise below, and use the words 'database' for a store of data, and 'DB program' for the program which does the manipulation work.

▶ Database – the data; database program (DBP) – the software that manipulates the data.

There are two levels of use of a DB program. First, it can be used as an immediate store of data, which can be viewed, added to, edited and manipulated directly from the screen, using immediate commands. This might be appropriate for a store of your contacts' names, addresses, telephone numbers, and so on. You use the immediate facilities of the DB program via its command system.

Second, the DB program is used as the basis for another program – written in a special programming language which is included with sophisticated database packages. This is usually a high-level language, which means that it is close to English, and easy to use and understand. Using this language, a program may be written to hold, manipulate and present data, perhaps in an industrial setting. A database of customized files is constructed for the application, and the program written to allow the final user to use the data in his or her own application. For instance, a library would hold data on books, members, due dates, and so on. The librarian may need to find out whether a given book is in stock. A special program would have been written to keep the files up to date, and allow the librarian to interrogate the database in a given manner. Operation must be simple, and not require any detailed knowledge of how DB programs work.

The simpler DB programs do not come with an associated programming language. You must choose a DB program to suit its eventual use. For instance, the secretary of a small club might want to keep a list of members' details, including their particular interests. It is probably not necessary to ask complex questions of this database; it is the holding of information in an easily accessible form which is crucial. This would use the simplest and cheapest type of DB program without any problems. An advantage of such programs is that they are considerably less complex to use than larger more sophisticated types.

Database structure

There are many different computer database products on the market, but their database files generally have certain common characteristics. A database is a file of 'records', each record containing one or more 'fields'. You can think of a database as a vertical collection of horizontal lines of data. Each horizontal line of data is a record which is split into fields, for example:

FIELD 1	FIELD 2
RECORD 1: P.J. Splash	32 Green Avenue, Taunton, Devon DD1 5ST
RECORD 2: K. Harcourt	156 Rose Road, Tring, Herts RR11 5DT
RECORD 3: etc.	

▶ Records contain fields by which the records are cross-classified.

As you can see, this is a database of names and addresses. Each record contains just two fields – the first field contains a name, and the second contains the address. In order to search for someone's address, the computer would simply look at the first field in each record, starting at the top, and compare this with the name being sought. When it finds the name, the second field of that record would be fetched, which is the address required.

This is probably similar to the way in which you would do the job yourself, except that if you were storing the data on file-cards, for instance, you would probably store it more 'intelligently' so that you could retrieve the data more easily. You would, presumably, store the data alphabetically, for instance, and then use this ordering of the data to help you find the target record more quickly.

Humans can 'flick' through cards and files easily, looking for the alphabetic area of the name, viewing the whole name 'by eye', extracting the surname part automatically, until the right one is found, and so on. Humans can even allow for spelling mistakes, changes of case (capitals or small letters), etc. Computers, however, have to be painstakingly programmed to perform this type of activity, and in fact rarely exhibit this degree of intelligence. On the other hand, computers can perform the task many times faster. A computer can search a large unsorted database of names and addresses, and find the correct entry more quickly than a human can, even from a fully sorted filing system.

▶ Selecting fields for a database is a very skilled activity and relates closely to the reason for using the database.

In the database above, the initials of the people are stored at the beginning of the first field, and are included along with the surname in the same field. If people are to be identified primarily by surname, it might be worth storing surname in a separate field from the initials. The surname field can then be searched on its own.

Similarly, the whole address is stored in just one field. If the information is to be retrieved by postcode, say for a mail shot, it would be much easier to store the postcode in its own field, which could be searched without looking at all the other information on the file.

The crucial point to remember is that the method by which the data is to be retrieved from the database determines the structure of the fields in the record. In order to construct a database, you should know how it is to be used before starting.

Good DB programs will allow very sophisticated modifications to be performed on the structure if you need to extract data in some new way, but just imagine the irritation of having to extract all addresses, from the above database, with a postcode starting with, say, DD. The whole address field would have to be extracted, taken apart, and the contents of the field fully examined for the occurrence of 'DD'. This can be done by a method known as 'string manipulation', which means analysing and dealing with strings of general characters – which is what addresses are. However, this method would be confused by any part of the address containing DD. For instance, suppose a family had named their house 'MADDENING'. This would throw up a match, and would be included as a positive result in the search for DD in the address.

Of course, you can think of ways to resolve most of these problems, but why bother? Just make sure that the database is well-constructed from the start.

Dividing the records of a database into fields imposes an order on the data. For instance, here, you could allow one field for the house number, one for the street, one for the town, one for the county and one for the postcode. It would then be easy to find all people living in a given town, or street, and so on.

 Before reading on, note down the problems which might be met during data extraction arising from incorrect entry of data.

Data entry

The DB program helps you to store data in the database, and tries to make this as simple as possible. All you have to do, in fact, is to think of a name for the file you wish to create, think of the field types, and the machine will construct the database ready for you to type the data in directly. However, suppose that you spell the county of Oxfordshire as 'oxfordshire' or 'Ofordshire', accidentally – an extraction process seeking all addresses in Oxfordshire will fail to find them all. It would be looking for 'Oxfordshire', precisely.

This is the type of problem which you will encounter in all database applications – data verity is crucial. The machine cannot be expected to have any idea of what you meant to say – it only knows what you have typed in.

▶ Data verity: accurate input is necessary for accurate output.

 Your local public library, and perhaps your college library, will almost certainly have a database including details of its library stock which can be used by readers looking for   •

particular books. Next time you are in the library, use the database to see how it works. Take note particularly of the various different ways in which you might discover whether a particular book was held by the library. Then try to work out what fields are used on the records.

Flat files and relational databases

A flat-file DB program is one where database files are separate, and generally only one file can be open and used at the same time. A relational database is one where files can contain data fields whose contents are extracted from other files, and where more than one file can be open and in use at the same time.

For instance, in an accounts program several ledgers will be open at once, and a current profit and loss statement will be constructed from all these files – taking data from wherever it needs to find it. Similarly, in a library system, there might be a file of members, a file of books out, a file of books in stock, and a file of books on order. The program may wish to construct a new file using data from some or all of these files. An example might be a file of members, with a list of books they have on order, books they have out, and books in stock which are by the same author as the ones they have out at present. This would make use of several files at the same time. The next step might be to send a standard letter to each of the members, supplying them with this information.

These two examples relate to several files during their action, and in the second case a new file is being constructed which itself relates to several files.

In sophisticated systems, the relations between files are kept fully updated as new data is entered. For instance, the file of information to be sent out to library members could be kept up to date as books are taken out, returned, and new books arrive. These standard letters could go out once a month, and would be absolutely up to date when the librarian 'presses the button' to start the letter-writing process.

Relational databases are required in most applications other than very simple stores of straightforward data which will only be searched for simple information. For instance, a telephone directory is a flat file, even if it does need updating regularly. Similarly, the plethora of electronic personal organizers, which replace diaries, have a simple database function, which records information by date and time, and holds name, address and telephone number data. This is generally a simple flat-file application.

▶ Flat files in a database can usually only be opened one at a time, and hence entries have to be made separately for each file, and each file searched separately. In relational databases several files can be open at once, updated at once and searched at the same time.

 Think of a particular application for a database. It might be to keep the membership records of a club; it might be to keep records of the stamps in a stamp collection. Any example will do. What fields would you want to define for the database? Would you need a flat-file or a relational database for this purpose?

Programming languages for databases

In any general application where a database is maintained, the information may be needed in many different ways. It is not possible to standardize for database usage. For instance, a computer-parts retailer will need to seek a given spare part, check its price, find whether it is in stock, and where exactly it is in the warehouse. At the same time, if the part is sold, the retailer needs to keep a record of the fact that there is one less in stock, and note if it needs reordering. A record must also be made of the financial transaction. A doctor, on the other hand, needs a file of patients, their recent ailments, family history (cross-referenced, perhaps, to related ailments), hospital visits, last time a medical was performed, and so on. This is completely different from the 'sales- and stock-control' function of the computer-parts retailer.

How can such diverse applications be catered for by a single program? The answer is to include as many general methods of arranging and manipulating the data as possible, and then allow the users to write routines utilizing these high-level and sophisticated facilities for their own needs. This is not to suggest that a retailer, or doctor, i.e the end user, is only going to be able to use a database if he or she learns to program in the DB program's special language. Rather, it allows a computer specialist to purchase a suitable database product, and write the required program in a fully customized manner, with ease.

Some special applications already have commercial programs written for them, which can be purchased directly, and fitted to the actual site. For instance, there are commercial programs which can be bought for doctors' practices, for specialized retailers, for solicitors' offices, and so on. Sometimes these programs are constructed using a general programming language, but often they will use a DB program with its related programming language to construct the final applications program. There are many advantages to this, due to the large variety and richness of the functions and facilities already available in the DB program itself.

Using a typical database program

The way in which a DB program is used depends upon the front-end processor it presents to the world. As always, there are two styles – command-line processing, and graphics and WIMPs.

Either way, the first task is to decide what data is to be stored, how many different files are needed, and how the records within the files must be split up.

Bound up with a DB program is the issue of the way in which the screen is handled, both during data entry, and while the database is being used. Though the computer specialist will not mind how this is achieved, the eventual user of the database will want the simplest presentation possible. For instance, if names and addresses are to be entered and split into a number of fields as data is entered, a screen which has those fields clearly delineated would be useful. At the same time, the cursor on the screen should be confined to just those fields, and nowhere else, and characters typed in should be able to be edited before passing on to the next field, or record.

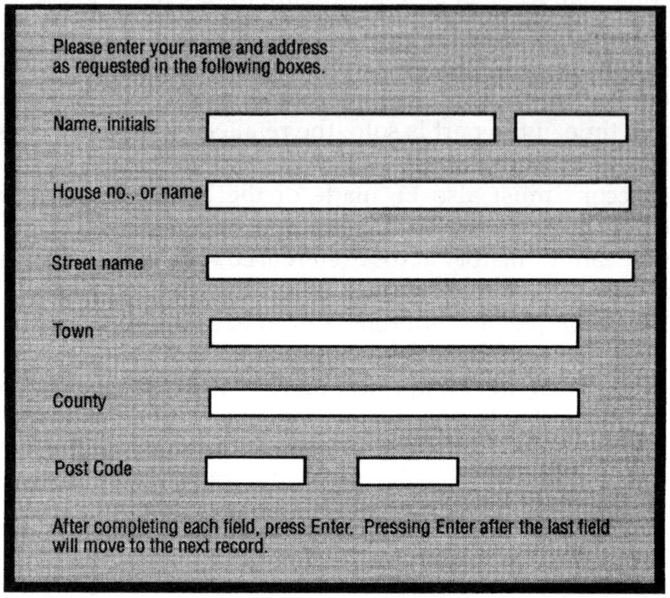

Figure 5.7 A typical data-entry screen display on a database

Figure 5.7 indicates a possible data-entry screen layout. It should be possible to construct this type of screen with ease, using the DB program's facilities. The fields are properly delineated, with details of what is to be entered, and there are other instructions to remind the user of what to do. Each time a field is filled with appropriate data, and **ENTER** is pressed, that data is stored in that field of the current record. At the end, the process repeats for the next record. There is just one thing missing – can you see what it is?

What's missing is that there is no apparent end to the process – how does the user exit this process, perhaps to pass to the next stage of the routine? This can be allowed for in various ways. For instance, pressing a control key on the keyboard might be used as an exit. If so, this should be included in a note on the screen.

These are all examples of familiar good practice and are attempts to make the process of interacting with the machine as painless and as foolproof as possible. This type of screen handling is usually well-catered for by modern databases, and some similar layout will be offered as part of the normal working of the DB program itself, in certain modern products. The principle is to make the handling of data as simple as possible.

Interrogating the database

All DB programs allow quite complex logical questions to be constructed to extract data. For instance, in extracting data from the name-and-address database, you may wish to find all people with addresses in Oxfordshire, but not with postcode starting with OX1.

We will suppose that the database fields are split up to contain the fields shown in Figure 5.7 – that is, eight separate fields. The county is separate, as is the first part of the postcode. This makes queries such as this very easy to apply.

In order to achieve the result, we must first open two files. The first is the name-and-address file itself, the second is a new one, with the same structure, but which will only contain the restricted information being sought.

A command is then issued to find all records where a condition such as the following is true:

County-field equals Oxfordshire, and first-part postcode not equal to OX1

This is called a 'Boolean condition' and, as the main file is searched from top to bottom, the two fields containing the county and the first part of the postcode are read, and this condition applied. If it is 'true', then that record is stored on the new file, if not, the record is skipped, and the process repeated to the end of the file.

This principle of applying logical, or Boolean conditions, to processes is a fundamental part of all computer programming. The decision process here is dependent upon the actual condition, and allows complex and 'intelligent' computer processing. It mirrors the way in which we use logic in our everyday lives.

► Boolean conditions are the definitions used to interrogate a database: for example, 'All mice which are not fieldmice' or 'All sweets which are also wrapped' – see Chapter 10.

Sorting and indexing

An important principle in the storage and presentation of data is that of the order in which records are kept. We generally keep alphabetic record of text data. In the sample databases given here, no particular order has been mentioned because different fields would impose different physical orders on the data.

In order to print the whole database of names and addresses in alphabetic order by surname, it would first be necessary to re-arrange the database in that order, and then perform the print. Again, if the whole database were also needed by postcode, or county, the same operation would have to be repeated. If these different orders were needed on a continuous basis, it would be appropriate to write the original file to several separate files, each with its own order. When the file is to be added to, or edited in some way, all these files would have to be updated at the same time to ensure that everything was kept up to date.

This process would be simple and quick in a small application, but if the database contained millions of subscribers to the tele-phone network, for instance, it would be wastefully slow. A better way of tackling the problem is to keep just one main file, and store a special set of 'index' files. An index file is a small file containing just the data from the fields which are to be sorted into order, along with the relevant record numbers. This smaller index file can then be sorted, and several different index files kept for different sort orders of the original file. If a particular order is needed, an appeal is made to the appropriate index file, which is used to pull out the numbered records from the main file in the correct order. All the smaller index files are kept up to date by a DB program, automatically, as the main file is updated. Note that the index file contains as many records as the main file, but much less data overall, which makes it far easier to handle.

Data combination and transformation

In using the data in a database, it is often necessary to combine information, and transform it according to mathematical or logical rules. For instance, the raw results from a scientific experiment may need many mathematical transforms to be imposed on them, in many different ways, and the results stored in various files. It is important that a full set of scientific and other functions are available for these purposes. A good DB program will include all the trigonometrical and general arithmetical functions, for instance, along, perhaps, with many statistical functions, and so on. This allows a program to take in raw data, transform it mathematically, and store it in files as results.

In a relational database, with a full high-level programming language, almost anything is possible in terms of data combination and transformation. In fact, it is often argued that almost any industrial and commercial computer application can be realized by using a full DB program, and nothing else. Many customized systems are realized using a DB programming language.

Database programming languages are full-featured languages in their own right, and should not be considered merely as a secondary add-on to a given DB product. In fact, this area of language products is so important that it is sometimes called the next generation of computer languages – the so-called 4GL languages (or fourth generation languages).

Finally, there is a type of standard language emerging for database programs, which is called SQL – Structured Query Language. This language has been around since the 1970s, and is used extensively in commercial applications. Many databases allow commands and programs to be constructed using this system for extracting and manipulating data, and relating database files together for general applications. You should be aware of its existence, though exploring its use is beyond our scope. If you use a database, you should look up SQL in a library, and see how it could relate to your application.

► SQL- Structured Query Language is the emerging standard for languages used for databases.

Points to look for in a database program
- Ease of initial use for simple applications.
- Good screen handling during initial use, and to set up applications.
- Relational database – allowing plenty of files to be open.
- Full-featured DB programming language, with full set of functions.
- Easy use of indexing with automatic updating.
- Plenty of indexes open at the same time.
- Plenty of Boolean conditions for search queries.
- Whether or not SQL can be used.

In a previous activity, on page 96, you identified a purpose for a database, and thought about the fields you would define for it. Take the same example. Use computer magazines or catalogues, and make a provisional choice of two database packages which seem suitable. Take a sheet of paper and divide it into two columns, one for each package, and write down their respective attributes. Use the points in the box above and decide which product seems most suitable.

DRAWING AND COMPUTER-AIDED DESIGN (CAD)

In many ways, this topic opens up a part of computing which is separate from the applications which we have looked at so far. The applications mentioned previously are based on the storage of text and numerical data. Screen presentation, though important, is secondary – it is merely a method of communicating text. Drawing programs, on the other hand, are concerned with graphical and geometrical patterns and with the screen presentation of information, and its application to 'hard copy' or print.

▶ Drawing programmes are all about screen presentation and the production of hard copy.

Even the simplest drawing programs can be used for some kind of graphical design, and as such are part of the field of CAD – computer-aided design. CAD also includes technical draughting (drawing to scale) and mathematical modelling and simulation. However, CAD usually has an element of drawing, or manipulating graphical patterns and figures, and we will look at this now.

There are many types of drawing program on the market, from simple, freehand-drawing packages to complex technical draughting packages. There is a blur now between sophisticated drawing packages, and technical-draughting software. However, the simpler programs are more suited to artistic drawing, and the draughting packages to producing professional technical drawings. That is not to say that the smaller packages cannot be used to produce accurate, general technical design – there will just be fewer technical facilities available.

All packages should be able to allow some freehand drawing, and all should be able to import graphical images from outside. This could include images prepared on other drawing programs, chosen from a clip-art library, or imported via a hardware interface such as a scanner, a video camera, video recorder, CD-ROM drive, and so on.

▶ Inputs from freehand drawing and from magnetic or electronic memory.

The commands for a drawing package are now almost entirely entered using a GUI interface. It is in this type of application that WIMPs come into their own.

▶ GUI interfaces are almost essential for drawing programs.

When a drawing package is started, it will display a blank area within which the drawing is to be made. An existing image may be called up and edited, or a new drawing made from scratch – or a mixture of the two. There are many drawing aids available to the user to help in producing accurate and varied graphics, mixed with text and imported objects as desired.

Drawing from scratch is done using standard lines and figures, and these are drawn one by one in the drawing area in order to build up the final image. As each part of the drawing is produced, it is considered to be a single object. For instance, a drawing of a cylinder might consist of an ellipse at the top, two lines for the sides and a half ellipse at the bottom. This would be considered, initially, by the package as consisting of four separate objects. They can be grouped together, of left separate. As far as the final hard copy production is concerned, it is irrelevant. The importance of separating objects comes in later modification, where one or more of the objects can be edited or moved, if required, without affecting the rest.

A typical screen from a well-known general drawing package is shown in Figure 5.8.

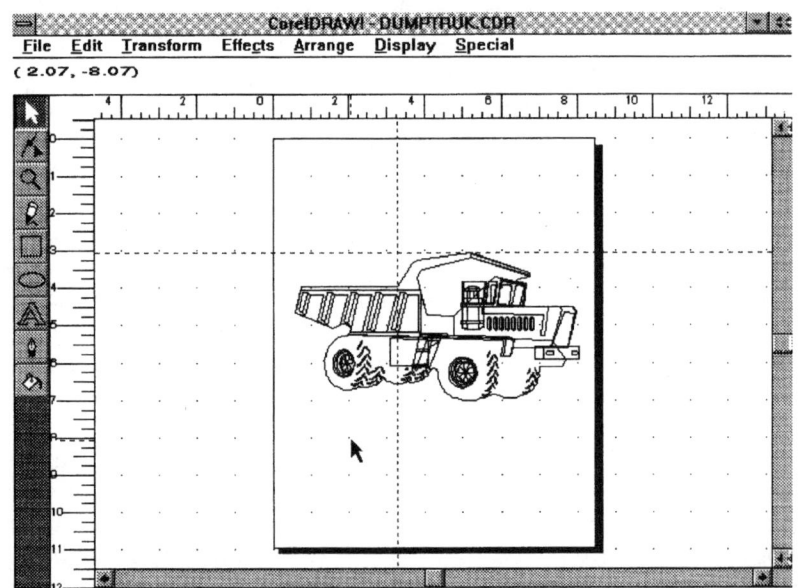

Figure 5.8 Screen display from a typical drawing package

Here, a drawing area is surrounded by command and indication graphics. There is a ruler at the top, and at the left-hand side – in inches in this case, though the units can usually be specified by the user. Further to the left is a vertical range of nine icon areas, called drawing 'tools'. They allow different types of drawing technique to be employed, such as straight line, circle, and so on. Above the main screen, below the main banner, is a line of pull-down menus, as well as a pair of coordinates which refer to the current pointer position. At the right-hand side, and bottom, there are positioning strips which allow the drawing to be moved around the screen. In the centre of the screen is the drawing itself, with the pointer appearing at bottom left, and a couple of dotted reference lines drawn across the picture. We will look at these various areas in the following paragraphs.

Ruler

Drawings often have to be created to conform to given dimensions, or an accurate scale. The ruler, and the accurate readout of positioning, allows technical specifications to be adhered to in producing a given drawing. The dotted reference lines shown can be brought in by clicking the mouse on the ruler, and dragging the mouse over to where the line is required – that is, moving the mouse while holding its button down. Many such lines can be brought into the drawing to allow the operator to line items up correctly. Here, two lines have been used to help the draughtsperson to position the text box accurately. The position of these lines can be read off directly on the rulers, or the cursor can be placed on the lines, and the cursor position read off accurately.

Drawing tools

A drawing package tries to help in the drawing process in as many ways as possible. Standard tools are available to draw squares, rectangles, circles, ellipses, and parts of these figures in many different ways. Straight lines can be drawn, or freehand linear sketches. Similarly, a line which has already been drawn can be modified by curving it, breaking it up, and so on, using one of these tools. The 'A' tool allows text to be added to the drawing. There are usually many different fonts and types available, and the size of the result is completely flexible, as is that of any drawn object. The tools shown in Figure 5.8 will differ from package to package, but the main attributes will be found in most of them. For instance, in order to operate accurately on just part of the drawing, it can be 'zoomed' in. That is, a small portion of the screen can be selected to be blown up to fill the drawing area completely, thus displaying that part in greater detail. The magnifying glass icon (shown) is used for that purpose.

The tool at the top, labelled with an arrow, is used to pick a given object, or set of objects, to be modified in some way. For instance, the line thickness, its colour, the type of line, can be chosen at will. If a closed object is picked, the bottom icon, showing a pot of paint, can be used to fill it with any of a large variety of colours and patterns. This can even include a brick pattern, tiles, textures of various kinds, and so on.

Pull-down menus

The seven pull-down menus at the top of Figure 5.8 allow general commands to be chosen for the drawing. The 'file' menu usually contains commands for saving the work to a file, opening a new file, printing, exiting the package, and so on. 'Edit' allows selected objects to be removed, duplicated, stored separately, and changed in various ways. 'Transform' includes such changes as stretching and mirroring, and the other icons allow many sophisticated options to be chosen from special methods of displaying the work on the screen to placing an 'envelope' around the object, whose shape can be changed in complex and general ways.

Again, different packages will supply different drawing options, and the complexity of the package determines how flexible you can be in producing finished work.

Using a drawing package

Although the operator would normally work on a drawing in the form shown in Figure 5.8, it is also usually possible to display the finished version on the screen. This is illustrated in Figure 5.9, along with some of the aspects introduced above.

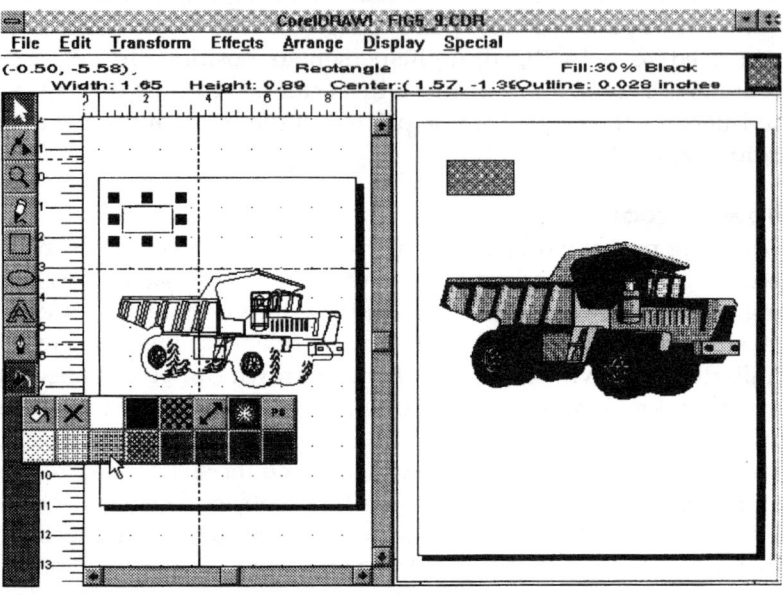

Figure 5.9 Wire-frame (left) and preview (right) displays for a drawing program

The left-hand drawing shown is a 'wire-frame' version, and the right-hand one is a 'preview' version of the drawing being made. The wire-frame drawing is fast and easy to deal with, and allows the draughtsperson to draught the work quickly, without worrying about the full detail of, for instance, which lines are hidden, or what sort of fill a given region has. Once the wire-frame has been constructed, the attributes of the various drawn objects can be determined. There are four objects here, and each has a different outline and fill.

The geometric shapes have been formed by using the mouse to select a given tool, such as ellipse, and then by moving and clicking the mouse. By this means, the drawing is formed with great speed on the drawing surface. The operator is now adjusting the fill patterns in the figures. Before achieving this, however, the object being dealt with must be picked by clicking on any part of its outline in the wire-frame section. Once picked, it is denoted by being surrounding by small black boxes, as shown in Figure 5.9. The small rectangle has been selected, and its attributes are shown at the top: rectangle, with dimensions and coordinates of centre, as well as thickness of outline, and at the far right a sample of its current fill.

The next stage is to move over to the paint-pot tool icon, and click on it. This reveals the pull-down menu showing fill options which cuts across the screen. The options include different densities of monochrome or colour fill, and a number of different standard patterns. It is also possible, in some packages, to draught a new fill pattern from scratch for customized purposes. The pointer is shown about to select the 30 per cent black fill instead of the brick-shaped fill which is in the rectangle at the moment.

After the fill has been chosen, the wire-frame image will remain unchanged, but the preview section will change to show the new situation. This is a WYSIWYG presentation, as mentioned on page 76.

The final result will be able to be printed to a graphics printer, perhaps in colour, or plotted on a pen plotter. The advantage of the latter is that lines are drawn accurately, instead of in small dots. A plotter is good for wire-frame technical draughting applications such as architecture, where lines are primary. A graphics printer, however, is essential for general artistic design work, as a plotter cannot fill areas as densely, or as quickly, as a printer.

► The wire-frame is for quick and easy drafting. The preview is WYSIWYG and shows how the drawing will appear when printed.

Technical drawing

Figure 5.9 gives some flavour of how a general drawing package would work. A good technical drawing package would be expected to include the ability to arrange the drawing as a set of layers, each one containing associated objects. For instance, all the text might be confined to one layer, and this layer could be viewed separately, and be subject to global changes without affecting other parts of the drawing. Also, a standard background drawing could be held on one layer, and the layer above could contain additions for a given application.

Technical drawing involves placing dimensions on the drawing, which can be handled automatically – this is called 'autodimensioning'. Corners can be rounded, and sophisticated packages include a full three-dimensional facility, with hidden-line removal, rotation, and so on.

A full library of technical objects for different applications should also be included. For instance, for use in the building industry, a full set of standard objects might include kitchen and bathroom units, furniture, various different external finishes, and so on.

► Technical drawing packages allow drawings to be built up as a series of layers, and allow accurate dimensioning.

CAD and CADCAM

Computer-aided design (CAD) includes these drawing packages, plus the full gamut of scientific and engineering analysis systems. An example of such software would be 'FE analysis' or finite element analysis. In this technique, a three-dimensional drawing of a mechanical object is split into small elements, and simulated forces applied to the object in certain places. The package analyses the stresses and strains on all of the small elements, and presents the information so that a designer can view the effects before actually building the object. By this means the designer can, for instance, discover the regions on the object which would be subject to the worst effects of stress and strain, and redesign those regions to reduce the effects. The more elements used in the analysis, the more accurate it is, but the more time and processing is needed.

Another example of a general CAD package would be the electronic-circuit analysis program. There are several aspects to this type of software. There is the part which aids a draughtsperson to

► CADCAM: computer-aided design and computer-aided manufacturing.

► FE analysis (finite element analysis): allows the stresses and strains on components to be analysed and measured.

draw electronic circuits, and then produce the printed circuit patterns to be printed onto circuit board. This is a comparatively straightforward draughting function, and any package will also include many clip-art objects for standard electronic components, to save time. There is also software which takes in a circuit designed by an electronic engineer, and simulates its operation. Voltages and currents are theoretically applied to the circuit diagram, and the results presented for checking. This is a powerful on-line program which an engineer can use, almost as if it were a wordprocessor for electronic components, to aid in the design process itself.

It is in this realm of aiding designers in the creative side of their work that the future for CAD lies. As in so many cases, however, this blurs with other computer software. For instance, a spreadsheet can be a CAD system if it is being used to simulate technical calculations which give a designer assistance during the creative process.

It should not be forgotten that the purpose of CAD is often to design an item for building or manufacture. CAM (computer-aided manufacture) effectively closes the gap between the designer and the machinery which will produce the final article. In fact, to go further, sophisticated packages will include modules which actually produce a file of instructions for a given automated, or numerically controlled (NC) machine. The designer draws and calculates the dimensions of the item to be produced, and the computer outputs a file of instructions, or in some cases media such as punched tape, which can be fed directly into an NC machine. If the computer is connected directly to the NC lathe or milling machine, then even this intermediate step is eliminated. This is the final goal of CAD-CAM. Much modern manufacturing machinery already has an allied computer system controlling it.

Output and file storage from CAD

There are two types of output from these packages – file and hard copy. There are many different formats of file output, and modern packages can convert from one format to another to allow portability from the one package to another. In performing this task, given the complexity of graphics data, some degradation of the image can result.

In general, there are two main types of file storage of graphical data. The first type is sometimes called the 'BIT image'. This simply breaks the image down into a specific number of separate dots, and stores the position and colour of each such dot. This is similar to the grain in a photograph. Indeed, in the same way as a photograph, if a BIT image version of a piece of graphics is enlarged, the dots also increase in size, and the image becomes less and less accurate. Essentially, once a picture has been stored in BIT image form, its maximum resolution has become fixed.

The second type of storage, which has many names, stores the image in a form of mathematical instructions from which the image can be reconstituted. This is sometimes called 'vector format' The problem is that different packages use different methods of

▶ The term CADD is sometimes used – it stands for computer-aided design and drawing (or draughting).

▶ File storage for graphical data: BIT image storage (storage as dots); vector format – storage by mathematical instructions to recreate image.

encoding the mathematical formulae from which the image can be reconstituted. However, the vector format allows the image to be recreated as large or small as required, without losing resolution. Enlargement simply means using the mathematical formula to produce more pixels to make up the presentation being demanded. Geometric transformations are also much easier to perform, and more accurate, as it is just the mathematics which is being transformed in a well-defined manner. The image itself is produced only at the end of the process, and is always as accurate as the electronics and mechanics can display.

Hard-copy output via printer or plotter has already been mentioned on page 79, but this is not sufficient for the commercial printing industry which expects very high-quality colour-separated film-based images. A good package will be able to provide this type of output, given a suitable quality of hardware. Colour is separated into constituents, each to be printed separately, and a separate monochrome image formed for each. A printing company then produces the final product by ink-printing each of the images in its own colour, thus building up the final image. While using the drawing package, the operator simply chooses colours which look good, and the software does the rest.

▶ Hard-copy output.

Points to look for in a drawing package
Basic points:
- Full WIMPs presentation.
- WYSIWYG view of the drawing when required.
- Plenty of different tools to ensure that all effects are possible.
- Good geometric facilities to ensure that drawing can be performed with technical accuracy.
- Full support for printers of all kinds.
- Full colour support, with a good WYSIWYG view of the colours, which should be easy to pick and adjust at will.

More advanced points:
- Support for layers.
- Full-scale and dimensioned accuracy.
- Plenty of technical help, such as autodimensioning.
- Good support for plotters, and other professional output devices.
- Modules to produce CAM output for automated machinery.
- Good clip-art libraries for different industries.
- Envelope and curve manipulation tools to allow the draughtsperson to design and modify for general effects.

 Choose an application for a general drawing package. Then use computer magazines or catalogues to make a provisional choice of two packages. Divide a sheet of paper

▶ Application of a computer within the running of a business.

into two columns of attributes, one column for each package. Then use the points listed in the box above to decide which is the better package for your purpose.

Accounts programs

There are many levels of accounts program on the market and, for some applications, a fully customized accounts program can be built up using the high-level language of a database program.

The lowest level of business accounts program allows day-by-day transactions to be recorded in the equivalent of a day-book. It will keep a constant tally of income and expenditure, and VAT. All transactions can be presented on the screen at any time, and some analysis of the type of income and expenditure is possible, as is some record of the bank account. This is very rudimentary, but is of immense help to a single, sole-trader business who wants accounts to be accurate, and simple to operate.

Accounts information

As soon as the level of business is above this lowest level, it is necessary to keep the three main ledgers – sales, purchase and nominal. The sales ledger is a complete list of all income transactions, kept under customer names. The purchase ledger is a list of expenditure items kept under the heading of creditor name. The nominal ledger keeps a list of all the above transactions, and any others which do not fit in, kept under general business headings such as 'stationery' or 'vehicle maintenance'. Thus transactions which appear in the purchase and sales ledgers will also appear again in the nominal ledger. The nominal ledger allows the business to analyse the various ways in which income and expenditure occur.

The information stored in these three main files is used to prepare reports such as the balance sheet and the profit and loss statement. Each quarter, the VAT account will be needed, and at the end of the year a full set of accounts will be prepared. As long as the transactions are all entered accurately, the rest is performed by the machine. Each time a transaction is entered, the operator must enter the financial details, plus a sales and purchase heading under which it is stored, and also a nominal heading. The machine then stores the information to the appropriate ledgers, and may also perform some other intermediate storage and analysis, though this is largely kept to a later time, when reports are required.

Integrated into this basic package may also be stock control, and employees' payroll. A payroll package needs to be periodically updated by the original software publisher to ensure that the internally stored tax tables are accurate. This is a good reason for choosing a large well-known software publisher for a full accounts system – the backup is more reliable.

Reporting from an accounts system

When a report is requested, the system looks into the ledger database, pulls out data, performs calculations, and arranges the result on the screen. This is rather like a combined spreadsheet and database application. Indeed, the more sophisticated spreadsheets can be programmed to perform accounts in a similar manner to the larger DB programs.

The range of management and other reports which are available in a package may be an important influence on the decision to purchase a given package. All packages will be able to prepare the standard accounts – balance sheet, profit and loss, VAT account. In addition, there will be a 'trial balance' facility, which effectively accumulates all transactions to date, and presents them by nominal heading. This allows income and expenditure to be viewed along a bottom line containing the difference between these two. It allows the current cash state of the business to be viewed at any time required.

▶ Computer-produced business accounts.

Other management accounts may provide lists of debtors (i.e. those who owe the business money) the due dates for their payments, who is overdue and by how long, and so on. In addition, statements may be printed showing this information, to be posted to the debtors. An analysis of creditors (i.e. those who are owed money by the company) may also be available. An analysis of the profitability of the business may be available, perhaps graphically, and split into areas of the business, thus showing which areas are more profitable than others. This all relies on the way in which data is input, and how it is stored in the fields and records of the database files. The more complex the queries on the database, the more information is needed, and the more fields required in the records.

Data backup
Another important issue is that of the backup storage of data. The business will come to rely on the automated accounts, and if data is lost it can be serious for the running of the business. In general, all the paper vouchers such as invoices, statements from suppliers and so on should never be discarded. The whole system can be recreated from this basic hard copy raw material – though restoring this will be very expensive for a large company. The next line of defence is the frequent production of account reports, which hard copy can be used to input the state of the accounts again if there is a major disaster.

▶ Hard-copy backup.

However, the most important line of defence against accounts-data loss is simple peripheral memory backup (i.e. on disk or tape), with plenty of copies, and previous versions of copies. This allows 'instant' re-creation of lost data. The main operating system of the machine can be used simply to copy all data files onto a floppy disk or data tape at frequent intervals. A good accounts program should have a peripheral memory backup system which can be operated from within the program. This is easier for non-computer personnel to use.

▶ Peripheral memory backup.

In a small company, this may mean taking copies once a week, though there is little extra overhead in doing it each day, before shutting down the system. In a large company, daily, hourly, or even continuous backup of data is performed. In the very largest systems, where the data is literally the financial lifeblood of the system, there is multiple hard-disk storage of all data, on line. If a disk unit fails, its data is still available on other units. There are special standards for this type of system, which are complex and expensive, and it is even claimed that in some situations the software and hardware are designed to allow a faulty disk unit to be removed and replaced, and brought back on line without shutting down or interrupting the system in any way.

To return to the more common system, which relies on off-line backup, it is important to use a regime of multiple-aged backups. The operator may keep, say, three data tapes for backup. The first tape is used to take a copy of the whole system on the first day, the second on the second day, and the third on the third day. This gives three days' history of the system. On the fourth day, the first tape is overwritten, still leaving three days' history intact. This rolling backup ensures that if there is a corruption which is not noticed for a day or two, an uncorrupted though slightly out-of-date version is available to recreate the system, along with the later hard copy. These copies are called 'grandfather', 'father' and 'son'. The system is not restricted to only three days, of course, nor even to days – the same system works for weeks, or even hours.

Every so often a complete backup is taken and stored, without being overwritten until it becomes completely out of date. For instance, once a year, at year-end, a complete copy of the system is taken. At any future time, the complete end-of-year situation can be recreated immediately and examined electronically.

This type of regime gives some comfort, but is still not foolproof. It is also not confined to accounts programs – it is applicable to any system where data must not be lost.

▶ Multiple-aged backup: grandfather, father and son.

 List some of the ways in which data could still be lost in the above system of multiple-aged backups.

Points to look for in accounts programs
- Large storage of data – the package should not be restricted to a small number of transactions in total.
- Separate sales, purchase and nominal ledgers.
- Ability to add on other modules, such as payroll, as required.
- Good screen presentation, with plenty of checks for the data entered.
- Easy entering of data, with plenty of help advice when required.
- Full range of management and accounts reports.
- Reliable backup from the software publisher.
- Efficient backup of data to ensure that the business accounts are never lost.

 Use computer magazines or catalogues to make a preliminary choice of two accounts packages suitable for a small business. Divide a sheet of paper into two columns for attributes, one for each package, and use the points in the box above to decide which is the better for this purpose.

Chapter review

- Applications packages are standard programs meant to solve a particular class of problem.
- WP – wordprocessing – uses the computer as an intelligent typewriter.
- A WP has a blank screen on which the user can write text.
- DTP – desk-top publishing – is a more flexible WP, allowing graphics and more general presentation of text.
- A DTP program allows graphics to be mixed in, and text to be of any size and type and be laid out in a general fashion.
- WP and DTP programs are becoming more alike.
- A spreadsheet is a program dedicated to the display and manipulation of numerical information.
- A spreadsheet supplies a blank screen sectioned into cells, each of which can hold a number, a numerical formula, or text.
- A spreadsheet can be used to construct numerical models such as cash flow forecasts.
- A business graphics program is usually integrated with a spreadsheet to allow graphical presentation of numerical information.
- A database is a computerized file of information.
- A DB program is a piece of software which allows a user to store, organize and manipulate data in a database.
- A DB program allows the user to construct files of data organized into records, each of which has several fields.
- A DB program may be flat file or relational – in the latter case the records and fields of one file may refer to other files.
- A DB program often comes with its own high level language to allow general applications to be written using the DB program's facilities.
- Accounts programs are examples of general business packages.
- Drawing programs include CAD – computer-aided design.
- The screen/keyboard layout for a package is termed its 'front-end processor'.
- Package front-end processors can be based around command-line processing or a GUI, as for an OS.
- Spreadsheets and WPs may also have dedicated high level languages.

- Drawing programs allow general artistic graphics to be constructed, and/or technical scale drawings to be produced.
- CAD also includes graphical analysis programs.
- CADCAM combines design with automatic manufacture of an item.
- CAD/CADD can output to a screen, printer and plotter.
- A typical business package would be an accounts program to keep daily financial transactions, and produce business accounts.
- Backing up data is crucial in general, and chronologically ordered backup should be practised in sensitive systems.

▶ **Now that you have completed this chapter, look back to the objectives at the beginning and check that you have accomplished each of them.**

(ACT) This chapter has covered only some of the more popular applications of computers. Use your computer magazines to identify other applications. For one of these, draw up your own 'Points to look for' list which might help someone to make a choice between rival packages.

6 Binary, memory and addressing

Chapter objectives

By the time you have read this chapter, you will understand:

▌ how digital devices are organized

▌ number bases

▌ binary numbers

▌ how computer memory is organized and addressed

▌ how to use different number bases in addressing

▌ how computers contact their memory addresses

▌ the computer's memory map

▌ the following key words: logical, physical, matrix, number base, decimal, binary, octal, hexadecimal, address, memory map, address decoding.

ORGANIZING DIGITAL DEVICES

In Chapter 3, we showed how digital computers rely upon on/off switch elements, sometimes in their millions. We will look now at how all this binary data is organized within a system, how memory storage works, and how the processor reads and writes data to and from the memory-storage switches.

In order to make contact with the BIT stored in a given switching element, it would be possible to have a specific electrical wire connected to it, which the processor could look at and determine whether the switch was ON or OFF – i.e whether the BIT was a 1 or a 0. However, the disadvantage would be that the number of electronic wires would soon become unwieldy – not to mention the number of pins on the average MPU chip! We will see, shortly, how the number of lines connected to a set of memory locations can be minimized. Also, in organizing the memory BITs, the programmer needs a logical method of labelling them, so that they can be involved in computer programs.

Logical and physical organization

There are two answers to the question of how BITs are organized. They are the 'logical' and the 'physical' answers. The 'logical' aspect tells a programmer how to regard the matter from a software point of view. The 'physical' aspect is the one which an electronic engineer would consider when designing or interfacing to a system.

▶ This chapter expands upon the way in which the hardware of computer memory is arranged and realized, and on binary notation. It explains the shorthand used for the large binary numbers which the machine itself reads. We then apply this shorthand to addressing memory and explain the internal memory map of the machine, and how it is contacted by the electronics.

Data is organized into memory locations, as we saw in Chapter 2, and each location is given an address – just as the houses in a street are distinguished uniquely by a number or name. A programmer would need to know where to store data, and to be able to keep track of these addresses. This is a purely software, or logical, concept, and in a sense is not the lowest level of explanation – it glosses over the hardware, or physical, question as to how the electronics perform the task of ensuring that the programmer can contact data by its address locations.

In order to see how the hardware of an electronic computer organizes data into many millions of memory locations, with a minimum of electronic lines, and how it allows the programmer to contact them, we have to look at two important concepts which form the basis of all electronic memory – namely, 'matrices' and 'address decoding'.

Matrices

Matrices form naturally in nature, as well as in the organization of human-made environments. For instance, a honeycomb is a matrix – a two-dimensional matrix of small pockets. If bees stuck the pockets together in a long one-dimensional line, their hives would be very different! They would be unlikely to keep as many pockets together in one place, and it would take longer, from entering the hive, to find a given pocket – unless the hive was open all the way along, which would be a bad idea from the point of security. Organizing the pockets into a two-dimensional surface makes the system much more compact and efficient. Similarly, when we plan a city from scratch, it is arranged on a grid system. Grids or matrices are used in filing systems, and in many other situations where a number of items are associated together.

If you have 100 BITs to organize, it is logical to arrange them as a matrix of 10 by 10, i.e. as a square of side 10 units. Then each BIT is labelled with a row and a column.

► Matrices (singular: matrix) – grids. The grid on an Ordnance Survey map is a matrix. It allows you to use map references to give an 'address' to any place on the map.

COLUMNS

	1	2	3	4	5	6	7	8	9	10
1	x	x	x	x	x	x	x	x	x	x
2	x	x	x	x						
3	x	x	x							
4	x	x	x							
5	x									
6	x						x			
7	x						(ROW 6, COL. 7)			
8	x									
9	x									
10	x									

ROWS

Figure 6.1 A ten-by-ten matrix of switches

Figure 6.1 shows the organization of 100 switches, each of which can be ON or OFF. The rows and columns are labelled with the numbers 1 to 10. Any given switch is labelled with a row number and a column number. For instance, the switch in row 6, column 7 shown is labelled as '(row 6 , column 7)'. If we decide always to put the row first and column second, we could shorten the switch's name to (6,7).

In order to tell whether switch (6,7) was storing a 1 or a 0, we could simply send an electronic signal to column 7, and see whether the electrical signal is conducted through to row 6, or not. As long as we only apply the signal to column 7 while we look at row 6, we can be sure that none of the other switches is contributing to any signal we find on row 6. This is crucial to reading the state of a BIT location. By looking in this manner, we can read sequentially the data BITs in the whole matrix. Only twenty lines are needed to do it (i.e. ten row plus ten column locations), and not a hundred. This is a good start at reducing the number of lines required, and this type of matrix is used, for example, for a keyboard. In this case, each key you press makes an electrical switch.

The labels above use 'ordinary' numbers. In fact, in computing, we use binary numbers to label locations and, before proceeding, you must know how the binary system works. This system will be used throughout the book, and is universal to both hardware and software.

Number bases

We are used to counting in 'base ten'. That is, we count 0 1 2 3 4 5 6 7 8 9, and then we shift to 10 and start over again and count 10 11 12 13 14, etc. to 19, when another 10 is added to make 20. When we reach 99, we shift up to 100 and start again, and so on. We shift 'up' by 10 after reaching every tenth digit (i.e. 9, 19, 29, etc.), and are said to be counting in tens or in base ten or in decimal. It is important that you note how we start counting from '0', and not '1'.

These principles are the same when counting in any other base – for instance, this is how to count in base seven:

0 1 2 3 4 5 6 10 11 12 13 14 15 16 20 21 22 23 24, etc.

Where have the numbers 7, 18, etc. gone? In fact, they are still there – '7' has been replaced by '10', and 18 by '24', and so on. To check this for yourself, starting with 0 in the number sequence above, point with a finger and count in normal base ten until you reach the number in the list which coincides with your count of '7' and then '18'.

This can be incredibly confusing – how can 18 and 24 be the same? In order to help, you should not label the numbers in the base–seven list above quite the way they look. For instance, what would you call the eighth number in the above list? Have a look! It can't be called 'seven' because it is a 'ten'. And would you say 'ten' or 'one-zero'? 'Ten' is completely wrong, it gives the false view that the 10 in this list is the 'ordinary' number ten – i.e. the number of fingers and thumbs on two hands. In fact the eighth number in the list is actually 'seven' – real seven – that is, the number of days in the week. As you can see, all the old numbers are still there but are labelled completely differently, after the first sequence of seven. However, the numbers still have the old meanings. For instance, the number of fingers and thumbs on a hand has not changed just because in base seven decimal ten is called '13' – i.e. 'one-three' (NOT thirteen!), which equals one seven plus three units (equals ten).

 Counting in base five, write out the first twenty-five numbers, starting at 0.

Numbers have immutable underlying meanings, which mean they cannot change, but by changing the 'base' we can relabel them. Frankly, base seven, is rather awkward, and does not have any real application in computing – or in many other areas, either. However, the following systems are tremendously useful in computing:

>   **Base two – called 'binary'**

>   **Base eight – called 'octal'**

>   **Base sixteen – called 'hexadecimal'**

Indeed without them the whole subject would be much more difficult to write and talk about. The reason stems from the difficulty that humans have in understanding long lists of binary digits. Octal and hexadecimal provide a shorthand for such lists.

The number of digits needed in a given base is equal to that base. For instance, ordinary base ten (decimal) numbers need ten digits:

>   **0 1 2 3 4 5 6 7 8 9**

Base seven needs seven digits:

>   **0 1 2 3 4 5 6**

Binary numbers use just two digits:

>   **0 and 1**

Octal numbers use eight digits:

>   **0 1 2 3 4 5 6 7**

and so on.

Hexadecimal numbers, therefore, must use sixteen digits, but we only have ten numerical digits available in decimal – 0 1 2 3 ... 9 – and so we have to invent six more: A B C D E F. Thus, hexadecimal numbers use these sixteen digits:

>   **0 1 2 3 4 5 6 7 8 9 A B C D E F**

As with base seven above, when the base number is reached, the next number is written as '10', and pronounced 'one-zero', in order

► The most important number bases in computing are binary, octal and hexadecimal (hex).

to signify moving 'up' to the next base level of counting. Thus, in octal we have:

0 1 2 3 4 5 6 7 10 11 12 13 14 15 16 17 20 21, etc.

In hex (which is short for hexadecimal):

0 1 2 3 ... 9 A B ... F 10 11 12 13 ... 1A 1B ... 1F 20, etc.

Again the basic meanings of the numbers themselves remain unchanged, but they are labelled differently. For instance, 'one dozen' is written as '12' in decimal, '14' in octal, 'C' in hex, and, for your information, '1100' in binary. Remember, once again, that 0 is the first number in all number systems.

To see how these bases are used, we will now look specifically at binary, which is at the heart of the system.

 Hex is very important in computing, and you should practise counting in the system now by writing out the first 150 or so numbers in hex, starting with the list above. This will help you to become familiar with the system for future use.

BINARY NUMBERS

To count in binary, simply follow the same principles as above. Increment the least significant digit (or LSD – i.e the right-hand most digit) until the number base is reached and then carry one 'up' the scale. Of course, as the base is only two, you end up 'carrying' up the scale rather a lot!

For instance, the first two numbers in binary are the same as in any other system:

0 and 1

Then you must carry to produce:

10 and 11

as usual. Next you carry again to produce:

100 101 110 111

You will notice that each time you carry, subsequent counting consists of going through all the previous numbers again, but with the left-hand BIT set to a 1 – the left-hand BIT is called the most significant BIT, or MSB.

► LSB – least significant BIT; MSB – most significant BIT.

This is the way in which binary counting is done in general – count through all the numbers until all the BITs are set to 1, and then add another MSB, set to 1, and start again.

 Carry on the sequence above, counting in binary from the number 111 above until you reach 1111. Again, you must become familiar with the way in which counting in this system goes.

Very often, in computer applications, there is a fixed length of binary number to consider, with leading 0s filling the more significant positions. For instance, counting a six-BIT number would go as follows:

000000   000001   000010   000011   000100   000101

 Finish off this six-BIT binary sequence before carrying on – make sure you end up with sixty-four numbers in total.

In order to find the decimal equivalent of a binary number, remember how decimal numbers are analysed. For instance, starting with the least significant digit, the number 38592 would consist of two units (or ones), nine tens, five hundreds, eight thousands and three ten-thousands.

Thus, the least significant digit is the number of 'ones' (or units), the next most significant is the number of tens, then the number of hundreds, and so on. Each time you move left by one digit, you increase by a power of ten – starting with ten to the power of zero, which is mathematically equal to the unit 1. Note that raising any number to the power '0' produces the number '1' – the reason is beyond our scope, but you must remember this point.

For binary (base two), the system is similar:

2^6 2^5 2^4 2^3 2^2 2^1 2^0

1   0   0   1   0   1   1

This binary number is 1001011, and, reading from right to left, has one unit (two to the zeroth power), one two (two to the first power), no fours (two to the second power), one eight, no sixteens or thirty-twos and one sixty-four. Thus the number equals $1 + 2 + 8 + 64 = 75$, in decimal.

▶ Raising any number to the power '0' produces the number '1'.

 Confirm the following conversions of binary to decimal for yourself:

10 = 2

101010 = 42

111011 = 59

10000001 = 129

 The reverse process to convert a decimal number into binary is not quite so important but if you are arithmetically minded, try to work it out from the following hint.

Hint: It is a matter of dividing by two over and over again, and noting down the remainders from right to left. Try it with all the numbers in the activity, and then try reversing 69 to get 1000101. Another, quicker way to look at it is to start by finding the highest power of two which will go into the number – in the case of 69 it is 64 as 128 (the next power) will not go. Then, subtract 64 from the number, and look at the 32s, 16s and so on down the powers to see which will go, subtracting each time. Note a 0 if they will not go into the number, and 1 otherwise – again, try this on the numbers in the activity to see how it works.

Simplifying long binary numbers

To simplify long binary numbers, we can group them into threes or fours. This is how octal and hex numbers arise.

► To simplify long binary numbers we convert to octal or more usually to hexadecimal.

For instance, the first eight binary numbers (with octal equivalents given underneath) are:

000	001	010	011	100	101	110	111
0	1	2	3	4	5	6	7

Note how the complete set of triplets of binary numbers converts naturally, and completely, into the set of octal digits.

The first sixteen numbers are:

0000	0001	0010...	1010	1011...	1101	1111	in binary
0	1	2	12	13	16	17	in octal
0	1	2	10	11	14	15	in decimal
0	1	2	A	B	E	F	in hex

Again, this shows how the complete set of quartets of binary digits converts completely into hex digits.

You should spend a minute or two filling in the gaps in these lists, for practice, and then keep a list of binary, hex and decimal equivalents by you for future reference.

Now look at a long binary number, written as triplets, with their octal equivalents:

101	110	100	010	000	010	101	111	101	101	100	001
5	6	4	2	0	2	5	7	5	5	4	1

You will agree that the octal 564202575541 is quite complicated, but not nearly as bad as binary:

101110100010000010101111101101100001!

Now look at the same binary number in hex – but first it must be grouped into blocks of four. This is because a four-BIT number produces exactly sixteen (two to the power of four, or 2×2×2×2) different patterns, or numbers, and each one of these has a unique hex equivalent, as we have seen:

1011	1010	0010	0000	1010	1111	1011	0110	0001
B	A	2	0	A	F	E	6	1

Again, BA20AFE61 is a large number, but much easier to write, say and even remember than the binary – it is more compact than the octal too. Hex has another advantage over octal – each digit represents a NIBBLE (see page 11), or half a

BYTE – thus a BYTE can be exactly represented by a two-hex-digit number. Because of this, we do not need to refer to octal again in this book – we will deal exclusively with hex for representing binary from now on, in company with the majority of the computer industry.

If we come across binary numbers which do not have quite enough BITs to split into exact quartets, we will simply add up to three leading zeros, in the most significant positions, to ensure that they do. For instance:

101 will be rewritten as 0101 and be called '9' and

101101 will be rewritten as 00101101 and be called '2D', and so on.

 Convert the following into hex:

10

1001

111101011

001110111

ADDRESS LABELLING

► *N* BITs can take up 2 to the power of *N* different binary patterns. So, for instance, an eight-BIT set can represent 2 to the 8th power ($2 \times 2 \times 2 \times 2 \times 2 \times 2 \times 2 \times 2 = 256$) different binary numbers. These start at 00000000 and run through to 11111111. You should be able to check this for yourself, if you have the patience!

Now consider the matrix in Figure 6.2.

	0(00)	1(01)	2(10)	3(11)
0(00)	x	x	x	x
1(01)	x	x (0101)	x	x (0111)
2(10)	x	x	x	x
3(11)	x (1100)	x	x	x (1111)

Figure 6.2 A four-by-four matrix

This matrix happens to have sixteen locations, which is four squared (i.e. four multiplied by itself). This means that four rows by four columns will arrange the locations in a natural grid. In fact, there are other ways to arrange the matrix – for instance, eight rows and two columns. Again, eight times two makes sixteen.

 Write out the other methods of organizing these switches into a matrix.

As you can see, this time the first row and column are labelled with a '0'. By now you should be used to starting at 0 and not 1 in digital counting.

Each row and column is labelled by a two-BIT number, and if we stick to using row first and then column for labelling each switch, a four-BIT number arises to label each switch address, which could be represented by a single hex digit.

As you can see, some of the switches in Figure 6.2 have been labelled with their four-BIT labels or 'addresses'. For instance, the bottom left-hand switch is labelled with 1100 – you do not need the brackets, this is a perfectly good four-BIT binary number. Each switch address starts with the two BITs on its row, and ends with the two BITs on its column.

 Fill in the rest of the switch addresses, along with their hex equivalents.

Matrices do not need to be square, nor do they need to be completely filled up. For instance, if you have 1,000 switches to address, you cannot have a square matrix – 1,000 does not have an exact square root (a number which multiplied by itself gives 1,000).

 Before reading on, see if you can design a matrix to label the 1,000 switches.

In fact, there are many answers to this question, and the electronic designer might decide, for particular reasons, to use a matrix of, say, 32 by 32, or 35 by 35, or 30 by 35, and so on. Then there will be more spaces for switches in any of these matrices than will be filled by the 1,000 switches available – there will be some unused addresses. In addition, this system still uses a fairly large number of electronic lines – imagine how this will increase considerably when addressing a memory matrix of many millions of locations. We will see, on page 123, how this can be handled.

The memory map

Any computer system is arranged in such a manner that different regions of internal memory are used for different functions. As we saw in Chapter 3 the way in which this internal memory is arranged is called a 'memory map'. Remember that internal memory is, for instance, where the program that is currently running is situated, and from where the processor fetches its instructions. A part of the memory map is also devoted to the reset, and other, vectors. Another part may be used by the video interface, and so on. It is useful, from the point of view of memory organization, to divide these regions off, as well as labelling them with binary addresses, for a programmer who has to work down at this level of software.

When the processor puts an address out on the address bus, it looks at the data bus to see what comes back, and this has to be the

▶ See Figure 3.8.

▶ Buses carry information from place to place in the system. In this case, when the MPU wants to know what data is at a given address, it places that address on the address bus and waits for the data at that location to be sent back along the data bus.

contents of the memory at that specific address appearing on the address bus. It is the job of the hardware designer to ensure this is the case.

Logically, the memory is divided into regions by binary addresses. In order to see how this is done, we will look at the organization of a typical eight-BIT MPU system.

An MPU is classified by, among other things, how many lines there are in its data bus – thus, an eight-BIT MPU has a data bus width of eight lines.

Eight-BIT MPU chips generally have sixteen address lines, along with their eight data BITs. Thus, when the MPU puts out a sixteen-bit binary pattern of electrical signals on the address bus, it expects a BYTE of data back along the data bus.

Consider the memory map in Figure 6.3.

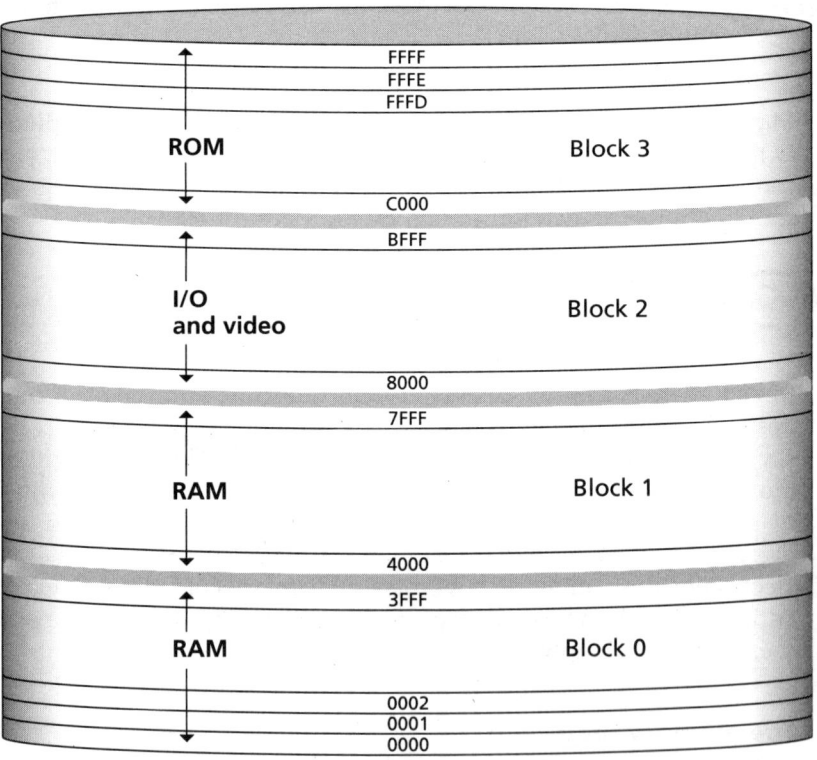

Figure 6.3 Memory map for an eight-BIT system

This figure shows how the memory is split into four regions, though these addresses are actually continuous from bottom to top – the split into regions is just for convenience of use and labelling. The memory elements are all 1 BYTE in capacity, and they range from address 0000 to FFFF, in hex. Translating these addresses into binary gives:

hex:	0	0	0	0	F	F	E	F
binary:	0000	0000	0000	0000	1111	1111	1111	1111

Thus, we can see that sixteen address BITs (and lines) are needed for this map, and the pattern of BITs on the address bus can be written as a four-digit hex number. The address regions chosen for the system are RAM memory in the blocks 0 and 1 from address 0000 to 7FFF, I/O and video devices in the block 2 from 8000 to BFFF, and finally ROM from C000 to FFFF.

This constitutes a total number of memory locations equal to the number of binary patterns it is possible to have on sixteen lines. This is equal to two to the power of sixteen, or 65,536 – which is generally referred to as 64K (i.e. 64×1,024). If this were all arranged as a matrix, as previously discussed, it would have to have 256 rows and 256 columns, and hence 512 electronic lines, which is hardly practical. Somehow, we have to find an electronic circuit which can take in a sixteen-BIT binary number, and select a unique memory location without having hundreds of electronic lines connected from the MPU to the memory matrix. This is solved by the concept of 'address decoding'.

► A 64K memory has two to the power of sixteen memory locations = 65,536.

► Address decoding reduces the number of physical connections required in a memory.

 Consider a machine which has only 32K of memory. What is the minimum number of address lines needed to address the whole memory? Write out the lowest and highest address in binary and hex. Split the memory into two equal regions, and write out the top and bottom addresses in each of these regions.

Address decoding

The actual organization of memory into regions, or blocks, is achieved by electronic means. The electronic system used is called 'address decoding'. The memory blocks are physical blocks of electronic memory, and in order for a given block to be selected, it must be fed an electronic 'select' signal. It is important that just one block receives a select signal at any time, or there will be conflict.

The address decoding takes in a few of the upper address lines, and converts, or decodes, each binary pattern which appears there into a unique block select signal. At the same time, the rest of the address lines are fed to the block itself, and the pattern on those does the job of selecting out a specific memory location within the block.

The maximum number of blocks possible depends upon how many upper address lines are used – there is a unique block for each possible binary pattern on those lines. Similarly, the maximum number of memory locations in a given block depends upon the number of lower address lines fed to it.

The complete binary pattern on the upper and lower address lines taken together is the binary address of the single memory location being contacted.

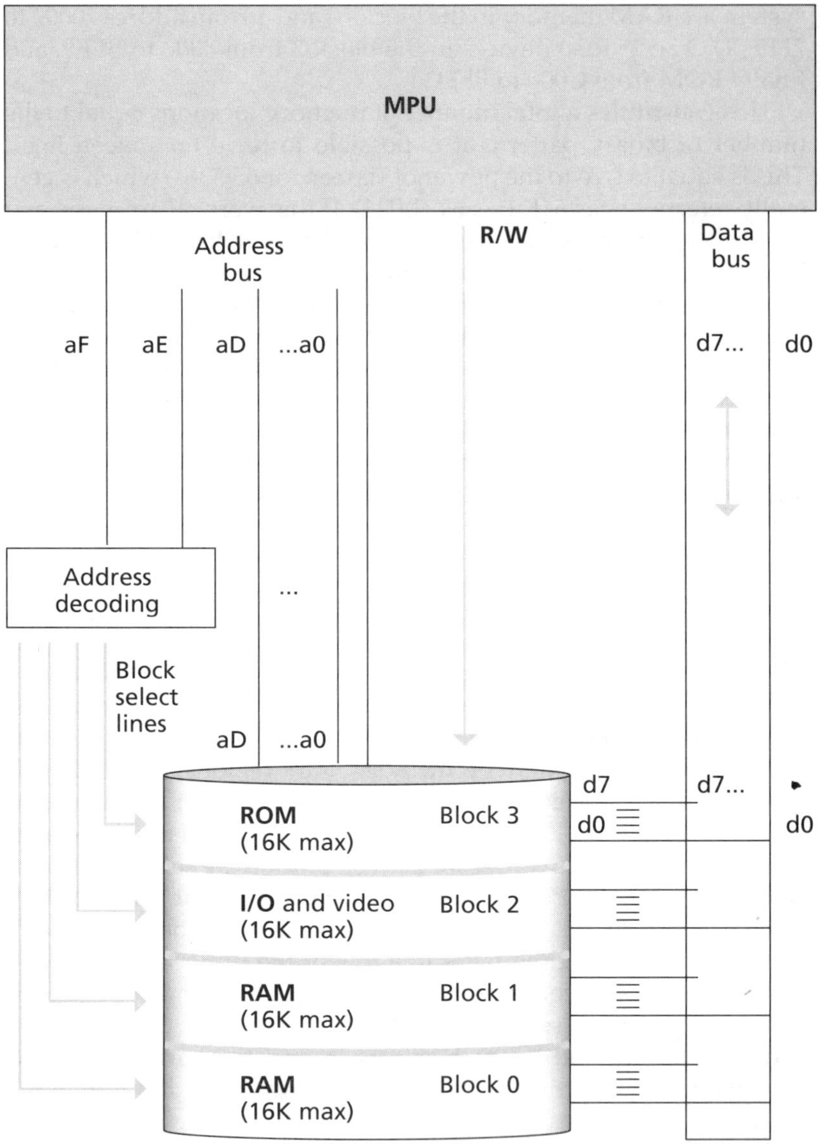

Figure 6.4 Address decoding

► Note that all the devices in the memory map have their data bus lines connected to the data bus, but they do not interfere electrically as only one memory location is electrically activated at any instant.

In Figure 6.4 the MPU's address lines are labelled a0 a1 a2 ... aE aF, and the data lines are labelled d0 d1 d2 ... d6 d7. The upper two address lines, aE and aF, are fed to the address decoding block, and the rest (the fourteen lower lines) are fed to the memory, I/O and video matrix. This means that there will be four possible patterns on aE and aF taken together, giving four possible memory blocks as shown. Similarly, the fourteen lower lines will allow each block to contain a maximum of two to the power of fourteen (ie 16K) memory locations.

The top two address lines control the most significant two BITs of the memory addresses. For instance:

6FA7 is equal to 0110111110100111

As you can see, the top two BITs are 01. This is one of the four possible patterns which can appear on these address lines, and each such pattern causes just one of the four block-select lines to become active. Here, 01 is the binary number for '1', and thus block 1 will become active, which is the second block from the bottom, and contains RAM. A location within the ROM would be contacted, for instance, at address CA3F, which is equal to:

1100 1010 0011 1111

and has 11 in the top two BITs, which is the binary number for '3' – hence block 3. No other block is switched on at the time, to prevent interference. At the same time as the address, the MPU is either placing a BYTE on the data bus to be written into that unique memory location (if it were a RAM location), or requesting the contents from it to be placed on the data bus for the MPU to fetch.

Another electronic line, called the 'read/write' (or R/W) line is used to command the memory location either to take in the BYTE from the data bus (write), or put out its BYTE contents onto the data bus (read), for the MPU to read in. When the MPU sets R/W to 'read', it is expecting to read a BYTE from the address. When in 'write', it is writing data into the memory location. Of course, some locations can only be read from (e.g. ROM) and an attempt to write to them will have no effect – they will simply remain unchanged.

▶ Read: an instruction where the MPU takes in data from the data bus. Write: an instruction to put data at a particular address. Read only memory (ROM) means you can't write.

The R/W line is a part of another bundle, or bus, of lines called the 'control bus'. This is somewhat complicated, and varies from MPU to MPU, and system to system – it contains lines such as the electronic clock, the reset line, and so on. Its description is beyond the scope of this book.

The matrix concept is still used here to reduce the number of lines required, and each block has its own electronics, and internal address decoding to achieve this in the most efficient manner possible, and with the least number of lines.

Also notice that in each location, eight BITs are ganged together, as it were, and hence we are no longer contacting a single memory switch at each location, but rather eight at once, to retrieve or store a complete BYTE. By increasing the width of the data bus, and ganging together even more data BITs with each read or write, much faster data communications can be achieved.

 How many upper address lines would have to be fed to the address decoding if it was activating eight blocks of memory? Assuming sixteen address lines as above, how many lower address lines would be fed to the blocks themselves, and how much memory would each block contain, maximum? If the MPU uses twenty address BITs, how much memory could it address in total? How about if it has thirty-two address lines?

Modern computer memory

Modern computer systems have, typically, between 1 and 32 mega BYTEs of internal memory, and twenty or more address lines, though both of these numbers are increasing all the time. A quick calculation will show that twenty address lines is only good enough to address (2 to the 20th) 1 MB of memory. To solve this problem for such MPUs, some clever electronics is used to switch in other pages of memory, and the operating system carefully manipulates these pages to store data and program elements in a hierarchy of memory layers. Some processors have up to thirty-two address lines, and they can address up to four giga BYTEs of memory.

Modern computer systems have many more data bus lines – sixteen and thirty-two are very common, while larger widths are also in use. As we have seen, this means that more BITs of data can be fetched and stored per address cycle, and each address location contains more than eight BITs. However, system memory is still classed by the number of BYTEs it holds. The BYTE is the basic element of memory capacity.

If you open up a computer case, you will be able to identify the memory chips fairly easily. They form a matrix of identical chips, arranged in rows. Alternatively, they are confined to small vertically arranged rectangular boards of identical chips. Either way, the memory needs to be arranged in blocks, and address decoding is used to ensure that the physical hardware chips are present at the correct software addresses for a programmer. Once this has been arranged, a programmer working at this low level needs to know no more than the actual binary, or hex, addresses of everything in the computer. There is no need for any knowledge of the way in which the electronics arranges the memory to be there.

As you can see, arranging addresses and memory maps is where software and hardware meet on an equal basis.

Chapter review
- Memory is organized as a matrix of electronic on/off switches.
- Binary is counting to base 2. We normally count to base ten (decimal).
- Binary can be represented easily using base sixteen, or hexadecimal (hex, for short).
- An N-BIT binary number can hold 2 to the power of N different patterns.
- A four-BIT binary number, or NIBBLE, can be represented by a single hex digit.
- An eight-BIT binary number, or BYTE, needs two hex digits.
- A memory map having 65,536 (2 to the 16th power) addresses can be uniquely labelled using sixteen address BITs, or two BYTEs, or four hex digits.

- 'Address decoding' is the electronic circuitry which activates the appropriate memory locations being addressed by the processor.
- The 'address bus' of the system is used to transmit addresses.
- The 'data bus' communicates data to and from address locations.

▶ **Now that you have completed this chapter, look back to the objectives at the beginning and check that you have accomplished each of them.**

Chapter objectives

By the time you have read this chapter, you will understand:

▌ types of electronic memory and how they work

▌ types of magnetic memory and how they work

▌ the comparison between disks and CD-ROM

▌ memory capacities and speeds

▌ how systems are organized

▌ the following key words: RAM, dynamic, refresh, static, battery backup, CMOS, ROM, mask, EPROM, EEPROM, PROM, SIMM, SIPP, PCMCIA, magnetic memory, peripheral, read/write head, cylinder, Winchester, track, sector, formatting, TPI, header, DOS, interface, open architecture, PSU, closed architecture, data tape, CD-ROM, access time, cache.

TYPES OF ELECTRONIC MEMORY

Chips

Electronic memory is currently formed as microscopic devices on the surface of a special material called a 'semiconductor'. Silicon is the most widely used semiconductor. The digital switching properties of these semiconductor devices are hardly dependent upon size, and so a one-millimetre wide transistor will perform, logically, as well as one which is one metre wide or one millionth of a metre wide. Thus, the devices can be made as small as practicable, and packed in dense arrays on a chip.

An important characteristic of memory devices is the information carrying density of a given chip – i.e. the number of locations which can be formed in a given size.

Electronic memory is usually internal to the machine, connected to the CPU or MPU via busses. We will look now at some typical classes of electronic memory.

Random access memory (RAM)

This is used for the internal memory of the computer system. Its contents are lost when the system is switched off. RAM consists of an array of switches whose states may be written to, and read from, by the processor via the busses. The way in which the memory switches are formed determines the physical type of RAM produced. Some of these types are described here.

▶ **In the last chapter we considered the way in which memory is organized and labelled. We also looked at the electronics and logic of addressing. This chapter deals with real electronic devices found in the majority of modern computers. This includes the internal electronic memory connected directly to the processor, via the busses, and peripheral memory such as disks.**

Dynamic RAM

In this type of RAM, the memory switches consist of a single transistor and a single electronic capacitor. The memory element is the capacitor which stores electronic charge, and whose state may be read and written to by the transistor, which is selected via the address decoding and the address bus. The advantage of this type of memory is the very large capacity of memory which can be formed onto a single chip – the extreme simplicity of the memory element itself allows millions of memory elements to be formed in a small space. However, the disadvantage is that the charge in the capacitor leaks away in a fraction of a second, and so needs to be continually refreshed.

Dynamic memory refresh is a straightforward process, and is simply controlled by the electronics of the memory chip and the system. However, it is no good if the chip is quietly refreshing a given set of memory elements at just the instant that the MPU needs to be in contact with it. Refresh must, therefore, be synchronized with the processor's needs. This is an important part of designing modern computer equipment, as dynamic memory is very common at present.

▶ Dynamic memory refresh.

Static RAM

This type of memory element consists of an electronic circuit with rather more than just one transistor and a capacitor. Its advantage is that it does not need to be refreshed. Once set, it remains static until changed, or until the power is switched off. Unfortunately, it is not possible to cram nearly as many static memory elements onto a chip as dynamic memory elements, and as such these are not normally used in high memory capacity applications. However, such chips are easier to use for small controllers, for instance, and due to the lack of a need for refresh, can be used in super fast applications where the RAM must always be fully available.

Battery backed-up RAM

As its name suggests battery backed-up RAM is capable of being maintained by a battery while the main power supply is off. This type of RAM is used in systems to store set-up data which the system is to remember for use each time it is restarted. This saves the operator from reminding the system of the basic devices present each time the system is restarted. You will see it referred to as 'CMOS' memory. This comes from a common technology used to form the transistors and other elements on the chip. They are called 'complementary metal-oxide semiconductors' (CMOS). This technology happens to

▶ Static RAM and battery backed-up RAM do not need to be refreshed.

be particularly low in power usage, thus allowing even quite a small battery to back-up such memory devices for a period of years. The same technology is used in electronic watches and calculators to save power.

ROM – read only memory

As explained on page 125, this type of memory cannot be written to, and thus is used to contain programs and data which are to be present and unchanging within the computer. There are several types of ROM.

Masked ROM

Integrated circuits are made using a photographic process to create special surface semiconducting regions. This is why chips can be so small. By using a microscope in reverse, a large drafted pattern can be photographed down to a minute scale. The screens used for this process, through which light is passed, are called 'masks'. In a certain sense, it is the set of masks which actually contains the design of the chip – the rest is mechanics. When a program or a piece of data is to be stored on a masked ROM, it is converted into binary data, and then into a pattern of fixed switch positions – some 'on' and some 'off'- to be read, eventually, as 1s and 0s, and hence fetched as data or program instructions by the processor. One of the masks used in the photography effectively contains this pattern, hence the name 'masked ROM'.

EPROM – erasable programmable ROM

This type of chip contains a memory matrix which can be written to, often using special voltage levels, in order to accept binary data. The data is then available to the normal address and data bus of the system, but the data cannot be changed by the electronics of the system. EPROM chips can be erased fully for reuse or modification, usually by removing a cover from a window on their top surface, and beaming ultraviolet light into it. This knocks out the electrons stored in capacitors within the memory matrix, and returns the chip to all 1s, or all 0s. This system forms a very useful method of quickly prototyping software, and plugging it into a system to try it out. Normally, such chips are pin-compatible with an equivalent masked ROM chip. When the program is correct, the EPROM contents can be converted into a large volume of masked ROMs for the computer manufacturer to plug straight in.

EEPROM – electrically erasable programmable ROM

As its name implies, erasing is an electronic process, as is programming. This is obviously more convenient than using ultraviolet light for erasure.

PROM – programmable ROM

This term is often used to mean 'fusible link' ROM. This is a chip with the memory switch elements all formed in the 'closed' condition by electrically conducting links. Given the BITs to be stored, a special electronic interface uses a high voltage to blow selected links. This opens just the required switches, forming a pattern of 1s and 0s. This type of memory is also good for prototyping, and it is characteristically a very high-speed type of memory. As such, it is useful for applications other than normal computer memory. For instance, if it is necessary to produce a given pattern of outputs, for a given set of binary inputs, PROM can be produced to do this. An obvious example would be in address decoding where a given pattern of address inputs must produce a specific pattern of outputs on the data lines of the chip. This must be performed very fast in order not to introduce delays in memory read and write cycles.

► EPROMs, EEPROMs and PROMs can be written to, but only by using special procedures. Unlike RAMs they are not altered during the normal use of a computer.

Memory upgrades

There are subsystems, or modules, of memory components which can be purchased to fit into a computer system. For instance, IBM PC-type computers can have high-capacity memory boards fitted into the expansion slots on the motherboard. The motherboard also usually has special slots for small vertically mounted memory modules called SIMMs or SIPPs (single in-line memory modules, or pin packages). These range from 256K BYTEs per board, to several MB. The number of available slots determines the maximum capacity of the computer. This is a more efficient way of allowing for extra memory than by full memory boards, or by allowing the plugging of individual chips into the motherboard itself. The former uses up valuable expansion slots, and the latter takes up space on the motherboard, making it large and unwieldy.

► Memory boards and modules.

Specialized memory upgrades

Some machines do not allow the user access to the interior, and memory upgrading may only be possible by a dealer, or the manufacturer. Other machines, to which internal access is also not possible, still allow memory upgrading to be performed, usually by plug-in memory modules. This is particularly true for the new gen-

▶ PCMCIA is the standard for slots designed to take external hardware.

eration of small personal computers, called, variously, laptops, notebooks, palmtops, and so on. A standard type of hardware interface is emerging in the IBM PC standard of machine, referred to by the initials PCMCIA, which stands for Personal Computer Memory Card International Associates, who have defined a hardware definition of a type of slot into which external hardware can be plugged. This might include disks, extra ROM packs containing software, and extra internal memory, as well as general I/O devices. In addition, most small machines allow for proprietary memory modules to plug into special memory upgrade slots in the computer case.

One of the problems of a small machine is that its internal RAM memory may not be of sufficient capacity to run modern sophisticated software efficiently. This problem can be solved by supplying the software on ROM to be plugged into the machine via a slot. The internal memory is then not cluttered with the actual program itself, but is free to store data.

Memory and power-consumption limitations

Another problem is in the area of power consumption – very small machines are often designed to be operated 'on the move' using internal batteries. However, disks, being mechanical devices, require comparatively large amounts of electrical power. The solution is to produce RAM modules organized in the same way as a disk. These are variously referred to as flash-RAM cards, RAM-disk cards, and so on. These cards are designed to be permanent stores of data, and as such may contain a long-lasting battery to keep the memory elements powered, and prevent the usual loss of memory on switch-off.

▶ Flash RAM cards/RAM disk cards: memory upgrades often used on small machines such as personal organizers.

Another advantage of using RAM in place of disks is a considerable increase in speed. Basically, the MPU is fetching data using a fast electronic system from RAM – there are no moving parts.

One of the greatest advances in computer technology is in the field of the small machine. You can see this clearly by examining the popular computer magazines. This is not just true for IBM PC machines – Apple, for instance, produce notebooks in their Macintosh series.

The dynabook concept

One of the dreams of the computer world is to produce a machine which is about the size of a paperback book, with the entire top surface devoted to display and operator input, and having a near infinite memory capacity. This has been named the 'dynabook'. It would be able to communicate intelligently with the owner, who could use it to store a complete library of books, many thousands of hours of digital music, any current working papers and notes, personal storage such as diary, contacts, personal finances, and so on. One of the main elements missing at present is that of sufficiently high-density memory.

Molecular storage

An important frontier in the search for low-power, high-density memory, is that of molecular storage. The concept is to store the BITs at the molecular level within a crystal matrix – the density of such memory could be truly immense, and should require ultra-low power.

 Buy a popular computer magazine and look through for adverts selling memory components. Note the number of different types of memory, including modules, which are on sale. See if you can work out a rough price per K, both for ordinary internal RAM upgrades, and for specialized memory modules. The latter normally works out more expensive.

MAGNETIC MEMORY

We have used the term 'electronic' memory for the devices introduced above. We will now look at memory which relies on magnetism. This is most generally used to produce 'peripheral' memory, which is used to store large volumes of data which can be fetched by the computer system, and stored in internal electronic memory for immediate use by the MPU.

▶ Magnetic memory: normally used for peripheral memory – tapes and disks.

Magnetic disks

The most common peripheral memory is that found on magnetic disks. These were introduced in Chapter 3 and historically started life as large 'hard', or inflexible, metallic disks, coated with magnetic material, and usually fixed within large computers. Several such disks were often ganged up vertically, with multiple read/write heads, and these packs were removable in a cylindrical plastic pack, in large computer systems. This allows library storage of data. Data tapes were used for even greater capacities of data and library storage. However, tape-based data is only available in a strictly sequential fashion, as such tapes are slow in comparison to random storage devices such as disks.

The major innovations which heralded the current era of personal computing were the invention by IBM of a compact hard-disk drive, which they called the 'Winchester' hard disk, and the invention of the flexible or 'floppy' disk.

Hard disks

The capacity of a hard disk, and indeed most magnetic media, depends upon the fineness with which the magnetic 'gap' in the record/playback (or read/write) head can be fashioned, and how close to the magnetic surface the head can be held. In the Winchester disk, a head with a fine gap was held 19 microns from the magnetic surface to produce a very compact but high capacity disk drive. Because the head was so close to the disk, the whole drive had to be manufactured to be enclosed within a hermetically sealed case, to prevent dust and debris from becoming stuck between the head and the disk. This is still true of most personal computer hard disks today. However, capacities have increased from around 10 MB to sizes in excess of 1 giga BYTE, and physical size has dropped considerably. Most hard-disk drives for personal computers also have multiple disks, spinning together, with multiple heads.

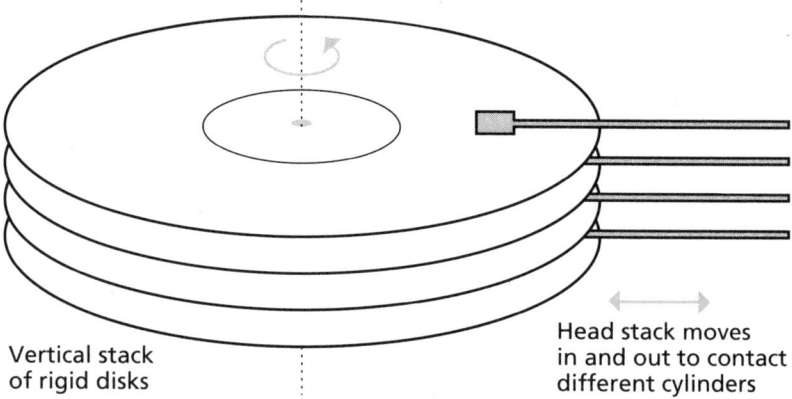

Vertical stack
of rigid disks

Head stack moves
in and out to contact
different cylinders

Figure 7.1 A stack of hard disks

Figure 7.1 shows how a stack of disks spin in order to bring different parts of the disk to the heads. The heads read and write to a vertical 'cylinder' of magnetic information at any instant, and move in and out, together, in very fine steps to contact inner or outer cylinders.

Floppy disks

The floppy disk is similar, but started out using an eight-inch flexible plastic disk, held in an envelope with a window through which a single read/write head contacted the surface of the disk. It revolves more slowly than the Winchester, and is self-cleaning to a certain extent, and so does not need a special enclosure. Again, the evolution of the floppy has increased capacity considerably, and reduced its size first to 5.25 inches, and latterly to 3.5 inches.

However, the exact physical characteristics are irrelevant to most users – all they know is that once a disk is installed, they can read and write data to it using applications programs, or the operating system.

Disk data organization

Disk data is stored as magnetic patterns – representing BITs. The problem is to index the information to ensure that all the information stored on the disk is easily and quickly found.

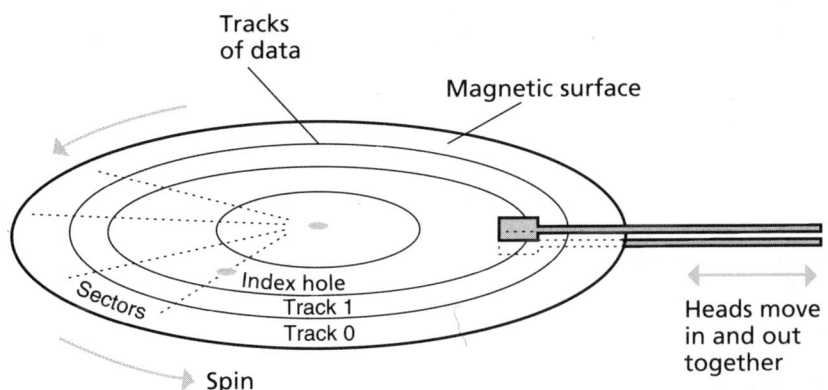

Tracks
of data

Magnetic surface

Sectors

Index hole
Track 1
Track 0

Spin

Heads move
in and out
together

*Figure 7.2 The surface of a
magnetic disk*

A flat featureless magnetic surface would not be easy to index, and finding the position of data stored on it would be difficult and thus slow. To ease the process, and store data in a consistent easily retrieved manner, the magnetic surface is split into concentric rings, called 'tracks', and each track is split into sectors. On the disk shown, there is an indexing hole which signifies the start of the first sector on each track. As the disk spins, the hole is detected by the electronics using a light shining through to a light cell.

The division of the disk into tracks and sectors is performed entirely by magnetic patterns – they cannot be seen with the naked eye. As the tracks are not mechanically marked on the disk surface, their positions rely on the head moving in and out, as shown, by repeatable and accurate mechanical steps to contact the tracks.

Formatting a disk

Before a new disk can be used, the magnetic indexing information must be stored on its surface. This is called 'formatting', and the operating system will have a special command which allows you to format new disks – both hard and soft. However, most machines are supplied with the hard disk already formatted, and the average user may never have to perform this operation. You should be aware that disks which already have data on them will lose it all if they are formatted again.

Once the disks are formatted, the data to be stored on them can fit neatly into blocks, each one filling a given sector, and perhaps ranging over many different tracks. The exact placing of this data on the disk surface is easier to keep track of in these blocks, and indeed the 'addressing' of each sector block of data is stored in a special region of the disk in track 0. The operating system is responsible for all this, and for keeping track of the data in general, and we will see how this works later.

A typical 3.5 inch floppy disk might hold, nominally, 1.44 MB of data, over both sides, upper and lower. Each side will store eighty tracks of data, with eighteen sectors per track each holding 512 BYTEs (or half a K). The data is packed quite tightly – typical track densities are 135 tracks per inch (TPI) which means that a little over

▶ Formatting: preparing the disk to store information (rather like setting up a system of pigeonholes). The disk surface is divided into tracks and sectors.

▶ If you format a disk, you will lose all the files already on it. Beware !

half an inch of the disk's radius is used on each side to contain the data. This ensures that the lengths of the tracks do not differ too greatly from inside to outside.

In addition to the data BITs, each sector has a 'header', put there by the formatting, which is used to identify the sector start. Also, there is some special checking data to ensure that the data has been stored accurately – we will look at data-checking techniques later. Furthermore, there are gaps between the sectors to allow physical separation. With the unused portion of the disk surface inside and outside the tracks, you can see that a large part of the disk surface is not used for data.

Reading the disk

For the floppy in Figure 7.2, two heads are used to contact the two sides. As for a hard disk, they move in and out together, and hence a cylinder for a floppy consists of at most two tracks, and here there are eighty cylinders, each holding two tracks' worth of data – or two times 512 BYTEs times eighteen sectors. Thus, each cylinder holds 18K of data.

This type of magnetic organization is similar for most disks, and though the densities are higher for hard disks, the principles remain the same.

► Disk capacity.

 How much data is stored on a cylinder of a hard disk having seventeen sectors per track, six heads, and the same number of BYTEs per sector as above? Rounded to the nearest whole number, how many MB does the whole disk hold if it has 600 tracks per disk surface? How many cylinders does the whole disk have?

Logical storage of data

The above explains the 'physical' or hardware characteristics of how BITs are stored on a magnetic surface, and we will now look at the 'logical' or software way in which data is stored.

BITs are grouped together into BYTEs, and stored as 'files' of BYTEs. For instance, if you are using a computer to write a letter, the characters and spaces in the text are stored as ASCII codes, BYTE by BYTE. When you wish to store the letter for later, you must first give it a name for later retrieval.

► DOS: disk operating system.

The operating system contains a section called the disk operating system (DOS) which is responsible for handling files – storing and retrieving them, for instance. Using the electronic interface with the disk, the DOS splits the file into blocks, and stores these within a set of sectors.

Each sector has a unique address – thus, for a 1.44 MB floppy, there are nearly 3,000 sectors over the two sides, each with its own address. Every time a file is stored onto the disk, free sectors must be found, and the file split into blocks, each one capable of being stored in a sector. The file name is then stored on the disk, in the first track on the disk, followed by the addresses of the sector blocks, in order, into which the file has been split. By this means, at a later date, a given file can be found and retrieved by name. The name is the most important part of a file, as far as a user is concerned. It is called up by name, and stored by name. The user simply relies on the operating system to do the detailed handling.

► So far as a user is concerned, filename is the most important identifier of a file. The DOS uses electronic addresses to store and retrieve the file.

PERIPHERAL MEMORY INTERFACE

Between the internal computer system and the external peripheral memory devices, there is an electronic interface which handles requests by the operating system for a given block of peripheral memory to be read into internal memory.

The interface may be an extra board, plugged into the expansion slot on the motherboard, or it may be a set of chips already contained on the motherboard. A set of cables connects the peripheral memory device to the electronic interface.

Peripheral memory interface in open-architecture machines

In 'open-architecture' machines, that is those where the user can open the machine and modify it, the peripheral memory interface is usually a special plug-in board. For instance, Figure 7.3 shows the internal structure of a typical open-architecture machine, such as a desk-top IBM PC format of computer.

► All desk-top IBM PC format machines are open architecture, and there is a great wealth of interfaces, upgrades and external devices of all kinds available cheaply and widely for this widespread standard of machinery.

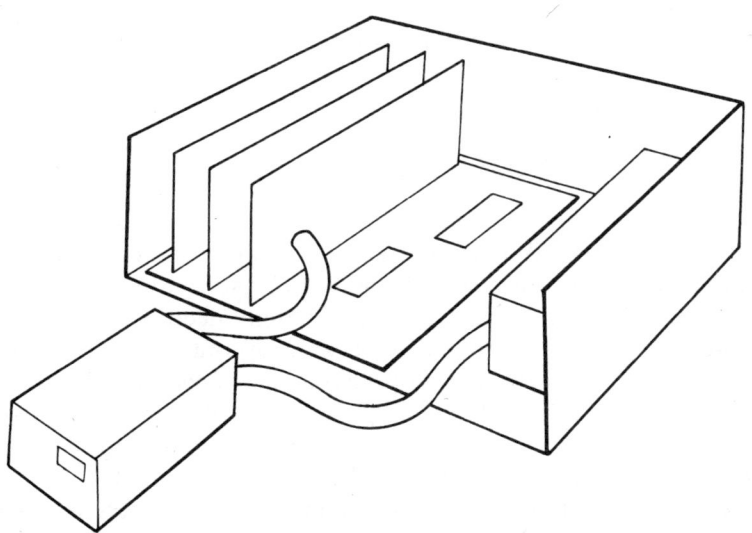

Figure 7.3 The inside of a typical IBM PC open architecture machine

The whole machine is contained in a metal box, with a motherboard on the floor of the box, a PSU (power-supply unit) at one end, and a set of plug-in boards placed vertically in expansion slots. One of these could be for one or more floppy and hard disks, though there is sometimes a separate board for each type of disk drive. There are many manufacturers of IBM PC format boards, and they all have their own designs and facilities.

Changing the hard or floppy drives simply entails opening up the case, unscrewing the existing drives, unplugging them, and then replacing them with a new drive. Most drives, hard and floppy, are designed to fit in the same, or a smaller space, and it is easy to purchase special cages to hold them in place, if one is not present. The accent is increasingly on ease of modification, up and down the scale of facilities.

Peripheral memory interface in closed-architecture machines

In machines which have a 'closed architecture', such as the smaller machines mentioned earlier, we have seen that expansion of the facilities comes from plugging devices into sockets provided by the manufacturer on the outside surfaces of the machine. This can be perfectly acceptable, but may be a little limiting for two reasons. First, plugging interfaces straight into the internal structure of the machine will often produce the fastest type of interface, though not always. Second, there is a limited number of interface devices available for closed-architecture machines as they are not so easy to interface. It is generally recommended that if a closed-architecture machine is to be used, it should be carefully specified for a given level, and replaced if a higher grade of machine is needed. Of course, an open-architecture machine is easier to specify at a low level initially, and upgrade without replacement as progress is made.

Closed-architecture machines include most laptops and similar non-desk-top machines, as well as series of machines such as the Apple Macintosh which are specifically designed to be closed architecture.

DATA TAPES AND BACKING UP DATA

Backing up, or library storage, of the data on a hard disk can be a problem. Even small machines will have thirty or forty megabytes of data stored on a hard disk. If this is to be stored in a library as a backup in case of hard-disk failure, you might need twenty or thirty high-density floppy disks. Also, backing up onto floppies is awkward, and time consuming – floppies have to be fed in and removed over a protracted period of time. There are two mass-storage technologies which are available at present – the data tape, and the writable CD-ROM. CD-ROMs are described on page 139.

▶ Digital tape.

A fast digital tape drive can be used to solve the problem by storing the contents of the whole hard disk on a single data tape (see Figure 7.4). The process may take ten or fifteen minutes, but proceeds completely automatically once set to run.

▶ Mass backup storage.

The procedure for taking and keeping backups of data is to keep several tapes of varying ages. The first time a backup is taken, a new tape is used. The second time a backup is taken, a second new tape is used, so that there are two backups in existence – the first is called the 'father' and the second the 'son'. A third tape might then be used for the next backup, and this becomes the 'son', with the old 'son' becoming the 'father' and the original tape becoming the 'grandfather'. The frequency of backing up is dependent upon the

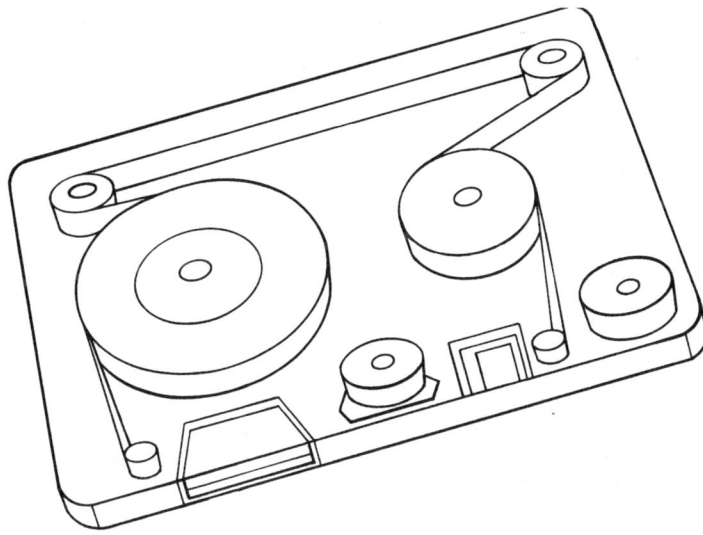

Figure 7.4 A data tape

flow of data in the system. Some much-used systems need backing up every night, just before shut down, others every week, and so on.

Other tapes may also be kept for greater security still. For instance, every month a backup could be taken on a new tape, and this could be stored in a library, and not overwritten, perhaps for a year. In this manner, a tape exists for each month of the previous twelve. This allows the history of the system's evolution to be examined, and allows for any consistent errors to be discovered.

COMPACT DISK READ-ONLY MEMORY

▶ See Chapter 3.

We are used to hearing music which has been digitized and replayed on a compact disk player. However, such devices only store strings of 1s and 0s, whose binary numerical values are converted, at high speed, into voltages of a proportionate value, and fed to an amplifier.

These binary numbers could just as easily be data or programs from computers, and indeed the same compact disks are used for this purpose.

Again, a special drive and interface is needed, but otherwise they are the same as magnetic disks. The data stored on their surface is in the form of bumps and shallows which are illuminated by a laser, as the disk spins. The resulting dark and light pulses are picked up by light cells, and converted electronically to binary signals. The individual cells are very small, and so a large amount of data can be stored on the surface of a compact disk. Currently, a normal audio disk can store around 600 MB.

Generally, data disks are called 'CD-ROMs' – which is short for compact disk read-only memory. However, it is now possible to both read and write to CD-ROMs, which allows very high density disk storage of data. This capacity will increase in the future, and many giga BYTEs of data will be able to be stored and retrieved by the user. A giga BYTE (GB) is a thousand MB. It would seem that the days of the slow and rather more mechanical data-tape backup storage devices are numbered.

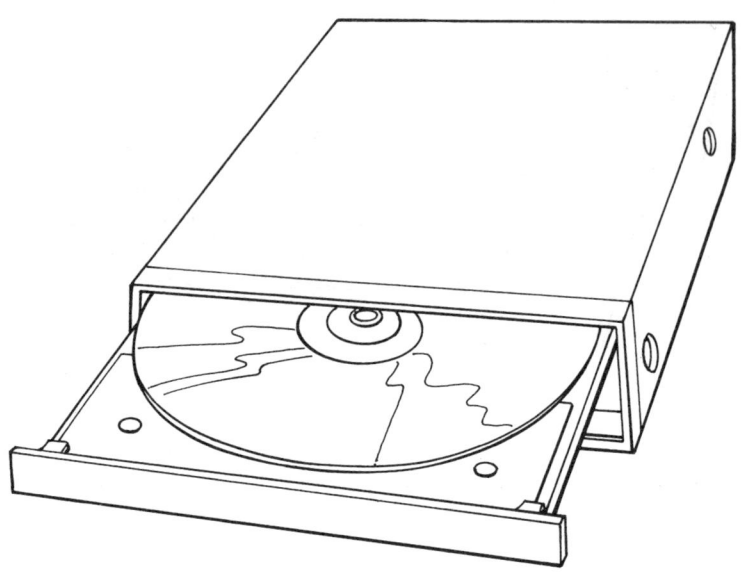

Figure 7.5 A CD-ROM drive and disk

Many large storage items are available on CD-ROM. For instance, complete encyclopedias, large catalogues of information on specific subjects, games, educational programs, and many of these are 'multimedia' products. That is, they do not just contain information in text form. They also have high-grade photographic and graphical images, and high-quality sound. It should not be long before all programs come on CD-ROM, and the floppy-disk method of distributing programs can die. Already, modern sophisticated software, even for wordprocessing, comes on several high-density floppies, and this is becoming seen as a cumbersome and slow way to receive applications.

Most CD-ROM drives have a socket in the back, or an internal amplifier, to allow loudspeaker systems or earphones to be plugged in. In this way, the sounds stored on a CD-ROM can be heard. In addition, because of standardization of storage, normal music disks can also be played on the drive, with suitable software in the host computer.

In the future, CD-ROMs will become more and more popular as means of distributing large volumes of data. For instance, the complete national telephone directory for the UK is available on CD-ROM, and in the USA there is already a move to give telephone company customers a free CD-ROM drive, and the directories on disk, as this is generally cheaper, and better for the environment, than the production of printed-paper telephone directories.

▶ Free computers in France. For a long time now the French telephone company have been giving away free computer terminals under the 'Minitel' system. The original idea was to save the telephone company from having to provide directories and directory enquiry facilities. As the terminal is connected to the telephone system, it is also possible to send any other type of data to the users. As the users are just about everyone in France, this is an alluring market for advertisers, and providers of information in general.

CAPACITIES AND ACCESS TIMES

As we saw in Chapter 3, floppy disks have typical capacities of from a few hundred K to a few MB. Hard disks have typically from a few tens of MB to many hundreds or a few thousands of MB. It is difficult to be accurate about these capacities as they are changing rapidly, but you can see that, essentially, there are a couple of orders of ten between the capacities of floppies and hard disks.

CD-ROMs start at around 600 MB, and larger disk systems can contain large numbers of giga BYTEs.

Small data-tape drives normally store several hundred MB on a small tape cartridge, and are good for backing up hard disks.

The times for access to data also vary considerably across these various memory devices. Access times also depend considerably on where the data is stored physically on the magnetic surface – some places take longer to reach with the read head. This reaches gargantuan proportions when a data request is received for information at the centre of a spool of tape. The whole tape must be rewound to reach it!

Access times are generally given as averages. For instance the average access time for a hard disk might be quoted as 19 ms. This means 19 'milli-seconds' or 19 thousandths of a second. This might seem quite fast, but bear in mind that the block of data might be distributed over the whole disk – some in sectors on the outside tracks, some in the middle, and some in the centre. Also, there is the question of the amount of data being retrieved. Once the data has been contacted, it must be read off the disk – this also takes a finite time.

Access times for a floppy are longer because the disk rotates more slowly, and the heads move in and out more slowly. Access times are typically around five to ten times slower for a floppy than a hard disk.

A CD-ROM is a very slow device in comparison. It has access times to find a block of data which are around 500 ms (half a second). The information is stored in a continuous spiral from the inside to the outside, and in fact the spin rate of the disk changes as the laser-read head moves in and out in order to keep the data stream at a constant speed.

Of course, a tape has access speeds which are entirely dependent upon the organization of its data. If data requests can be confined to a given area of the tape, and not dotted about from end to end, speeds of access will not be too low. However, as a mass storage device for random retrieval, it falls far short of practicality, and is not generally used in this way.

In comparison with the above, internal electronic memory is extremely fast indeed. For instance, the delay between a BIT being requested from a memory chip, and the BIT appearing on the data bus can be as short as a few billionths of a second – that is a few 'nano-seconds' (ns). In fact, main microcomputer memory is typically 50ns to 100ns, but mainframe-memory components are an order of ten faster. However, such memory is more power hungry, and not as physically compact. It is also too fast to be taken advan-

► Capacities.

► Access times.

► Caches.

tage of by current micros, except in specialist areas such as 'caches'.

A cache is an area of RAM, sometimes formed on the MPU chip, in which the processor stores what it thinks is the next section of the current program. If it is right, then fetch and execute cycles are speeded up considerably – if not, it has to flush out the cache, and start again. The result is a fairly useful overall increase in speed of processing, with no software change.

MPU AND SYSTEM LEVELS

The memory capacity of a given processor, and its ability to transmit large numbers of BITs to and from memory devices is what is used to classify systems into different levels.

The very first chips were actually four-BIT MPUs, which quickly progressed to eight-BIT units. The 8080 MPU, and its more powerful derivative the Z80 (produced by a company called ZILOG), formed the basis of much of the microcomputing in the early years of personal computing, along with the eight-BIT 6502 chip.

► From four-BIT to sixteen-BIT.

The most significant event in the field of microcomputing came when IBM decided to enter the personal computer market in the 1980s with a machine caled the 'IBM PC XT'. They decided to start with an INTEL chip called the 8088, which was basically a sixteen-BIT chip, but only internally to the MPU – its external-data bus was still eight BITs. This was soon superseded by other manufacturers producing true sixteen-BIT machines, based around chips such as the 8086, which was a true sixteen-BIT MPU, but software compatible with the 8088.

IBM continued to dominate the personal computer market, and many other manufacturers simply produced machinery to the same standard, but gradually better and faster, though software compatible. This allowed many software houses to standardize, and sell their products to the largest body of computer users in history.

IBM set the initial standard, and other machines made to that standard are known as 'clones'. At the same time, Apple brought out its range of Macintosh machines, based around the sixteen-BIT 68000 series of MPUs, in direct competition with IBM, and using a completely different software standard, which was later copied, in essence, to fit onto IBM machinery.

The 8086 was soon followed by the 80186, the 80286, the 80386 and the 80486, which were designed to increase instruction throughput, and could run at faster and faster clock speeds – up to around 50 or 60 MHz (million cycles per second). Most software remained compatible through this range, but a new range of machines was produced called the 'AT' series using the 80286, and beyond, and much modern software needs at least this level of machine to run correctly.

Just as the original IBM standard was copied, so the INTEL chips have been copied by 'second source' manufacturers, and as each new level of chip is brought out, second sources fight with each other to produce the product cheaper. This is all generally good news for the consumer.

If you scan the magazines, you will see that the 80386, and 80486, levels of MPU exist in two versions – the 'SX' and 'DX'. The latter is the more powerful version.

After the 80486 became the standard, INTEL brought out the next level of MPU, the 80586, but called it the Pentium – they decided not to brand it the 80586 as a court in the USA ruled that a number could not be copyrighted.

The Pentium MPU can run with a processor clock speed of a minimum of 60 MHz, which will increase to 100 MHz and beyond, contains in excess of three million transistors, and runs a sixty-four-BIT wide data bus. It also uses sophisticated multiple caches to try to predict the next area of program and data which will be needed, and thus gain fetch and execute speed. Also, the old microprogram method of decoding the fetched machine-code instructions has given way, to a certain extent, to hardware electronic circuits that do the job faster.

Floating-point arithmetic and the maths coprocessor

Another important concept in the evolution of the MPU has been the method by which floating-point arithmetic operations are performed. When we add, subtract, multiply and divide, we are automatically doing floating-point calculations. That is, broadly, the result is represented by a number which may have a decimal point with any number of digits before and after it.

Classically in computing, the floating-point, and other 'scientific' operations and functions are performed by modules consisting of small programs devoted to these operations. Essentially, floating-point operations have been a software problem. Such operations are widespread in computing, and so attempts have been made to incorporate floating point directly onto the MPU chip, or at least provide for it in some special fast hardware which would not involve the execution of any software elements. Thus the programmer could simply call up these operations automatically, and the operations themselves would be executed at considerable speed.

The 80XXX series of MPUs (where the Xs represent two or three digits, depending upon the level of the MPU) were designed to interface directly with a special chip called a 'maths coprocessor' which would provide these operations in hardware. The 80486DX and Pentium levels of MPU have incorporated this maths hardware directly onto the chip.

The advantage of these hardware maths elements can best be seen when complex graphical software is being executed. In such programs, there is a vast amount of calculation being performed continuously, and coprocessor hardware speeds this considerably.

Developments in systems

Systems are becoming faster and use more and more sophisticated processors. Also, I/O facilities are becoming more complex. For instance, small computers, which imitate notepads, can be communicated with using a type of pen, written over the surface of the display. The machine tries to decode the actual writing itself, in order to interpret the user's commands. The goal is an ever more intelligent and natural interface with the machine.

As you look at the magazines, you will see a range of clock speeds being advertised for machines. As explained before, this is not always the best parameter for judging machines, except for computers which use the same processor. A 25 MHz 80386SX machine will not perform as fast as a 33 MHz 80386SX machine, but both will be eclipsed by a 25 MHz 80486DX machine – particularly in mathematically based software for which the 80486DX has its own on-chip floating-point coprocessor. Essentially, be sure to compare like with like.

▶ Now that you have completed this chapter, look back to the objectives at the beginning and check that you have accomplished each of them.

Chapter review

- RAM – random-access memory – is volatile as its contents disappear on switch-off.
- ROM – read-only memory – is always retained.
- ROM can be programmable, and thus hold programs and data permanently.
- As disks spin, the magnetic data on the surface is read and written to by a read/write head which moves in and out across the magnetic surface.
- A magnetic disk is organized into concentric 'tracks', and 'sectors'.
- Memory capacity in general is usually denoted in BYTEs, K BYTEs (KB) and mega BYTEs (MB).
- A closed architecture machine is one where the owner is discouraged from opening the processor box, open architecture is the opposite.
- Data tapes are magnetic tapes for holding and backing up large data capacities.
- CD-ROM is a high capacity laser-read data disk.

 **Operating systems and software**

THE OPERATING SYSTEM (OS)

Unless the computer is specifically dedicated to a given task, such as controlling a video recorder, or collecting weather data for onward transmission, the user will interact with the machine via an operating system of some kind. As you know, this will normally be via a keyboard, a screen, and perhaps a mouse, or something similar. Essentially, when you are looking at a screen, and interacting with it, it is the OS you are communicating with, and the OS does the job of making the actions work. The commands you type into the machine when it is not running one of your application programs, are OS commands. Of course, if the OS is entirely graphic, you may not actually be typing commands at all. Everything might be done using a mouse, and a bunch of icons. However, the principle is the same.

You give high-level commands, from the keyboard or mouse, such as 'run a given program', 'clear the screen' or 'give me a list of all the files I have stored on the hard disk'. The work which goes into actioning these 'simple' commands includes storing and retrieving indexing information, fetching files from the correct place on disk, starting and monitoring programs, writing data to the

▶ The user of a computer communicates with its operating system, using high-level commands.

▶ **This chapter looks at typical operating systems, and the commands and facilities you should expect to see.**
We will also expand further on the types of programming language available: starting with high level programs and seeing how they are turned into machine code for the processor to execute.
Chapter 9 looks at machine code itself.

video memory, monitoring the keyboard and mouse continuously, and so on. These are boring mechanical tasks which are usually quickly and accurately performed by the OS.

Imagine having to keep a full and continuous note of all the sector addresses of all the blocks of data you have stored over many millions of BYTEs on your hard disk, let alone having to consult this list to call up a given program or piece of data at high speed. The OS performs such involved, boring, low-level jobs, and many others, automatically, leaving you free to use the computer like a tool, without having to be unduly concerned with how the hardware is controlled. To this extent, therefore, the OS distances, or separates, the user from the computer itself. Most uninformed users will not realize that they are interacting with a program called the operating system – they just see the whole package as 'a computer'.

► Using high level commands leaves all the tedious work for the operating system to do.

Also, in some applications, the OS may not even be 'seen' by the user. Computers can be set up, using the operating system, to execute a given applications program immediately after switch-on, rather than giving the user the option of choosing the application. For instance, a computer can be set up, on switch-on, to go straight into a wordprocessing program. As far as general users are concerned, the machine is only a wordprocessor – that is all they ever see. Only an informed user will know how to exit the WP program, and go into some other application using the OS.

Judging an operating system

► Two categories of operating systems:
• single processing
• multi-processing (or multi-tasking).

Modern operating systems fall into two main categories. These are single-processing systems, where just one job is being performed at any time, and multiprocessing, or multi-tasking systems, where several programs may be run apparently simultaneously. In addition to this is the consideration as to whether a given OS supports networks of computers.

Given that these main categories describe classes of operating systems, there are some important criteria on which a given system may be judged, particularly by the user. These criteria fall roughly into areas which may be described by the following qualities:

1. accessibility
2. extent
3. speed
4. standardization.

Other criteria might include whether it is supported on a given manufacturer's machines, whether it is expensive, takes up a large amount of disk space, and so on. However, from the user's point of view, the four numbered points above are crucial. We will look at those now.

Accessibility means the ease with which the facilities offered are accessible. For instance, if the user has to remember and type a special eight-digit code for each function needed, it would be difficult to use the machine efficiently. Simple 'mnemonic' command words for functions are important – that is, words which mean something to the operator, and are easy to remember. Also, it is important to be able to access the operating system itself with ease.

Extent means how comprehensive the OS is. If it does not include a whole class of important functions, which other OS's do offer, it will not be acceptable to the user.

Speed is important – you should not have to sit in front of the machine waiting for interminable amounts of time for simple operations to be called up and performed. A good OS is efficiently written, and works as fast as possible.

Standardization is very important. It is useful for a user to be able to transfer, without relearning, from machine to machine. Thus, recent OS's generally try to use standard command words with which people will already be familiar.

These point to the main advantages of a good OS in actual day to day use. Other criteria are important, but less obvious to the person sitting at the screen and keyboard.

Types of operating system

There are several types of operating system, defined by various attributes. For instance, we will look at the main two types of screen and interaction methods employed by different operating systems: 'command-line processing' systems and 'graphical-user-interface' systems.

► Types of OS:
• command-line processing
• graphical user interface (GUI).

Another major OS attribute is whether it is 'multi-tasking' or 'single-tasking'. A multi-tasking OS is one which is capable of running two or more programs at the same time. A single-tasking system allows just one program to run at any time. That program must be completely shut down before another can be started. Most microcomputers run single-tasking OSs, but multi-tasking systems do exist, and to some extent the 'GUI' and 'windows' approach to software, introduced on page 67, allows some multi-tasking. Minis and mainframes, however, are designed to run many terminals and users at the same time, running any programs they wish.

Single-tasking

A typical microcomputer system is physically only able to run a single task at any instant. The illusion of running more than one program at a time is created by 'time-slicing' the operation of the machine. A given amount of time is allocated to each program. For instance, each might be allocated a hundredth of a second. The first program is then processed for that time, then the next program, and the next and so on until the first is started again. In this way small parts of each program are run at high speed, and consecutively, to give the illusion, to the much slower human observer, that all the programs are running simultaneously. When a given time-slice comes to an end, the values associated with its program are stored in a special 'control block' in memory. The control block for the next program is then retrieved and used for its time-slice before being

▶ Time-slicing is a way of using machine time more efficiently when several programs are run on a single-tasking system.

stored again to make way for the next. This continues until the first program is retrieved again, and so on round the cycle.

The problem, in small systems, is to find enough memory to retain a copy of each program in store, so that each can be run quickly as its time comes round. A possible solution to this is to bring the programs in from disk each time, but this slows the operation down considerably.

▶ Time-sharing.

Systems which employ these, or similar tactics, are sometimes called 'time-sharing' systems, and they are a common feature of large systems serving many users. In fact, large computers effectively have more than one processor within their program-execution unit, and as such have a hardware advantage in terms of serving many users.

As you can see, time-slicing uses the computer's memory quite intensively, and the speed with which the operation proceeds is dependent upon how fast the processor can read and write data, as well as performing executions. In general, only the fastest processors are worth using in this mode.

Networking

A further attribute which should be considered for an OS is whether or not it is capable of running on a network of computers. Many standard OSs (single- and multi-tasking) come in forms which apply to network operation, and in addition there are various special OSs which are designed from scratch to service a network of computers.

In this chapter, we will be considering single-user OSs, but much of what is presented transfers to other types of OS without modification.

NON-GUI OS COMMANDS

▶ GUI: graphical user interface.

Non-GUI processing is sometimes termed 'command-line processing', and we will see why now.

▶ Prompts: the computer asks you do to something.

If a GUI is not being used, the chances are that upon switching the machine on, the screen puts up various information on its set-up process, and then sits waiting for keyboard input with a cursor flashing its position by a 'prompt' character. This might look like:

    C >_

Characters typed in at the keyboard appear after this prompt, on what is termed the 'command line'. The cursor moves to keep the user informed as to where, on the screen, input will appear as it is typed in. The prompt does not just show position, it usually has some information about the other main task of the OS – that of keeping track of files on disk. Here, the prompt contains a letter. All disk drives in the machine, of which there are often two – one hard and one floppy – are given labels. Labels are usually single letters. Here, the prompt is informing the user that the current 'logged' disk is disk 'C'. This means that commands and program files can be retrieved from the C disk directly. Let us see what this means. Remember that different OSs may use different names for commands, though most have some resemblance to the following.

At the prompt, you could decide that you wish to see a list or 'directory' of files which are resident on the current logged disk. Alternatively, you may wish to log in a new disk, and operate on that one instead. For the moment, we will stick with the C disk.

Generally, a request for the directory takes on the form of a **DIR** command. This is simply typed in, in upper or lower case, at the prompt, giving a display such as:

► Looking at directories.

    C > DIR_

The cursor, shown as a lower dash, moves over to the new typing position as **DIR** is typed in. At this point, you have the choice as to whether to change the command shown, or even correct its spelling. Before the computer will accept this command, and execute it, you must finish typing it, including corrections, and then press a key on the keyboard called the **ENTER** key. It is usually over to the right of the letter keys, and is usually rather larger than the other keys. It may be labelled **ENTER**, or **RETURN** or simply have an angled arrow on it. Either way, the computer does nothing until **ENTER** is pressed. At that point, the command cannot be changed, or modified, and the computer executes it directly.

The result is likely to be a single long vertical list of file names which is longer than the typically twenty-five lines of the average VDU. The list scrolls off the top of the screen, and much of it is lost. There is usually a modified directory command which solves this problem. For instance, in the operating system called 'MSDOS' which controls IBM PC types, the **DIR** command can be changed to:

    DIR/W

The /W is called a 'switch' and it switches the basic or 'default' **DIR** mode to displaying the files across the width of the screen as follows:

COMMAND. COM	DISKCOPY. COM	DOSKEY. COM	MARTDRV. SYS	DOSSHELL. INI
DOSSHELL. COM	FORMAT. COM	KEYB. COM	LOADFIX. SYS	MIRROR. INI
MODE. COM	MSHERC. COM	SYS. COM	TREEE. SYS	UNFORMAT. INI
ATTRIB. EXE	CHKDSK. EXE	COMP. EXE	DEBUG. EXE	DOSSHELL. EXE
DOSSWAP. EXE	EMM386. EXE	EXE2BIN. EXE	FDISK. EXE	FIND. EXE
LINK. EXE	MEM. EXE	RECOVER. EXE	RPED. EXE	SETVER. EXE
UNDELETE. EXE	XCOPY. EXE	COUNTRY. SYS	DOSSHELL. GRB	DOSSHELL. SWP
DOSSHELL. VID	GRAPHICS. PRO	HIMEM. SYS	KEYBOARD. SYS	RAMDRIVE. SYS

Unfortunately, if you are using MSDOS, you just have to remember this switch, and indeed many more commands and codes like it. This is one of the reasons for using a GUI instead of a normal OS: it is much easier to remember how to use the command structure as it is presented visually. However, it is also true that using the basic commands of an operating system puts you more fully in touch

▶ How filenames are composed.

with the system at a lower level. This is important for programmers, and technical users of the machine.

The list of filenames on the previous page include various types of file associated with the operating system itself. The filenames have two sections – the part before the 'dot' is an arbitrary name, chosen by the originator of the file. The part after the 'dot' is called an 'extension' and usually gives some indication as to the type of file, or its use.

For instance, anything with the extension **EXE** or **COM**, in MSDOS, is a program which may be executed simply by typing in the filename (without the 'dot' and extension) at the prompt. For instance, if you were sitting in front of the screen, instead of typing **DIR**, you could type:

FORMAT

followed by a press of the **ENTER** key. This would command the OS to look in the directory for a file whose name is **FORMAT** with a dot extension which is **COM** or **EXE**. If it finds one, it must consult the filename index, fetch the complete program into memory, and start the MPU at the top of the program. The program itself then takes over until it is complete, when the OS is standing by to restart. This program is used to prepare floppy disks for use in the system. It stores the magnetic indexing information referred to on pages 00–00, i.e. the sector headings.

If you look at the directory above, you will see there are many more commands which can be typed at the keyboard, one for each **EXE** or **COM** file shown, in fact. However, you will not see a command file such as **DIR.COM** or **DIR.EXE**. The reason for this is that **DIR**, along with a number of other much-used commands, are internal commands of the OS – they are stored within the OS program itself, and do not need to be contained in external command files, such as **FORMAT.COM**.

In general, OSs contain some basic common internal commands. External commands are supplied as separate command files, and there can be any number of these. Indeed, further external commands can be added, or specially written. The only proviso being that they are stored on disk with the correct extension.

Other internal commands which are commonly included in an OS are as follows, though different OSs may use different names for the actual commands illustrated here:

- **DEL** – which deletes files from the disk
- **CLS** – which clears the screen and places the cursor at the top
- **TYPE** – which types up the contents of a file to the screen
- **REN** – used to rename a file
- **COPY** – copies a file from one place to another – perhaps from a floppy disk to the hard disk

and so on. As you can see, the majority of commands are associated with the handling of files, and this is a common feature – it is the

DOS (disk-operating system) part of the OS which predominates. The manipulation of files is a central task of any OS, and when you sit down at a new machine, with a prompt showing on a screen, you should automatically type in **DIR** in the hope that the operating system being run recognizes this command, and you will be shown a list of the files immediately available.

File organization

Even quite a simple computer system can have many hundreds of files stored on it, and usually there will be in excess of a thousand. Every time a piece of software is purchased, it comes with many files for all sorts of different applications and options. Keeping track of these files, or even reading the filenames after a **DIR** command can be a formidable task.

In general, the OS offers a method of storing associated files within areas dedicated to different applications. For instance, a modern wordprocessing program will not come as a single **.COM** or **.EXE** file which you simply call up and run. It will come with perhaps a hundred files, made up of a main program, a number of peripheral programs, some example texts, a series of 'help' files where the manual is stored, special configuration files for different printers, and so on. If you were then to purchase, say, a business-accounts program, then a further hundred files might be loaded on, and they will intermix with the wordprocessor files. In principle, this does not stop the main programs from working, but there are several disadvantages of allowing these very different program files from coexisting side by side.

First, it is difficult to understand the directory if it contains two large applications intermixed – you may want to check that a given file is present, and it is hidden among twice the number of files that came with that application.

Second, there may be two files, one in each application, having the same name – this causes severe confusion, and will probably lead to one of the files being abandoned. Two completely different program writers, perhaps working in different countries, cannot be expected to allow for this possibility across the complete spectrum of available software.

Third, you may at some time wish to remove one of the applications from the machine – this is very difficult if intermixed with others.

There are other disadvantages too, and any decent OS will allow compartmentalization of applications.

In MSDOS, the disk can be divided up into separate directories, and even hierarchies, or trees, of directories.

► Disk trees.

Each disk has a 'root' directory, and, usually, a number of sub-directories. In fact, subdirectories can also have their own subdirectories, and thus any number of connected compartments can be created in a hierarchy, if required.

Each directory must be given a name, and directories can be used to separate applications from each other. In order to see the files in a given directory, the user changes to that directory, and then issues a **DIR** command, and just those files are shown.

This directory structure is not just for different applications programs, a directory can be created to keep files together for other reasons. For instance, a wordprocessor might be used to write several different types of document. All letters could be kept on a **LETTERS** subdirectory, all reports on **REPORTS**, and so on. The basic idea is to impose a neatness and organization on the collection of files held on a disk.

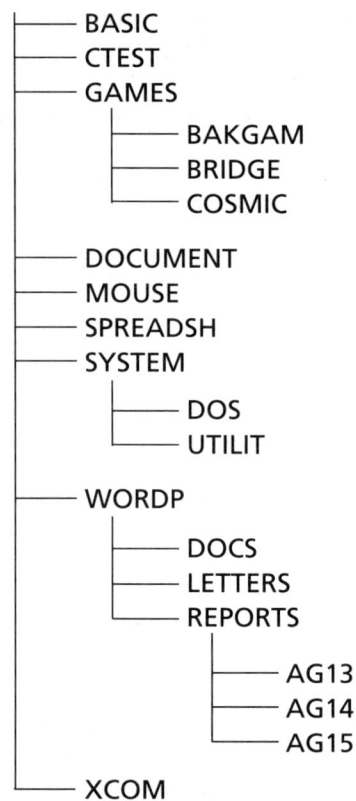

Figure 8.1 A hierarchy of file directories

Figure 8.1 shows a root directory at the top designated by a '\' symbol (a backslash), followed by various directories with names chosen to suggest their content. It is entirely up to the user to choose the names, and as long as each name conforms to whatever rules the OS demands, anything is possible.

As you can see, there are several directories with subdirectories, and even further subdirectories, making a large tree with any number of levels required.

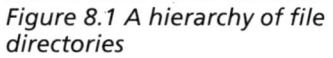
Making a new directory.

A new directory is made by using the internal command **MKDIR** which is short for 'make a new directory'. The new directory name is typed in after the command, and this new directory is created within the tree as a subdirectory of the current directory. In this manner, any number of directories can be made, with any branch structure required. There is also an internal command to remove directories.

Front-end processors

Unless a GUI is presented on the screen, as with the Macintosh, most OS commands are quite difficult to use and memorize fully. It is much easier to interact with the machine if a visual summary of all the available OS commands are shown on the screen, perhaps with some 'help' information on their use. There are many programs which try to provide this user interface, and they are called 'front-end processors'. They will place all the commands available on the screen, along with all the files available, and hence give a user a clear idea of the system's extent.

An approach to the supply of 'help' information, common also in applications packages, is that of 'context sensitive' help. At any point in the application, a special keyboard key (called a 'hot key') can often be pressed, and the commands and facilities available at that point are displayed, perhaps with invitations to access further help details by pressing other keys, or using the pointer to select them. Such facilities need not rely on hot keys. A menu of help options might appear constantly on the screen to allow the user to point to one, and delve into the details on the use of a given command, etc.

These front-end processors are particularly useful for OSs which allow 'trees' of directories to be stored in the machine. The complete tree structure can be shown on the screen, usually in a form similar to Figure 8.1, and the user can visually enter any directory, and view and manipulate the files in there using the basic OS commands. A mouse is useful here to point at directories, files and commands, and to this end most modern front-end processors look rather like GUIs.

Later versions of MSDOS come with a front-end processor called DOSSHELL, and the Macintosh screen is a natural GUI front-end processor. In fact, all Macintosh programs and applications have the same GUI look.

▶ DOSSHELL.

APPLICATION OF THE OS

Whatever form the OS of the machine takes, it is always in the background, either supplying large amounts of 'free' programming for applications programs to 'plug' into, or just staying quietly behind waiting to take over again when the current application is finished.

Either way, the user may never have to interact directly with the OS, if the machine is dedicated to a given task. For instance, in a telephone-sales setting, or at the customer-accounts end of a utility, there are perhaps hundreds of operators just using the machine to bring up customer accounts, or other details onto a screen to allow them to interact with customers at the end of the telephone. Such users never even see an OS working. It is up to computer services managers, and their staff, to ensure that the user is completely isolated from the system, to allow them to work at their jobs unhindered by the slightest whiff of technology. Computers in this setting are purely fast simple tools.

Small-business people, however, often find that they and their staff have to understand more about the computer. They need to be able to switch it on and start an application running. They will also have to format disks, load in new software, perhaps even read manuals and learn how to copy disks and files for backup. Such a setting cannot afford the luxury of a special department aimed at distancing the users from the technology. Fitting computers to a given work situation is a balance between the desire to use computers without facing technical issues, and the simple problems of budget and business size.

The OS has a major effect on all sizes of business. The small business must necessarily interact with it at every level, and the large concern uses it to develop applications for its non-technical users. The more efficient the OS the better, and in many ways the OS should be chosen to fit the application, though most smaller users do not have much choice in this area.

It is also interesting to compare the application of the GUI environment in these two cases, as there is an industry-wide movement towards WIMP graphics. In some cases, this can be a step backwards. The idea is that all GUI-based applications should look and feel the same. They all use 'buttons' to be 'pressed' by the mouse, or menus and icons to be selected for commands.

▶ For some applications GUI is an advantage, for others it is not.

For a general telephone sales or accounts screen, the addition of a mouse and icons would be a definite disadvantage to the users. They are far faster at using a keyboard and specially designed screen layouts to perform the task, instead of fiddling about with yet another input device. On the other hand, a small business may consider that it is easier to teach new workers how to bring up the main programs and applications which are used every day using a WIMP environment – it is certainly visual, and less reliant on keyboard skills.

These are some of the issues which have to be faced when selecting a system for a given business.

PROGRAM FILES

When we looked at file organization, we saw that many of the files contained programs which could be run directly by the processor. We will now look at how these files arise.

▶ Purchased ready-made or specially written.

In fact, the main method by which a machine acquires programs is simply by the user purchasing programs on floppy disks, and loading them through the floppy drive into a directory, or user area, on the hard disk. The programs can then be run directly. This is probably an adequate way for the majority of standard business users to acquire programs. However, in larger, or non-standardized applications, it is necessary to write, or commission, new programs.

▶ Interpreters and compilers: helper programs to convert higher-level languages into machine code.

The programmer will write programs using another program to help in this process. Such 'helper' programs are typically called 'interpreters' and 'compilers'. We will look at these on page 157.

In general, you should be aware that the program files which are used as direct commands, or are run directly by a GUI, are files containing machine code. That is, they are files of binary numbers which are interpreted as machine-code instructions by the MPU when fetched and executed.

This means that, for instance, you cannot use a binary program file from a Macintosh on an IBM PC. The reason is simply that they use radically different MPUs, and one does not understand the machine code of the other.

► Different kinds of machines understand different versions of machine code. This divides the IBM standard from the Macintosh standard.

The aim of the programmer is to produce a set of instructions which fits a given specification. The programmer is not interested in the binary numbers being produced, just the flow of logical instructions which solve the problem. It would be very difficult indeed if programs had to be written directly in binary – the programmer would have to remember a large number of totally incomprehensible binary numbers for instructions. These would have to be written in a list, and stored in a file. Even using hex to reduce the binary to a few digits would hardly be of much help. It is essential that the computer acts as an interface between the high level at which the programmer wishes to speak, and the final low level binary file, which is sometimes called the 'object file', or a file of 'object code'.

► Object file: file written in binary/machine code/object code.

Humans simply do not think in binary or hex, they think along human-language lines when solving or describing a problem. It would be useful if the computer could offer the programmer the facility to talk in a human language, and then take these instructions and code them automatically into the object code for MPU interpretation.

Another important reason for helping the programmer is that it is useful if the program could be adapted to run on any MPU system. In other words, the transfer of the program into object code should be done at the last minute, and performed differently for different MPU systems. This would allow programs to be universal, and capable of transfer, with appropriate coding, from machine to machine.

In reality, computer languages have been developed which go some of the way towards allowing programmers to list instructions in their normal language, but the process is not complete – computers cannot yet understand normal human language. High-level languages have some English words, and are highly stylized to force the programmer to think along specific lines while programming, and thus reduce the problem of coding programs into object code. Also, a given computer language will exist in many different dialects – it is not always possible for a given version available on IBM PC types to be transferred directly to another type of machine. However, the changes required to effect the transfer are usually fairly minimal.

Computer languages are evolving all the time – it is an area of computing which is changing continuously.

High-level languages

A program is simply a list of logical steps, or statements, which in-

► A program is a list of logical steps, or statements, which instruct a machine to perform a task, or solve a problem.

struct a machine to perform a task, or solve a problem. These statements must conform to the rules of the computer language chosen, and then the final program coded into machine code. If the language chosen uses human language components, it is 'higher' up the scale towards the human operator than machine code, which is lower down, nearer the MPU.

Some typical high-level language statements might be:

LET X = 3

PRINT "HELLO"

INPUT, Y

▶ Assignment statements: give a value to a variable.

Output statements: specify an output, for example that a word appears on the screen.

Literals: typed between double inverted commas – this is literally what will be printed (mistakes and all!).

Input statements: make a prompt appear and ask the operator to input something.

The first statement is an 'assignment' statement – it assigns the value 3 to the variable X. The second statement is an output statement – it asks the system to print the word **HELLO**, probably to the VDU screen. Here the word to be printed is contained within double quotes – sometimes called 'literals'. This ensures that the computer is told exactly what to print, and no more. Finally, there is an input statement. This suspends the program and waits for the operator to type in a value which the computer stores in the variable Y.

These statements have a certain clarity to a human user due to their English content. They are also quite easy to remember, and use. However, when the computer is asked to turn these simple statements into object code, a fair amount of work is required.

The word **PRINT** has to be identified, and compared with the standard list of statements available. The computer then sees that the **PRINT** statement has to have something after it to be printed, and it has to interpret the following "**HELLO**" as a literal word to be printed. It must then generate the machine-code statements which cause this to happen, including manipulating the VDU correctly. In fact, the machine-code program will probably interact with the operating system to present the word on the VDU. After all, the OS already has modules for VDU handling, and it is a waste of time to write this code again from scratch. This goes for many other ways in which the program might interact with the I/O of the system. For instance, if the program is to store and retrieve data from disk files, again OS modules are used to perform the task.

Compiler programs

▶ Compiler programs take as their input a high-level language file, and produce as their output a translation into machine code (object code).

The program used to change the high level statements into object code is called a 'compiler'. The input to such a program is called 'source code'. The compiler, therefore, is a program which uses a file of high level program statements, or source code, as its input data, and outputs a file of MPU-executable object code, which can be run directly as a program. In order to write programs in this manner, an 'editor' program is also required. This is a type of 'wordprocessor' – that is, it allows the user to type in sentences, correct them, and store them in a file. The editor does not 'understand' the sentences in any way, it faithfully and blindly stores them. The editor should be regarded as a type of blank sheet of paper for the programmer to use. Basically, the programmer cannot see the consequences of the programming while using the editor. The source program does not run until it has been compiled down to object code. Only then can mistakes be noted for later correction using the editor.

Interpreter programs

An 'interpreter' is a little more sophisticated. It combines editor and compiler in one. It produces a source file, but does not produce an executable file of object code. When a program is run, the interpreter simply interprets the source line by line into machine code, and the MPU runs the machine code in pieces. It allows a very fast method of 'debugging', or highlighting and correcting, a program, as the statements are continually being interpreted and executed. If an error is found, the exact statement being executed is quite clear. This is not so true of a compiled program.

However, a compiler will produce a faster version of the program, it is more efficiently coded and does not have to deal with source statements as it is running. In fact, one of the most efficient methods of writing a program is to produce and debug it using an interpreter, and then simply compile the finished source code. This gives the best of both worlds.

Specific languages

The program statements above are examples from a language called BASIC. This language was originally designed to be simple for beginners to use. It has evolved into one of the most widely known languages in existence. Its original conception had many limitations, and latterly these have been corrected so that it is possible to buy a version of BASIC which is as sophisticated and efficient as any other high-level language in the field. It is also one of the easiest to learn.

Other high-level languages which have been popular for many years include ALGOL, COBOL, FORTRAN and Pascal. These also use English language statements, and require interpreters and compilers. ALGOL has fallen out of favour, but looks similar to BASIC in many ways, except for something it called 'block' structure. FORTRAN was for many years the basic language of science and technology, COBOL the equivalent in business applications. Pascal is a more recent language, though now very well established, and is a modern naturally 'structured' language.

There are many other high-level languages, and each one has its own advantages and disadvantages. Once you have learnt one of these, the concepts pass quickly to the others, even though the languages can look quite different. For instance, they all have line after line of instructions, which the computer must execute from start to finish.

Other high-level languages are based on quite different concepts. These include PROLOG and LISP. These rely on a form of mathe-

► Interpreter programs allow for a file in a high level language to be written, and translated into machine code as it runs. This allows for quick checks and debugging.

► BASIC stands for Beginners All-purpose Symbolic Instruction Code.

► BASIC, ALGOL, COBOL, FORTRAN, Pascal: high-level languages with some features of ordinary English.

► PROLOG and LISP: examples of languages based on mathematical logic.

▶ More on programming in Chapter 10.

matical logic to perform the tasks, and have applications in the field of artificial intelligence.

We will look further at how to program in high-level languages in Chapter 10. However, before we pass to applications programs, and programming, we will look at machine code, which is the lowest level of programming, allowing the programmer to control the processor directly.

We have seen how the MPU fetches and executes binary instructions from memory, and we have looked at the structure of the memory itself. We will now look at the way in which machine code is structured, and how it can be written with the help of a program called an 'assembler'.

> Before reading on, you may find it useful to refer back to the binary and hexadecimal numbering introduced in Chapter 6, along with the memory-addressing information.

Specific processors' machine code

Machine-code languages vary considerably between processors produced by different manufacturers, and even for different processors from the same manufacturer. However, a given hierarchy of processors from a given manufacturer may provide partly compatible code. This is the case, for instance, with the INTEL series of 80XXX processors. For instance, code written for the 80286 will run on the 80386, but it is possible to write code for the 80386 which will not run on the predecessor.

However, there are general similarities between machine-code languages, even across the manufacturer spectrum, and we will look at some typical machine-code instructions in Chapter 9, and how they work. We cannot, here, look at a specific MPU's machine code, so the description below is 'generic', that is non-specific, but typical of processors in general. The aim is to introduce some of the background concepts of machine-code programming, at a simple level.

Much of the working of machine code involves internal registers within the processor. The processor will generally have a large variety of registers. One of these, for instance, is used to store the current position within the program – this is called the 'program counter'. Another is used to store the latest instruction fetched from memory, which is undergoing execution within the processor. This might involve fetching another piece of information, which again will be stored within a particular register. When the current instruction is complete, which may take several clock cycles if it is particularly complex, it is replaced by fetching the next instruction in line, and the program counter is incremented to reflect the current position within the program.

▶ To understand how the machine code of a given processor works, it is necessary to know what registers it has, how many BITs each holds, and how they work – its register architecture.

Reduced instruction set computers (RISCs)

Some processors are constructed to understand a very large variety of overlapping machine code instructions. The idea is to give the programmer as many different ways of writing software as possible. The set of instructions will include many simple basic instructions, which are fast to execute, and simple to use. In addition, there are various higher level instructions, each of which summarizes a set of many instructions which would otherwise have to be written to perform the same task. For instance, some processors have machine-code instructions for floating-point arithmetic operations. Such instructions are complex and slow.

In some ways, this overlapping of code has gone too far in modern machines. The instruction set is so complex that programmers only bother with a very small percentage of the instructions offered, and are still perfectly able to produce any type of software which is required. A lot of the design and silicon-chip surface is wasted.

The solution to this problem is to reduce the instruction set of the processor considerably. This has led to a group of machines called reduced instruction set computers – or RISC machines. This is not a new idea, but one which has been catching on recently. The codes involved are very easy to use, do not overlap unnecessarily, and run very fast – a single clock cycle is sufficient in most cases. Peripheral software, such as an operating system, is more complex because there are not so many ways of summarizing complex functions – each must be written in full. However, the increase in speed is well worth while, and this is an area which is expanding considerably.

In the next chapter we will look at some common machine-code instructions, prior to looking at programming in Chapter 10.

Chapter review
- A computer is usually running an operating system (OS) for all its normal housekeeping activities, including I/O of all types.
- An OS must be accessible, extensive, fast and standardized.
- Two OS machine–human interface types exist – command line and GUI.
- Command-line OSs require commands to be typed in.
- GUI OSs allow selection of commands by icons and a pointing device.
- The OS organizes filing of information on disk.
- An OS can be single- or multi tasking.
- An OS can be single-user, or multi-user.
- Files are organized by name and may contain data or programs, or both.
- Machine code is a low-level language which the MPU can run directly.

► Now that you have completed this chapter, look back to the objectives at the beginning and check that you have accomplished each of them.

- High-level languages allow a programmer to use near-human-language instructions.
- A machine-code program does not usually carry from one type of processor to another.
- High-level languages are usually portable, perhaps with a little modification, between machines.

9 Machine code

Chapter objectives

By the time you have read this chapter, you will understand:

- the meaning of machine code
- how machine code is constructed and stored
- some typical machine code instructions
- assembly language
- how to code a program, and convert it into binary
- the following key words: registers, program counter, index register, data register, OP code, mnemonic, addressing mode.

MACHINE CODE IN GENERAL – THE REGISTERS

The first step in understanding any machine code instruction set is to look at the internal processor registers which exist. It is upon these registers that the codes act. Three registers will suffice for now.

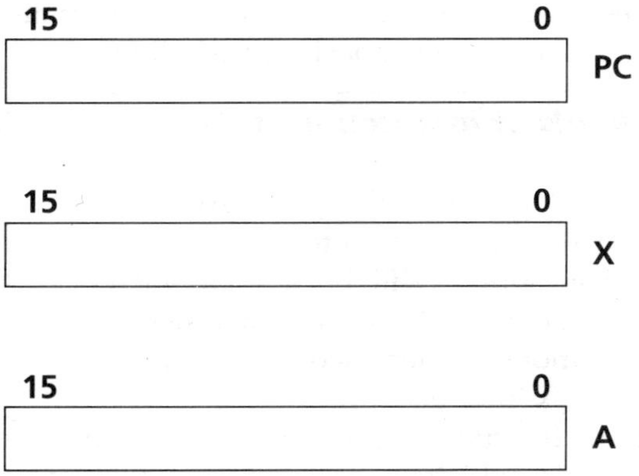

Figure 9.1 Processor registers

They are all sixteen-BIT registers, and are described as follows:

> **Program counter (PC)** – stores the address at which the next instruction will be found in memory
>
> **Index register (X)** – used by some instructions to compute an address from some base address
>
> **Data register (A)** – used for general memory requirements – sometimes referred to as an 'accumulator'.

Remember that these registers are defined as being internal to the

► This chapter describes typical machine-code instructions and how to use them. This is not a complete course in machine-code programming, but provides an introduction to the field which will make it easy for you to pick up specific machine-code languages if you need to. This chapter also gives further information on the way the processor works to control the system, and run programs in general. If you do not need this specific information at this point, you can skip the chapter entirely. The rest of the book does not rely on its contents.

▶ There are many more registers on a typical processor, of different types and lengths.

processor. They do not have memory addresses, and will be referred to by the shortened forms shown in brackets.

To start a program, all that is necessary is to cause the address of the first instruction to be loaded into the PC. The processor does the rest. It fetches the contents of that first location, and increments the PC by a count of 1. In decoding the instruction, it may find it necessary to fetch one or more further BYTEs of program before completing execution of that instruction – these are fetched one by one, incrementing the PC as they go. When execution is complete, the PC is used again to locate the next instruction, and so on.

The instruction types

The next step in appreciating the machine code of a given processor is to look at the types of instruction which are offered.

As you know from Chapter 2, a program consists of binary patterns, each being one or more BYTEs long. Each of these instructions is fetched, and causes the processor to perform some action. Each of the instructions included within a processor has a binary pattern to represent it. These patterns, usually written in hex for convenience, are called 'operation codes' (or OP codes), and are chosen by the designer of the processor. They are just labels, and may be quite random in their choice. Each instruction type, as we shall see, has several different forms, each of which is assigned a separate OP code. The processor is designed to take in these OP codes, decode them, and execute them accordingly. Before looking at the OP codes themselves, we will look at the type of instruction our theoretical processor can handle.

There are several classes of action which any processor can be instructed to perform, and some of the most basic are as follows.

The more common kinds of instructions to a processor

LOAD (LD) instruction. Commands the processor to input one or more BYTEs from a given source, into an internal register of the processor. The source will be a main memory location. It cannot be a location on the surface of a disk directly, for instance. Such locations are accessed via the operating system, and a hardware disk interface.

STORE (ST) instruction. Instructs the processor to send a given BYTE or set of BYTEs, which are stored in a processor register, out to a main memory location.

JUMP (JP) instruction. Loads the PC with a new address. This forces the processor to stop processing at the current position in the program, and fetch the next instruction from the new memory location. This is used to change the order of program execution.

INCREMENT (INC) instruction. Causes the current binary number within a register or memory location, to increment by 1 – i.e. it just adds 1 to the stored number.

DECREMENT (DEC) instruction. Decrements by 1 instead.

In what follows we will use the shortened 'mnemonics', shown in brackets after each instruction name in the inset. When we have looked at how these instructions work, we will look at the actual machine code which ties up with each of these instructions.

To extend the mnemonics further, we will use the following abbreviations.

Common abbreviations for instructions

LDA The **LOAD** instruction which loads two BYTEs into the sixteen-BIT data register, A.

LDX As above, but for the index register, X.

STA Stores the contents of register A out to a main memory location.

STX Stores X out instead.

INCA Increments register A.

DECA Decrements register A.

INCX Increments X.

DECX Decrements X.

JP Causes a program to **JUMP**.

JPZ Causes the program to jump only if the A register contains the number zero – hence the 'Z' in the mnemonic. Otherwise, the program continues with the next instruction in the list. Note that in our simple instruction set, we are only defining a conditional **JUMP** dependent upon the value stored in the A register, so the mnemonic does not have to contain the letter 'A' specifically. If there were more such conditional **JUMP**s, in the instruction set, which depended upon other registers too, the register would have to be included specifically in some way, to prevent confusion.

In addition to these basic instructions, we might add some arithmetic instructions such as **ADD** and **SUBTRACT**. There are normally many more such functions provided by modern processors. They can act as purely binary number operations, special decimal operations, or even full floating-point multiply and divide.

▶ These mnemonics are in assembly code: a code which an assembly program can convert into machine code.

Addressing modes

After looking at the registers and the types of instruction which exist, the next step is to look at something called the 'addressing modes'.

Most of the above instruction mnemonics refer to main memory. The question is, how do you define the memory locations referred to? This is where the concept of 'addressing modes' comes in, and the mnemonics above must be extended to indicate the addressing mode being used, and the address location being referred to. For instance, the **LOAD** instruction, **LDA**, can load A from several sources, and those sources are not made apparent in the mnemonics above.

We will look at four addressing modes here, and they are called, for our purposes, direct, immediate, inherent and indexed.

Direct and immediate addressing modes

Suppose A is to be loaded 'directly' from the memory location A34D, then the instruction could be written:

> LDA,A34D

Here, the first part of the instruction is the action to be performed (**LOAD** A) and the second part, after the comma, is the address where the data to be loaded can be found. Note that the LOAD instruction copies the data from location A34D, without modifying the contents of A34D – the **LOAD** modifies the destination (A) but not the source (A34D).

This **LOAD** instruction is said to define the address location of the data to be loaded 'directly', or by using the direct addressing mode – that is, the source address appears after a comma, after the mnemonic.

The index register will also have a form such as:

> LDX,M

where M is a memory address.

Now, how about loading A with a specific piece of data such as the number 0, or the number E3B5? It would be no good writing 'LDA,0' or 'LDA,E3B5' because this might be confused with loading A from the address 0 or address E3B5. We need another mnemonic to fit this mode of the LD instruction, and hence make it clear that the data following the instruction is to be loaded immediately. This might be:

> LDAI,0

or

> LDAI,E3B5

This is short for 'load A immediately with whatever comes after the comma'. It may be called an immediate load instruction – hence LDAI. X will also have such an instruction:

> LDXI,n

where 'n' is a piece of data in hexadecimal to be loaded immediately into X, without looking at any other memory locations.

► Main addressing modes: direct, immediate, inherent, indexed.

So far we have looked at two modes for addressing the data used by an instruction. These are called:

- the direct memory addressing mode – where the instruction mnemonic is followed by the address of the data required, and

- the immediate memory addressing mode – where the data itself follows the instruction mnemonic.

 Before reading on, could the **STORE** and **JUMP** instructions have the same addressing modes? If so, write down mnemonics which you consider to be suitable.

Inherent addressing mode

A further addressing mode where the source of the data is obvious from the mnemonic itself is called the 'inherent' mode. For instance, **INCX** and **DECA** do not need any further information – they contain everything required within the mnemonic – one acts to increment the X register, the other to decrement A.

Indexed addressing

Indexed addressing uses the index register contents as a base memory address from which a new address is calculated. This concept is useful, for instance, in processing a table of values. The first value might be stored in address 1A00, for instance, and the table might be twelve locations long. That is, it takes up locations:

1A00, 1A01, 1A02, ..., 1A0A, 1A0B

The index register could be loaded with the base address, 1A00, and all memory references for **LOAD**, for instance, be made by adding a number to the address held in register X – the number to be added is called an 'offset'.

Thus, the third address location in the table of values (1A02) would be referred to as:

- (contents of X) + 02
- which equals 1A00 + 02
- which equals 1A02

The '02' is the offset. The mnemonic we shall use for this operation will be:

► Offsets.

LDAX,offset

This means, load A with the contents of the address made up from the contents of register X, plus the offset appearing after the comma. By this means, the table can be based wherever the programmer wishes, and indeed can be moved around, without altering the program – the offsets stay the same, it is just the initial loading of X which is different.

Also, if the table is to be processed just once, the first action could be performed using **LDAX,0**, and then the **INCX** instruction would move the processing to the next member of the table by incrementing the contents of X. There are many ways to use this addressing mode, and it is a simple example of a whole range of methods of producing software without specifying actual address locations more often than is absolutely necessary, and hence allowing simple relocation of the code within the main memory map.

 Before reading on, write the **STORE** and **JUMP** instructions in indexed mode, and note their actions.

STORE and JUMP instructions

The **STA** instruction naturally works in the direct and the immediate mode at the same time, in a sense. A direct-mode **STA** instruction would store A directly into M, using the following mnemonic:

STA,M

Similarly, an immediate-mode **STORE** would do the same – that is store A immediately into memory location M – there is no other way to look at an immediate-mode store, and so this mode is redundant for the **STA** instruction.

The **JUMP** instruction is the same – the program can jump to a specific address, and start execution. This is direct addressing, and could be represented by the following mnemonic:

JP,M

This loads M into the PC, and the processor jumps to fetching instructions from address location M, thus forcing a change of position within the program.

JUMPS can also use indexed addressing. The **JUMP** would be to an address which is equal to the base address stored in register X, plus an offset. The following might be a suitable mnemonic:

JPX,offset

Similarly, the conditional **JUMP**s:

JPZ,M

and

JPZX,offset

respectively, which only occur when the A register is zero. The first of these causes a jump directly to location M, the second to a location with address equal to the contents of register X, plus the offset.

Operation (OP) codes

The above machine code concepts have relied on a mnemonic presentation of the machine code instruction which a processor can understand. However, the processor cannot directly understand 'JP,M' and 'LDAI,n' – these are human terms which help us to remember the actions which the associated instructions perform. The processor itself must fetch electronic signals along its data bus which are interpreted as 1s and 0s. Thus, the mnemonics must be converted into binary patterns, and then stored in actual electronic memory locations.

The first step is to convert the instructions into OP codes. This depends upon looking at the processor manufacturer's data sheets, and finding out which binary patterns do what. In fact, there are programs which do this for you automatically. They are called 'assemblers'. The mnemonic codes used so far are called 'assembly codes', and programs written in this form are said to be in 'assembly language'. Each processor has its own assembly language, and its own special assemblers which take in lists of mnemonics and convert them into binary patterns suitable for the processor to fetch directly. To see how this could be done by hand, we will look at the process in full.

The machine-code instructions so far defined are as follows:

► Assemblers are programs which convert mnemonics such as 'LDA1,n' into machine code/OP codes.

Direct mode	Immediate mode	Indexed mode	Inherent mode
LDA,M	LDAI,n	LDAX, offset	
STA,M		STAX, offset	
			INCA
			INCX
			DECA
			DECX
JP,M		JPX, offset	
JPZ,M		JPZX, offset	

Each of the mnemonics above must have a unique OP code associated with it. However, before we look at actual OP codes, it is necessary to know how many BYTEs each instruction is likely to take up. We will assume that the basic instruction types are all eight BITs in length – that is, one BYTE, but some of them are followed by further information. For instance, **LDA,M** is an eight-BIT instruction, followed by a sixteen-BIT address (M), so this instruction takes up a total of three BYTEs. However, **DECX** does not need any data, and a single BYTE will suffice. This is the reason why, after an instruction is fetched, more fetches may be needed before that instruction can be executed. In an eight-BIT machine, three separate fetches will be needed for an **LDA,M** instruction, while only one is needed for **DECX**. In sixteen-BIT and higher machines, more information is fetched each time, and there is a natural speed increase.

To bring these concepts down to the electronic level of the processor itself, we will choose some OP codes for the instructions introduced above. These are chosen entirely at random. It is up to the electronic designer of the processor to ensure that fetching one of these patterns causes the desired effect within the processor.

Note that in the following list of simple instructions, offsets in the indexed addressing mode are single BYTEs long. This means that the range of offsets possible are only from 0 to 255 (decimal).

Mnemonic	Op code (binary)	OP code (hex)	No. of bytes
LDA,M	11011001 M	D9 M	3
LDAI,n	11011010 n	DA n	3
LDAX, offset	11011100 offset	DC offset	2
STA, M	00101011 M	2B M	3
STAX, offset	01001001 offset	49 offset	2
INCA	11111101	FD	1
INCX	00001000 M	08	1
DECA	11000010	C2	1
DECX	11000001	C1	1
JP, M	10101010 M	AA	3
JPX, offset	10101111 offset	AF	2
JPZ, M	10101001 M	A9	3
JPZX, offset	10100000 offset	A0	2

As you can see, sometimes the processor fetches a single instruction, and can complete execution without further memory reference, and in other cases, up to two further fetches are needed first. This is a fairly restricted OP-code set. For instance, current sixteen-BIT and higher processors usually have a minimum of sixteen BITs for the OP code, thus allowing many more possible binary patterns, and hence instructions.

You can see that complex instructions are not only slow to execute because they involve larger amounts of calculation, they may also be slower because more information needs to be fetched.

A simple program

In order to bring these ideas together, we will consider how to code a very simple program segment. The flow chart for the program algorithm is shown in Figure 9.2.

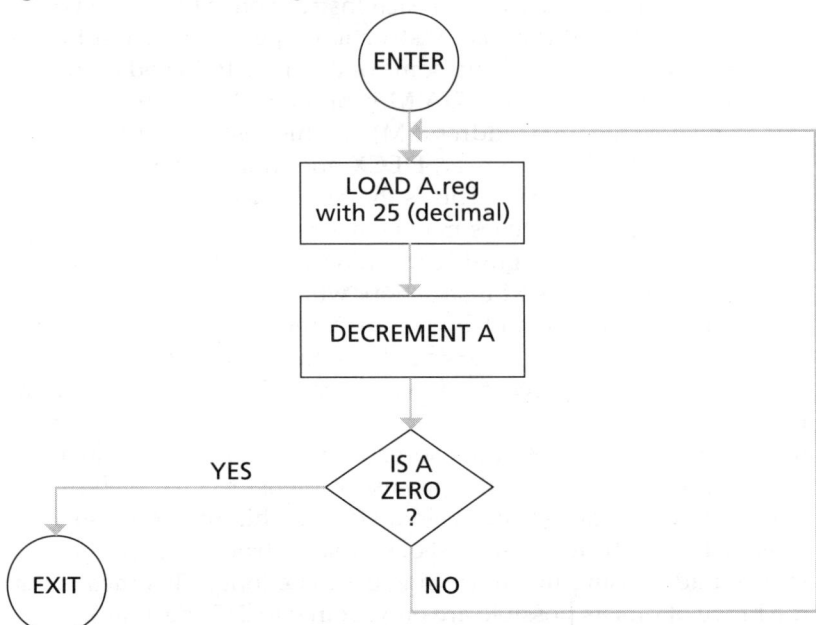

Figure 9.2 Algorithm for a program segment

In this figure, circles are used for entry and exit to the program segment. After the start, the first operation is to set the A register to the number 25 (decimal), or 00011001 (binary), or 19 (hex). This can be confusing, and it is important that you always remember to indicate the number base being used unless it is obvious. The next step is to decrement the A register, and check to see if it is zero, which it will not be at the start. Thus the 'no' branch is executed, and this loop begins again, and decrements A. This continues until the question has the answer 'yes', when this bit of programming is completed. What happens next is not our concern here, or indeed how the program was entered in the first place. We must now code the algorithm into OP codes, to be stored in memory locations.

The first task is to decide where in memory to store the OP codes. We will choose the program to start at address 0100 (hex) (we will see how this fits in on page 170).

The mnemonics for the program are shown below, where 'H' following a number means it is in hex:

```
        LDAI,19H

L1:     DECA

        JPZ,L2

        JP,L1

L2:     next part of program
```

Here, we have used labels (L1 and L2) instead of actual memory locations. We have to use labels as it is not obvious, until the OP code table is consulted, how many memory locations each instruction takes up, and hence exactly where in memory any of them will be situated. The assembler would be responsible for working out the actual memory locations, given that the program segment starts at 0100H. The first instruction is an immediate **LOAD** of A, with the number 19H. Then A is decremented, and if A is zero, a **JUMP** occurs to the label L2, which is at the start of the next part of the program. However, if A has not yet reached zero, the fourth instruction (**JP,L1**) is performed, which is an unconditional **JUMP** back to the decrement instruction, labelled L1. This loop continues until A is zero.

 Try to convert the above program into OP codes, before reading on.

We will now perform the task of the assembler, and code the program into OP codes, in actual memory locations.

To see how this will be done, we will start with the **LDAI,19H** which is converted, using the table, into **DA 00 19**. Remember that this instruction is defined as having three BYTEs, and so leading 0s must be packed in to ensure that the number loaded into A is a full sixteen-BITs long, and takes just the right number of memory locations. The full program, appealing to the OP code table above, is shown below. Note that all numbers shown are in hex, including the addresses showing where each BYTE of the program is stored.

0100:	DA	Load A with 0019H, or 25 (decimal)
0101:	00	
0102:	19	
0103:	C2	Decrement A
0104:	A9	If A is zero, JUMP to rest of program
0105:	01	
0106:	0A	
0107:	AA	JUMP back to the decrement instruction
0108:	01	
0109:	03	
010A:	etc.	Rest of program starts here

This is the lowest level of programming which we have seen so far. However, it is still comparatively readable, and is only an indication of the program which the actual processor will 'see' in memory. Figure 9.3 shows the actual memory map containing the program in binary exactly as the processor would see it at the electronic level. This is properly where the software and hardware meet.

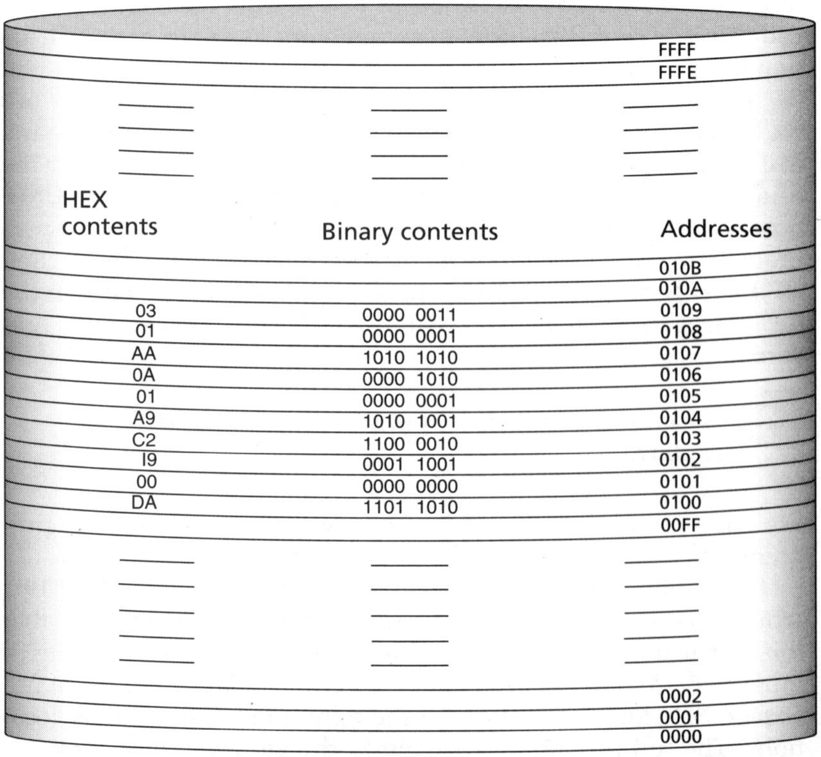

Figure 9.3 The contents of the memory map

In this figure, for simplicity, we have assumed that the map only has 64K of memory, which is rather small by modern standards. The map spans from the address 0000 to FFFF.

This shows exactly why there are so many 'tricks' to make the programming of a computer system understandable to human beings. This is really the lowest level in the machine, and via the address decoding, and electronic system itself, gives a good indication of the actual electronic signals which the processor itself will see as its program. It is this confusing image of 1s and 0s which is the reason for the full gamut of high-level programming languages which you will encounter in computing, and the many 'front-end processing' systems such as OSs which are produced to allow human operators to interact fast and easily with the machinery.

To make the above program run, the PC has to be set to 0100H. The processor then simply fetches and executes as shown, looping around the loop until A is zero, and then plunging on through memory, fetching and executing as it goes. Each full program must come to an end eventually, and the processor put into a special quiescent state, or be made to execute a tight loop, waiting for the next command from the keyboard. This type of housekeeping is often left to the operating system, unless the program is running in a small control setting, in which case the programmer has to address the problem of ending and starting programs, as well as everything else!

Separating program and data BITs
As you can see, there is no difference between the binary of a program and the binary of a set of data. For instance, a table of values, stored in memory, could just as easily be decoded, using the OP code table above, into program instructions. Of course, this would just produce a list of random codes, which would be meaningless. Indeed, some of the data BYTEs would probably not even have an equivalent instruction code, and would simply be left undecoded. The result would not run in a well-defined manner – anything would be possible.

The trick is to ensure that the program starts at a correctly defined address location, and the **JUMP**s and general processing never allow the processor to try to fetch instructions from memory locations which do not contain part of the current program. The problem is that unless fully controlled at all times, the processor just careers on, fetching from memory, incrementing the PC, fetching from memory, and so on. It is important to contain this activity by writing 'closed programs'. That is, programs which start and end properly.

Assuming that this is attended to correctly, the separation of programs and data is never an issue. Programs can stretch over any memory locations you like, as long as the **JUMP**s are written properly, and the program can use data stored anywhere else you like, as long as the **LOAD**s and **STORE**s, for instance, are controlled.

▶ Closed programs: programs which start and end properly.

In fact, starting a machine-code program is not simply a matter of loading a value into the PC – it must be arranged either by the operating system being used, or by a hardware arrangement rather like the reset system described in Chapter 3.

► **Now that you have completed this chapter, look back to the objectives at the beginning and check that you have accomplished each of them.**

Chapter review

- Machine code itself is composed of binary patterns, called OP codes, or operation codes.
- Machine code can be programmed in assembly mnemonics.
- Addressing modes control the way in which machine-code instructions use data and memory.
- Machine code acts largely on internal processor registers.
- Typical machine-code instructions shuffle data between internal processor registers and addressable memory.
- The separation between programming BYTEs and data BYTEs is automatic.

Computer programming

► **This chapter introduces two main concepts:**
• **system development**
• **the mechanics of programming itself.**

Chapter objectives

By the time you have read this chapter, you will understand:

▮ how high-level languages are constructed

▮ how program production is organized for a given problem

▮ the meaning of systems analysis

▮ SSADM – standard systems analysis

▮ the main types of data which appear in high level programs

▮ the use of flow charts

▮ logical, or Boolean, statements and conditions

▮ structured programming

▮ the meaning of modularization of a program

▮ object-orientated programming

▮ how high level programs treat filed information

▮ program conversion to machine code

▮ neural networks and parallel processing

▮ the following key words: systems analyst, code, development, program statement, variable, flow chart, bug, debug, maintenance, I/O statement, conditional statement, iteration, procedure, file, data type, integer, floating point, real number, array, string, literals, sequential, decision, loop, assignment, Boolean, structured programming, object orientated, OOP, subroutine, function, neural network, procedural, declarative, expert system, knowledge base, parallel computing.

SYSTEMS DEVELOPMENT AND PROGRAMMING

System development starts with some kind of definition of a problem, or analysis of a situation, so that it can be split into smaller, more manageable, problems. Analysis is very important in large systems, and formal analysis methods exist to try to standardize this crucial stage. Once the problem has been defined, and a method of solution found, programming can then be performed. We will look at two examples, one simple and one more complex, to illustrate analysis and system development.

As we shall see, classical programming involves splitting a problem or task into small pieces, each of which can be written as a

► Two main approaches to programming:
• the classical or procedural approach
• a declarative approach. There are also approaches which do not use programming as such: for example, neural networking.

single statement in a given computer language. This is called the 'procedural' approach. The computer can then work on these pieces in sequence, following the procedure, and thus perform the whole task. We will look at how to analyse a problem, and present the steps to its solution in a graphical form, using flow charts. The next step is to code it into the chosen language. We will look at high-level languages, and how to use them.

In looking at programming itself, we will see how high-level procedural languages are used, and how they compare with other approaches, such as the 'declarative' approach, which is described towards the end of this chapter.

Some systems do not use a programming language at all. For instance, 'neural networks' try to reproduce the way in which the brain solves problems – the system effectively writes its own program from experience.

'Good practice' in producing computer programs will be examined, including 'structured' and 'object-orientated' programming.

PROGRAMMING A PROBLEM

Computer programming itself generally concentrates on constructing a set of commands which force a machine to produce the solution to a given, clearly defined problem. For instance, if there were a set of mathematical equations to be solved, a programmer could be called in to produce a program which would take in the appropriate data, and output the solutions in a clearly defined manner. On the other hand, the programmer would not normally be the first person called in to produce, say, a complete system for a large company who wished to integrate accounts, shop-floor organization, employees' pay, stock control, etc.

► A procedural approach.

There are, therefore, two levels of problem (or system) for which computer programs must be developed. The first level is that of a compact, clearly defined problem for which a procedure, or set of computer commands, can be constructed to solve the problem directly. The second level deals with the general computerization of a large system, perhaps currently dependent upon manual methods which now require automation. This latter involves extensive analysis and interface with the users, before the actual programming effort can be started.

The steps in developing a computer programme

The steps employed in developing a computer program, whether solving a compact problem, or producing a larger system, are broadly as follows:

1 Analyse the problem.

2 Define the data, its storage and how it is input and output (I/O).

3 Produce a specification for program (or programs).

4 Construct an algorithm (or algorithms).

5 Code the algorithm in a form which can be processed by computer.

6 Produce and test the program.

7 Debug the program until apparently working.

8 Install the program.

9 Maintain the program in service.

As mentioned above, for simple problems, some or all of these separate steps might be performed entirely by the programmer. Furthermore, several of these steps may be abbreviated into a single task. However, for large and complex problems, even these steps might be subdivided, and the whole problem modularized and split among a large team of software engineers.

The above nine-point development list splits naturally into three separate areas of responsibility for specialized personnel. There is always some overlap, but the following cover most situations:

Systems analysis – Systems analyst

Program coding – Programmer

Installation – Systems engineer

These roles tie up with the nine development steps in the following manner:

Systems analysis envolves development steps 1, 2 and 3. These are the preprogramming steps which would be partly or all the province of a systems analyst, who would interface with a customer, learn the present system being used, and spend time recasting it into computer terms. The actual mechanics of the computer's language are not considered here, and these first tasks are largely language-independent.

Program coding involves development step 4, using the information from the previous steps, plus steps 5, 6 and 7. These are the province of the programmer, and would involve choosing a specific computer language, writing (or coding) the problem, and testing the program.

▶ Installation is dealt with in more detail in Chapter 12.

Installation involves the last two development steps, 8 and 9. It may not be taken by the programmer, but rather by a general systems engineer whose job would be to interface with customers, train them to use the system, and keep a careful log of required corrections to the system, to be passed back to the programmer. The systems analyst may also perform this last task, having already made contact with the customer and the system, and having become fully familiar with both.

To make the above stages appear more familiar, we will now consider a simple, compact example which incorporates them all.

An 'addition' program

We will look at the problem of taking in fifty numbers via a keyboard and producing the sum of the numbers. This is a small procedure, and may, in practice, form part of a larger program. However, we will assume that it is a complete program, and look at the nine development steps, in order. In addition, we will look at representing the flow of logic within the program graphically using a flow chart. This is an excellent and highly visual method of showing the logic in small problems, though it can become too cumbersome and involved for large programs. Other methods of representation have been developed for such situations.

The development of the program would proceed as follows:

Step 1 is to analyse the problem. This is simple – the numbers are input to the program, added up, and the answer presented to the operator.

Steps 2 and 3 involve defining the data, its I/O and the program specification. A formal approach, including enough information to construct the program, might be as follows:

> Take in fifty floating-point numbers, through the keyboard, ranging between 0 and 999999.99, accurate to two decimal places. Add them together, and print the final sum, to two decimal places, on the screen. Present enough information on the screen during the process to lead the operator through the process, and indicate when the process is complete. Present the answer in a clear form.

This is a fairly complete data, I/O and program specification for such a simple problem, and should be enough for a programmer to construct the complete program.

Step 4. aims to express a program algorithm as a list of commands, or 'program statements', written in a computer language which can be processed directly by machine. However, before that can be achieved, the basic logic of the program must be constructed. This is presented in diagrammatic form in Figure 10.1.

This figure details the processes which the program will execute, in enough detail for the programmer to code the problem directly. Each step is small and couched in computer terms. It can be written in a typical high-level computer language.

It is important to identify the variables used by the program for two reasons. First, these point to the interface with the user – the data and its I/O. Second, the program becomes easier to read if the variables are understood throughout. You should bear in mind that the computer primarily performs its action by manipulating these variables. In some languages, it is mandatory to declare, at the start of the program, exactly what variables are used, and what 'type' they are, as we shall see. The type of a variable describes the sort of value it holds. For instance, if it takes entirely whole-number values it is said to be of type integer.

▶ Steps 1, 2, 3.

▶ A floating-point number is one which may contain a decimal part – i.e. one that has digits after the decimal point. Such numbers are often called 'real' numbers, as opposed to 'integers' which are whole numbers.

▶ Step 4.

There are three variables within the program:

COUNT is used to store how many numbers have been added together it is of type integer.

SUM contains the accumulated sum of the numbers as the program proceeds, and is of type real.

CURRNUM stores the number which has just been input, and is also real.

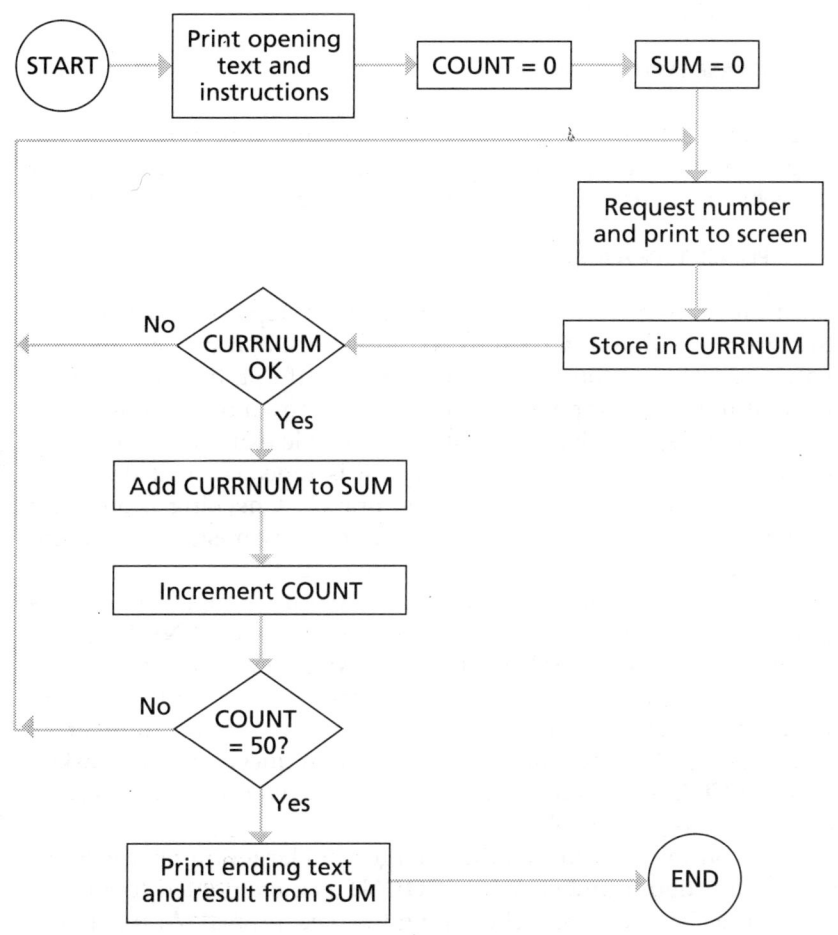

Figure 10.1 An algorithm for the number problem

The program starts by printing some explanatory text to the screen, such as:

PLEASE INPUT FIFTY NUMBERS, ONE AFTER THE OTHER AS REQUESTED

NUMBERS MAY BE WHOLE, OR HAVE UP TO TWO DIGITS AFTER THE DECIMAL POINT

ALL NUMBERS MUST BE BETWEEN 0 AND 999999.99

The next step is to set the variables which will be used in the program to some properly defined values – zero, here. Note that statements such as 'COUNT = 0' are not meant to be statements of fact, they are commands to actually assign a given value to a variable. Here, **COUNT** is being set to 0. All the 'equals' signs in the flow chart are commands of this type – they are called 'assignment' statements.

Then a request for a number is printed to the screen, which may look like this:

PLEASE TYPE A NUMBER

The operator then types the first number, and it is 'echoed' to the screen – that is, it is printed up so that the operator can be sure that it has been taken in correctly. The screen might then look like this:

PLEASE TYPE A NUMBER 34.8

The number 34.8 has been typed in. The next step is for the program to store this value in **CURRNUM**, and check that it is an allowed value, as noted at the start of the program. If not, then the request for that number is repeated. This check is shown on the flow chart by a triangular decision box with two possible exit directions. If the number does not conform, the request is repeated, if it does, the program passes on, down the 'yes' branch. Checking input, and perhaps giving a message to the operator of any mistakes, is an important part of making a program more usable.

Now comes the actual point of the program – an addition takes place by adding the current number, stored in **CURRNUM**, to the accumulative store in **SUM**. At first, **SUM** is zero, and the addition here simply leaves **SUM** equal to the first number. **COUNT** is incremented (increased by 1) to keep a record of the number of numbers input – it becomes 1 at this stage. A question is then asked to see if **COUNT** has reached 50 yet. The answer, here, is 'no', and the process repeats itself.

This continues, accumulating a larger and larger number in **SUM** until the fiftieth number, when **COUNT** is incremented to 50, and the last decision box branches along the 'yes' branch. At this point, **SUM** contains the answer.

The final action of the program is to print up a suitable ending, to remind the user that the program is complete, and to present the answer. The final line on the screen might read as follows:

THAT WAS THE LAST NUMBER, THE TOTAL EQUALS 25478.98

The program then ends.

As you can see, there is more to even a simple program than just the main operation, which is addition in this case. Several variables may be needed, various printing operations are required, and some error checking has to be done along the way.

Now we have to address the last five steps in the program development list on pages 174–5, to which you should refer quickly before reading on.

Step 5 involves writing the flow chart as a set of program statements which can be processed directly by computer. This is where the flow chart is converted, or coded, into an actual program – a very easy step here. It is already nearly in the form of a Pascal or BASIC program, and it would also be very easy to convert into code.

► Step 5.

Steps 6, 7, 8 and 9 involve feeding data into the program for a known numerical addition, and testing that the correct result is forthcoming. If there is a mistake, known as a 'bug', this must be corrected – we say the program is being 'debugged'. The program then has to be presented to the final user, and installed. If there are further modifications, or if later bugs come to light, the programmer will have to make changes to the program – this is called 'maintenance'.

► Steps 6 to 9.

It is sometimes regarded as surprising that software requires maintenance, just as hardware does. However, even the most popular and often-used programs are continually being updated and expanded, new versions are being produced, subtle bugs are being found and corrected. It is sometimes said that the end-user simply forms another stage in the debugging process.

► Maintenance.

► Maintenance is dealt with in more detail in Chapter 12.

As you can see, this simple program illustrates all of the steps described above for program construction and use. However, it is fair to point out that in this simple case, the programmer would just go ahead, produce a complete program, and present it to the user without bothering with all of the separate steps shown here. No flow chart would be drawn, for instance.

Program documentation

Another issue which has not been mentioned here is that of 'program documentation'. A complex program should be written in such a manner that its operational logic can be followed through by anyone who may meet the program in the future. This makes it possible for others to maintain and modify the code. Even the original programmer will tend to forget the logic unless it is very simple, or carefully documented. In this case, the flow chart is a full and comprehensible documentation of the program logic. Larger programs will also benefit from a flow chart, but should contain plenty of comments within the program itself. Some program languages have a natural structure which is easy to analyse and understand. We will see how this works later.

Before looking at a more complex problem, we will look at the basic program elements which have been used here.

Program elements

As you can see from this simple program, there are several types of program statement possible. The ones used here are:
• I/O statement
• assignment
• decision
• repetition.

I/O statement

The I/O statements here were a print to the screen (output), and an input from the keyboard.

Assignment

Assignment means setting a variable equal to something else – here, some variables were assigned actual values, including 0, and **SUM** was assigned a formula. The assignment for **SUM** would look like this:

SUM = SUM + CURRNUM

In this case, **SUM** is being set equal to itself plus something else. Each time this is done, the old value of **SUM** is updated by an addition of a new number, and the result stored as a new value back in **SUM**.

Decision

Decisions were taken depending upon a condition – in this case whether a variable had a given value. The result was a choice of one of two possible branches for the program to follow. This type of statement is sometimes called a 'conditional statement'.

Repetition

Repetition is not really a program statement, it is a method of processing. It is seen here by a loop in which fifty numbers were taken in and added together. The loop was entered at the start of the program, and not exited until a suitable condition was true. Looping is sometimes called 'iteration'. This simply means repeating a process until that process is complete.

These basic elements of procedural languages are common to both the simplest and the most complex programs. In addition to the above elements, there are ones which have to do with:

- manipulating files, and
- calling up separate program modules, or 'procedures'.

▶ As with the concept of program documentation, we will have to leave these elements until later in this chapter.

Before looking further into the actual methods of constructing programs, we will look at the systems-analysis stage in more depth. This can best be appreciated in a larger case, and we will look at a business example called 'order processing'. We will then look at a more standardized and formalized method of systems analysis.

ORDER PROCESSING: A BUSINESS EXAMPLE

A company buys and sells goods, and currently handles the process of dealing with customer orders manually. Various departments deal with different aspects of processing a given order. The tasks which are performed are as follows:

- An order is received.

- The name, address, telephone number and other details are recorded for future use, if necessary.

- The customer's credit limit and discount status are checked.

- The stock-control department is consulted to see whether the goods are in stock, and to check prices.

- The order is accepted in part or in full.

- If the goods are not there, they are ordered by the purchasing department.

- When and if the goods are in stock, the goods are issued to the packing department.

- The packing department packs and sends the goods, and then informs accounts of this fact.

- Accounts sends an invoice.

The main order processing procedure here is clear and it must not be confused with the ordering done by the buyers. Order processing refers to the important job of organizing the fulfilling of customer orders, which are the lifeblood of the business.

A successful business might have operated an efficient and largely error-free manual system for many years. The task of computerization is to apply machinery to the system in a sympathetic manner, with as little overall shock to the business as possible. The aim is to save cost, allow for a larger number of orders with the same staff, be more reactive to customers and provide much more up-to-date management information than can be gleaned from data which resides on sheets of paper in physical folders and books. The systems analyst now looks at the flow of information, and where data is to be stored. Definitions of files are constructed to hold the data, and how the data is to be used is considered.

Computerizing the system

The company has to automate the procedure for taking in orders, issuing product, controlling stock and accounting financially for the process. This might be informally summarized in a diagram such as Figure 10.2 (see page 182).

In this figure, when an order is received it is processed, goods are despatched and an invoice is raised. This is the purpose of the system, and the rest is there to support and organize this process. When an order from a customer is received, the customer master file is interrogated, and updated with customer details if necessary. This ensures that the company keeps a good record of all the firms it has done business with, and all of their details. This is important for despatch package addressing, customer care, and future marketing. The customer's credit limit and special discounts available to them are also found from the file at this point.

The next step is to check the goods, stock and prices file to see whether the order can be fulfilled. If required, the customer can be given price and availability. A stock-control system will keep this file up to date. If there is insufficient stock to satisfy the customer's order, a purchase order is raised by the purchasing department.

▶ In addition, there are many background processes not mentioned. For instance, the production of packing notes to accompany the goods, controlling stock throughout the firm, ensuring that orders are not lost while the buyers in the purchasing department replenish stock, accounting in the business ledgers, and so on. These are handled by separate systems which run along side order processing, and share information as required.

▶ Step 1.

▶ Figure 10.2 is not meant to be a complete procedure for solving the problem, indeed it is not really even a flow chart. It is a first step towards working out how the system might use information, and where that data could reside. It is a rough but highly visual method of showing how the system might be constructed.

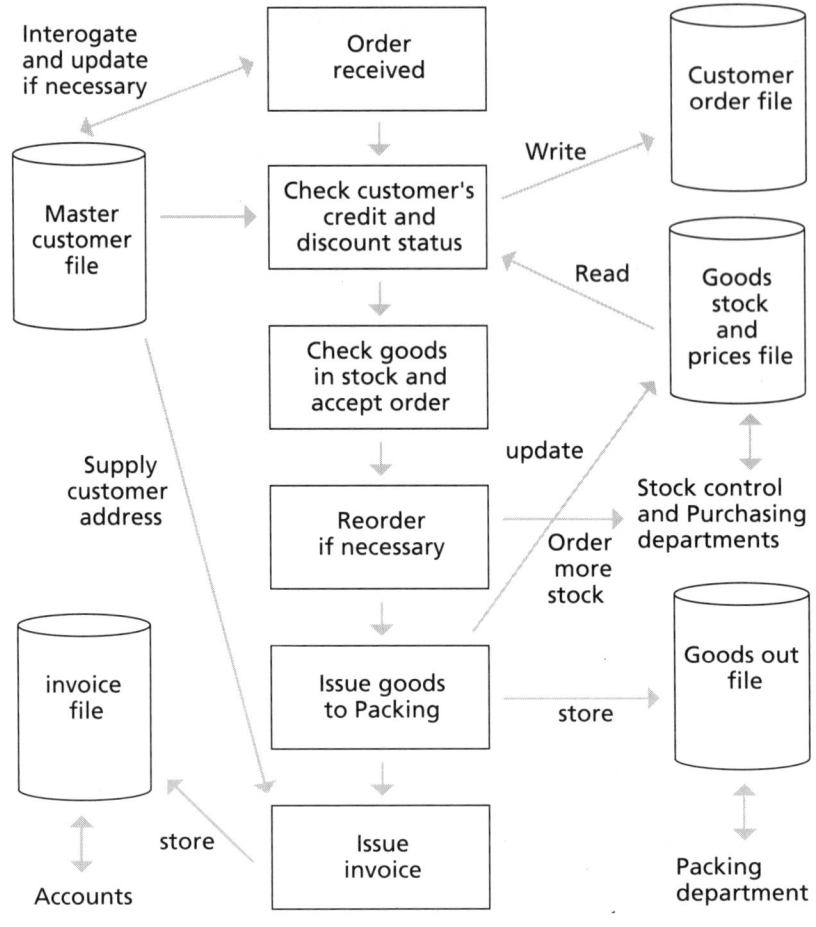

Figure 10.2 Some of the procedures associated with order processing in a business

If the goods are in stock, and indeed when they do become available, an order is given to the packing department to remove the goods from store, pack them up, and send them to the customer. This command is achieved, here, by storing the information on the goods-out file. The packing department will look through this file periodically, and pack the goods it finds requested there.

At the same time as the order is given to goods out, the goods-stock file must be updated to ensure that the goods sold are removed from the file to prevent their being sold twice. This function would probably be the duty of the stock-control department. Another important function of the stock-control department is to maintain a minimum stock, i.e. to re-order as soon as a stock level falls to or below the minimum stock level. In fact, the only time an order cannot be fulfilled should be when there is a run on that item.

The final step in the process is to issue an invoice. This is achieved here by storing invoice details, on the invoice file, constructed from a knowledge of the actual goods despatched. Accounts will attend to this in their own time, using the details on the master customer file. This will include chasing for the money when due, if necessary, and updating the business accounts with the transaction.

At any time, a manager can request reports on the number and types of order which the company has, the levels of stock, the amount of money owed in total, and to whom, and so on. It is generally the function of the 'MIS', or 'management information services' department to have programs already in existence to provide any type of analysis which is required, and they will be able to write more analysis programs on request. The MIS function uses almost all of the files shown on the diagram for analysis. Note that the main purpose of MIS is to help in the control of the business.

A small system might not actually have quite as many output files as are shown here. Output files include 'goods out', 'invoice' and so on. The goods-out information may simply be transmitted straight to the packing department as a paper docket, and the invoice might be printed immediately. However, somewhere in the system, these data will be stored for future analysis, and as part of the accounting system.

► This is not the only way in which the problem can be solved – there are usually many ways to construct files and processes to solve a problem. An experienced systems analyst will know how to achieve the end efficiently, but different individuals may have different approaches. There are more examples in Chapter 12.

 List the computer processes described in this example, and, as far as the main order-processing system is concerned, state which are:

(a) batch-processed

(b) real-time processed.

► Batch processing/real-time processing – see Chapter 3. On line/off line – see Chapter 3.

Which of these processes is on line and which off line?

File definition

The next step is to define the file structures for the five files mentioned in Figure 10.2. If you look back at databases in Chapter 5, you will already have some idea of how to define the files. In fact, this entire system could be constructed using a relational DB program, with its own high-level language in which to write the procedure.

► Step 2.

As an example of a file definition, each record of the master customer file would have at least the following fields:

NAME, ADDRESS, TELE NO., CUST., REF., CREDIT LIMIT, DISCOUNT STATUS

Each of the fields must be defined to be long enough to contain the longest example, and some of the fields may need to be broken down further, as discussed in Chapter 5. Other fields which might be added are the total number of orders received from this customer, date of last order, and so on. This would all help the marketing department to target the right type of customer for sales approaches in the future. At the same time, it is a good idea not to make the records too large and cumbersome, or the whole system slows down.

The essence of designing the system – and hence the files which are kept – is to be reactive to what is needed by the business. In other words, the needs of the users. For instance, if they prefer to have hard-copy dockets, printed in a specific format for a particular reason, then some special print statements must be incorporated into the logic, and the files defined to supply the information suited to the task. Similarly, if the marketing department uses its existing customer base in a given way, it is crucial that the fields in the master customer file reflect that need.

 Design a typical set of fields for the goods-out file.

Preparing for system programming

► Step 3.

Before a program can be written for the system, a lot of detail must be collated on the way in which the company works at present, and what its aims are for the future. All current documentation must be examined, and a decision made as to what will be kept, and what is no longer required. Large amounts of the documentation will be stored as files by computer, and hard copy can be produced as required.

In this case, there is a manual system in existence already, and its working must be analysed fully. This can be achieved by direct observation, by interviewing current users, and by the use of carefully prepared questionnaires. The techniques for systems analysis have been carefully studied, and standard, methods will be known to an experienced analyst.

In addition, the interface with the other systems must be defined – the goods-stock file, for instance, needs to be shared with the stock control system, which will also, presumably, be automated.

Once the logical flow of information around the system has been defined, a specification can be constructed from which a program can be written.

► Step 4.

A flow chart might be a good way of transmitting the overall process to a programmer, but there are other methods which are less cumbersome and more standardized as the detailed levels of the specification are described. Description of such methods is beyond the scope of this book.

A detailed definition of the way in which information is to appear on the screens of the system must be given to the programmer, as well as the exact manner in which print is to appear on any hard copy.

Essentially, the programmer needs to be given three basic things:

- I/O definition, in complete detail – with example drawings of the layouts of the screens and documents as the users interact with the computer.

- File definition – with actual analysis of the fields of the records of all the files, including field length.

- Process – which is the way in which the logic of the program proceeds, and uses the I/O and files.

From these specifications, the programmer performs the task of generating a program which satisfies these requirements in an appropriate language. During this process, there will be continuous consultation and liaison between programmer, systems analyst, any systems engineers, and the users. All will have constructive ideas for system development.

The systems analyst may also indicate the type of data which the programmer should use for initial testing of the program, though the programmer will test each part with data designed to be as searching as possible. When the complete system is tried out, it must be compared with the specification to ensure that, for instance, the screen and print layouts are as specified.

The final test, as always, comes after installation in the target site. The engineer assigned to installation and testing finds problems, and acts as the interface between the user and the programmer.

By these means, a computer system is produced which conforms to the business's requirements. In some cases the existing manual system will continue for a while in parallel with the computer system. This allows the computer system to be incorporated in a gradual and secure manner.

However, there are problems associated with this apparently ideal situation. For a start, considerably more human effort is required to drive two systems at the same time. Second, the two systems will inevitably be rather different, and they will often clash. Third, the systems can never be fully simultaneous or, for instance, orders and invoices will be duplicated, to the confusion of the customers and suppliers. In practice, some element of side–side operation is possible, but if the computer system is well founded, it will soon dominate as it is faster, more efficient and accurate, and provides much more information to managers for control of the business.

Standardizing systems analysis – SSADM

The development steps, used in this chapter so far, are not formally standardized, they just follow a typical, common pattern of system development. There are, however, formal, internationally recognized schemes for standardizing the task of systems analysis, and one of these is referred to as SSADM – structured systems analysis and design methodology. In general, such methodologies are not designed to apply to small compact problems. They figure, for instance, in the computerization of commercial systems which are currently run partly, or entirely, by hand. The second example above, of order processing, etc., is typical.

One element which has not been mentioned in the above programming and system examples is the 'feasibility study' phase. We have assumed so far that the introduction of a computer system, or program, has already been decided upon, and it was simply a matter of producing the final system. However, particularly in a large commercial system, there would normally be a feasibility phase during which a simple analysis of the situation would be considered,

► Step 6.

► Step 7.
Bugs appear at all stages of the development and testing, and are corrected as they appear.

► Steps 8 and 9.

► Steps 8 and 9 are also dealt with in Chapter 12.

► We will not look at the coding of this example – Step 5 – as it is rather large and complex, and requires the full specification to be developed before program writing begins.

► Feasibility studies usually precede any more detailed work in computerizing a system. A feasibility study is designed to establish where computerization is a practical option, i.e. whether it is feasible.

along with approximate specifications and costs. The result would be a report, the feasibility study, which would be used by managers to decide whether to commission a new system, and if so, to decide upon its general design and extent. The feasibility phase is often included within the SSADM structure.

SSADM consists of three 'phases', each of which is split into smaller 'stages'.

Phases and stages in structured systems analysis and design methodology (SSADM)

Phase 1: Feasibility study

Stage 01: Problem definition
The problem, which implied a computer solution in the first place, is examined and defined in sufficient detail to identify the 'need' for a computer solution.

Stage 02: Project identification
A simple analysis of possible solutions is constructed, including outline examples, specifications and some costing. Thus, several alternative projects are sketched out for solving the problem, assuming the need has been established.

Phase 2: Systems analysis

Stage 1: Systems analysis of operations and current problems
(Some of this may have been performed during feasibility.) The current system and its documentation is examined and analysed for both physical processes and data flows. This helps to form the background for the design, and ensures that nothing is missed from the final system. Current problems are identified at this point.

Stage 2: Requirements specification
At this stage the users are interviewed for their requirements, and the requirements defined exactly. This often tests the skill of the systems analyst considerably in tying down rather informal requests from non–technical personnel.

Stage 3: Selection of technical options
The means by which the computer will be implemented is decided here. As a part of this the users are asked for their preferences. At this point, the type of screen and printer, computer, communications and peripherals are identified.

Phase 3: Systems design

Stage 4: Data design
The types and origins of data which the system will take in, manipulate and output are identified. The more finely the data is described, the easier it will be for the programmer to include it correctly within the program.

Stage 5: Process design
The main flows and procedures within the system are described and documented here, so that a programmer can

construct algorithms for a solution. Attention is given to the way in which data is input and output.

Stage 6: Physical design
The main part of this stage is actually to design the program specifications for all the procedures and transactions within the system. In addition, program testing is planned, along with implementation and documentation for the users.

As you can see, the above steps have much in common with the more informal list of nine development steps described at the start of this chapter. A crucial point to make is that in general it is prudent and logical to define and design the system before actually buying anything. Unfortunately, this is often not appreciated by businesses, and the computer consultant is often confronted with an existing system which is grossly more complex, or considerably simpler, than is required to solve the problem. The feasibility stage, in particular, is an attempt to prevent such mistakes being made.

 Compare the earlier nine development steps with the six main stages in SSADM (leaving out feasibility). Against each of the six SSADM stages write down, by number, which of the nine development step(s) is/are included.

 Consider the order processing example above, and see how SSADM might be applied to it. Using the amount of information available in that example, write an analysis of the system, using SSADM as far as you can. How would you proceed to gain more information in order to produce a full analysis?

PROGRAMMING

After the analysis, the specified programs must be written in order to command the computer to perform the tasks. This requires a decision as to the computer language which will be appropriate.

Many systems houses have a favourite language, or languages, which their staff know well, and which they have chosen to be fairly widely applicable. There are several languages to choose from, and we will look a little at a couple of them. It is not possible in a short precis such as this to teach programming, and certainly not to describe more than one or two programming languages in outline form. However, the high-level procedural languages, though they do often look rather different at first sight, have many principles in common. Thus, it is generally agreed that once you have grasped the details of one, others are easy to learn. Common general high level languages which you will meet include Pascal, BASIC, C and perhaps Cobol. We will look briefly at the first two.

Programming languages

We have met examples of the lowest level of programming language, in the form of assembly and machine code. Programming the above examples requires knowledge of high-level languages where the basic electronic housekeeping of the system is not controlled by the programmer. The programmer needs a language which allows the problem to be expressed in full, quickly and efficiently, and then tested as fast and completely as possible.

An example of a programming language which is often the first one encountered is BASIC, though commercially you will probably encounter Pascal, C and more sophisticated commercial languages more often than BASIC for a number of reasons. However, you should be aware that there are many dialects of BASIC, and the better ones should not be considered as an amateur's or beginner's language. Sophisticated versions have procedures for any general problem which it is possible to construct. However, there are languages, and packages with associated languages, which will have the edge for certain purposes.

For instance, a file-based program would best be written using a database program to supply the basic file–keeping procedures which would otherwise have to be written specifically by the programmer. Similarly, tables of numbers and formulae for presentation of computer models of business situations are best attacked using a spreadsheet, and an associated programming language which uses its facilities. This saves having to write table- and graphics-handling routines specifically.

Thus, many business problems are programmed either by using the high-level language of a DB program to query the database of files, or by using Pascal, C, or other similar procedural languages.

We will now look at coding problems in this type of language, along with examples of common data types and statements. At the same time, we will look at program documentation and the two main program elements missed out before, namely: file handling and the use of separate program modules. When this has been examined, the next step is to see how programs written in this way can be fed into the computer for processing, which involves 'interpreters' and 'compilers'.

Learning a new high-level programming language

There are several aspects which you should examine when encountering a new high-level procedural programming language. These are listed in the box.

Aspects of a procedural programming language
Variables and data types
Most high-level languages allow variables to have several different types of value. For instance, variables may store integers (whole numbers), floating[nbh]point numbers (with decimals) called 'real' numbers, lists of general characters, ar-

rays (tables of data), and so on. This is the first thing you should look for when you learn a new language. As mentioned above, programs largely manipulate values stored within variables.

Statement types

The actual statements which are allowed within the language provide its vocabulary. Different languages offer different types of statement, some are very basic, and others allow much higher levels of program statement.

User input and output

This includes methods of printing to the screen and printer, and how the user can input information through the keyboard. All high-level languages handle this fairly effectively. They usually offer several ways of printing text to the screen and printer, though the use of graphics may be quite cumbersome. Others supply graphics functions as standard, with the ability to work in full colour, and any resolution. Similarly, high-level languages supply statements to allow characters to be taken directly from the keyboard, and often other input media too.

Filing information

Some languages have a very basic method of storing and reading filed information, others have a near database level of file handling. In general, a non-DB program will require a comparatively large amount of work to be done to store and read data, as well as to keep track of it. All the file handling will have to be constructed from scratch.

Available functions

Most languages supply the main standard functions found on a scientific calculator, such as arithmetic operations, square root, raise to a power, trigonometric functions, and so on. Functions are not always numerical. For instance, there are usually functions which can act on variables having character values – that is storing a set of characters such as 'HELLO'.

Advanced facilities

This includes the use of separate customized procedures. In many languages, a program can be constructed entirely from separate modules, each of which can be written and tested in isolation, passing information back and forth to other modules through a standardized interface. This is also the basis of 'object-oriented programming', known as 'OOP'.

Other advanced features include the ability to define and use what are known as 'user functions'. For instance, a more complex trigonometric function than the ones offered may be needed many times in a given program. It is useful if the programmer can define how the function is to work, and effectively add it to the repertoire of functions offered by the language.

There are many other features which you will discover as you learn to program.

We will now look at the elements of procedural programming languages in more detail, with some examples from typical high-level languages. The next step will be to examine how a simple program works, and then look at what constitutes 'good practice' in programming.

In the following paragraphs, examples of programming concepts are described around a couple of specific programming languages. This is just a sketch of the languages involved, and is designed to provide an introduction to the languages. If you wish to learn the languages properly, you will have to work on a computer with the chosen language installed, and work through the facilities, writing programs for yourself. There is no substitute for 'hands-on' experience.

Variables and data types

The names of the variables used in a program will often be names which mean something to the programmer. In general, variables can usually be any single letter, upper or lower case, or any combination of letters often up to some maximum length. In addition, certain special symbols can be mixed in – others may be excluded.

For instance, if an accounts program is working with a variable which stores the latest invoice payment being processed, it might be called 'INVPMNT', or 'INVPMT1', and so on. It is a nuisance to type out long variable names all the time, so a certain amount of abbreviation is common. However, choosing appropriate variable names is the first step in providing documentation within the program to make it comprehensible. If all variables are called 'X' or 'Y' or something simple, the meaning of the program is far less clear.

The values which a variable may take are usually as follows:

Integer – whole number value such as 2, –556, 87, 0.

Real – may contain decimals, or may not. For instance, 3, 4.8, –77, 67.88539, 10,000. They might also be expressed in 'scientific' or 'powers of 10' form such as '3.4 E 6', which means 3.4 times 10 to the power 6, or 3.4 million (3,400,000). You may be familiar with this notation if you have ever used a scientific calculator for large numbers.

Char or string – these values are simply single characters, or lists (strings) of characters. The word 'char' (short for character) is used to describe this data type in Pascal, while 'string' is used in BASIC.

Char or string entities might include any characters available, including numbers. A char constant in Pascal is identified by being enclosed in single quotes, while in BASIC, and others, the string is identified by double quotes. Also, BASIC variables can store strings of any number of characters, while Pascal can only store single characters in a 'char' variable or constant. Examples would be:

Pascal	Basic
'H'	"H"
'3'	"3"
'*'	"*"
	"34.985"
	"*** The rain in Spain.***"
	"*"
	"Hello"

The quotes are not included within the string – they are external delimiters only. They are sometimes called 'literals'. Note that some of the constants contain only numeric characters – this is not a number but a collection of digital characters and a decimal point. Variables which contain a string are distinguished in some special way in BASIC. For instance, a string variable name always ends in '$'. Thus, **CURRNUM** is a numeric variable, but **CURRNUM\$** is a string variable, and these two variables are completely different.

In Pascal, the char variables are made specific by being 'declared' as char type at the start of the program. Some other programming languages also demand that all the variables be declared at the start. This may seem a nuisance, but it promotes a structure to the programming which BASIC does not inherently have. This also helps considerably in documentation, and general readability of a given program – you do not continually have new variables popping up completely unannounced in the main body of a program.

Array – this is a table of variable values such as A(N) or B(N,M). For each value of N and M, there is a separate stored value. To understand the way in which this works, you should view the array 'A' as a set of component variables, one for each value of N (called the 'index') as follows:

A(0), A(1), A(2), A(3), A(4), ...

Each of these components has a value, and thus the array A stores a whole set of numbers, each of which has a specific numerical index, which appears within round brackets. The array may also contain char, or string, 'values', and again in BASIC would be called A\$(N), while it would be declared as of type 'char' in Pascal at the beginning.

The size of the array is determined by the maximum possible value of the index. A is a one-dimensional array. B, below, is a two-dimensional array, it is a matrix of components as follows:

B (0,0)	B (0,1)	B (0,2)	B (0,3)	B (0,4)
B (1,0)	B (1,1)	B (1,2)	B (1,3)	...
B (2,0)	B (2,1)	B (2,2)	B (2,3)	...
B (3,0)	B (3,1)	...		
B (4,0)	B (4,1)	...		
B (5,0)	...			...

Each of these components stores a single value, and as such an array supplies a large amount of indexed storage space, grouped together within a single entity. Its index can be operated upon by the program, and thus selection can be made from the table in a mathematical way.

Arrays can have more than two indices, to accommodate higher-dimensional matrices, and can store integer, real or char variables.

Another type of variable is the 'Boolean' variable, which can only have one of two possible values – true or false. We will look at this concept when we examine decisions, on page 202.

Statement types

In general, there are three basic types of language statement:

- sequential, for example, an assignment

- decision

- loop.

We have seen examples of all of these, and you should look back at the first flow chart in this chapter for examples (see page 177). An assignment, for instance, is the first type (sequential), a decision box is the second (decision), which also led to a loop (which is the third). We will now look at some typical statements in a high level language. Statements are to be regarded as the fundamental building blocks of a program. Each statement achieves a single objective which, when taken with all the other statements in the program, achieves the program's task.

In dealing with variables, the assignment statement is fundamental. An example in Pascal might be:

WEEKS := 52;

> Note: Read the ':=' symbol as the words 'set equal to' – also notice that Pascal statements in general end with a semi-colon.

This is a single statement which sets the variable 'WEEKS' to the value 52. Here, a special symbol ':=' is used to denote this command. In BASIC, the equivalent statement could be written:

LET WEEKS = 52

Throughout any high-level language, there are simple human-language words, such as 'LET' in this example, which are understood by the computer in a specific and well-defined manner. There are no subtle nuances in a programming language – a given word or symbol means exactly one thing, and nothing else.

'LET' is called a 'reserved word', or 'key word', and ':=' might be called a 'reserved symbol'. The compiler, or interpreter, which is used to convert this program into machine code will be looking specifically for these reserved words in order to perform the conversion. Having found the word 'LET', for instance, the BASIC compiler then expects to find a variable, followed by an '=' sign, and then a number or mathematical formula. If it does not find this specific pattern it reports an error, and the programmer has to rewrite the instruction in the required form. The compiler does not try to work out what was meant by the writer, it is simply not intelligent enough to make a guess. Also, the case of the key, or reserved, words is not usually important. Sometimes we will use upper case, and sometimes lower.

Note that even though we are comparing Pascal and BASIC here, they cannot be mixed. A BASIC compiler or interpreter will generally report an error if it encounters ':=', for instance, and a Pascal system will reject 'LET'.

Assignment, as we have seen, is also used to force a mathematical formula to be evaluated, and stored in a variable. For instance, in Pascal:

```
DAYS := YEARS * 365;
```

or in BASIC:

```
DAYS = YEARS * 365
```

▶ Incidentally, the word 'LET' happens to be a BASIC keyword which is optional. If a statement just consists of a variable followed by an '=' sign, and then a number or formula, the compiler assumes 'LET' is in front of it. However, '=' is also used in other ways, as we shall see on page 194. In Pascal, there has never been a need for LET anyway as the special equals sign ':=' denotes assignment unequivocally.

▶ Assignment.

These, and many other, computer languages use '*' as the multiplication symbol to save it being mixed up with the letter 'x'. Here, the variable 'DAYS' is being set equal to the value of YEARS times 365.

All the functions offered by the language can appear in assignments, for instance:

```
ANGLE := ARCTAN(B3);

AREA := SQR(7);

Z := Y * (A + B + C);
```

Again, note how variable names are chosen in all the above examples, where possible, to help in documenting the process which is being undertaken.

Other types of sequential statement are I/O statements, file-handling statements, calls to other modules, and so on. These will be described in later sections of this chapter.

Most computer languages supply a large number of reserved words and standard structures to allow decisions to be undertaken, and in many ways this overlaps with looping, as we saw in the flow charts on pages 172 and 182.

An example of a common decision statement would be the 'IF' statement, which is found in Pascal, BASIC and many other languages. It could be used as follows:

▶ From now on we will stick to Pascal, unless BASIC is mentioned specifically.

▶ Do not worry if your mathematics is not up to understanding the above functions. For our purposes you just have to understand the meaning of 'function', which is really just a special type of mathematical formula.

▶ Decisions and loops.

IF some condition is true THEN take some action ELSE take another action

The 'action' is any valid program statement, or even block of statements in some languages. The 'condition' is simply an expression which is either true or false.

An example **IF** statement might be:

IF YEARS = 1 THEN AGE := 'A' ELSE AGE := 'Z';

This **IF** statement illustrates the two uses of '=', which you must be careful to distinguish in most high level languages – even without the ':' sign. The first 'equals' is part of a question, namely:

'is the variable YEARS equal to the number 1?'

The second and third '=' are part of action commands – in fact, assignment actions, which set the variable 'AGE' to the char constant 'A' when 'YEARS' has value 1, and to 'Z' otherwise.

The two uses of the '=' are fairly natural in this statement, and the **IF**, **THEN** and **ELSE** are used in the same way as we use them in English, which is the whole point of a high-level language.

General structure of a program

As you should know by now, a program simply contains a list of instructions in an appropriate computer language. In BASIC, and other languages, the program requires no special header or initialization statements, it simply launches straight into the program statements. This has been designed to make it simple to teach, and to write short programs without preamble. Indeed, it does make for a very simple introduction to computer programming. However, the more structured languages, such as Pascal, do require initialization, or 'declaration' statements to aid in documentation and ease of transfer between programmers.

▶ Initialization/declaration: sets up program variables and helps documentation.

For instance, in Pascal, all the variables which are needed within the subsequent program must be named and their type defined at the head of the program. Thus, if an arithmetic program is being constructed to compute the sum of a set of numbers, the answer might appear in the real variable 'sum'. At the same time, the program may use an integer variable called 'num', and another real variable called 'fred'. These variables, along with a definition of their type, must be declared in the following formal manner:

```
var

sum, fred : real;

num : integer;
```

The reserved word 'var' introduces the variable declaration, which can contain any number of such declarations. Each declaration statement consists of a list of variable names, separated by commas, and followed by a colon, a data type and a semi-colon. As is always the case, the actual 'syntax' (the way in which computer language sentences are written) must be followed closely, or errors will result.

By this means, anyone can read a Pascal program and be sure of all the variables which will appear. As mentioned on page 00, in BASIC variables can pop up anywhere, with great ease, but little definition. Declaration ties the programmer down to careful definition. It does mean that during the writing of a program, new variables will be needed continuously, and they must be added to the growing collection of declarations. If an undeclared variable is used in a program, or if its type is misdeclared, an error will result.

Header for a Pascal program
The general form is as follows:

program	name (program parameters)
label	list of statement labels
const	list of constants
type	list of special data types
var	list of variables with types
	declaration of subprogram names and parameters
begin	statements
end	

▶ The order of Pascal declarations cannot be changed, but many of them can be missed out. However, the initial reserved word 'program', followed by a program name, and a list of 'program parameters' is necessary. It is also difficult to envisage a meaningful program without at least the 'var' section. Also, the section at the end which starts with 'begin' and ends with 'end' is mandatory – it contains the actual program. The others depend upon the sophistication of the program.

We will now look briefly at these various sections, culminating with the 'begin ... end' block.

program

The first line contains the keyword 'program' followed by a name for the program. For instance, if the program is designed to play chess, it might be named 'chess'. It is worth using words which mean something to an onlooker. A typical initial program statement for program called 'sum' might look like this:

program sum (input, output, sumfile);

Note the semi: which is needed to end the statement. The round brackets following the program name are mandatory. Within them the 'program parameters' include words such as 'input', 'output', 'sumfile', and so on. These words introduce the input and output channels found within the program. For instance, the simple word 'output' here usually means that some output from the program will be directed to the video screen. The simple word 'input' usually means that some input will be taken directly from the keyboard.

This is also the place where files used by the program are named. In this case, the program will be working with a file called 'sumfile', and while the program is running, it will 'hook' into the filing functions of the operating system under which Pascal is running, and ensure that the data file is handled correctly.

label

'label' declares any labels which are used to refer to particular statements within the program. We will not be looking at this part of the language.

const

'const' defines any constants which may be used within the program. It has the form:

```
const
        minim = 0;
        max = 32;
        fixedcost = 125;
```

Here, the constants 'minim', 'max' and 'fixedcost' are declared, and their values defined. Notice the semi-colons again.

type

'type' is used to declare special user-defined data types other than the usual ones such as integer or real. For instance, it may be useful to define a special data type called 'subint' which is just a small set of integers from the number 1 to some number stored in the constant 'limit', which would already have been declared and defined in the 'const' section. The full declaration would have the form:

```
const
        limit = 1001;
type
        subint = 1..limit;
```

Notice the use of double full stop to denote the word 'to' in the sense of 'from 1 to limit', where limit, here, equals the number 1,001.

var

The double full stop is also used when declaring variables or constants as arrays. For instance, the following would be a valid array declaration:

```
var
        temp : array [10..99] of integer;
```

This would declare an array called 'temp' with ninety elements, indexed from temp[10] to temp[99] containing integers. As you can see, the general form of an array declaration is:

```
array name : array[index range from .. to] of type;
```

declaration of subprogram names and parameters
The next section in the program structure above concerns the definition of user-defined subprogram modules such as special user-functions, procedures, etc. Here, in a predefined manner, all these constructs are defined so that they are available for use within the main body of the program. The exact form of this section of a Pascal program is beyond our scope, but, for your information, user-defined functions and procedures, etc. are introduced later in this chapter.

► For user-defined functions and procedures see page 209.

begin ...end
The final part of the structure is the program itself, which must be fully enclosed within the words 'begin' and 'end'. These words are called 'block delimiters'. Pascal is said to be a block-oriented language, and in general will contain many blocks within the main outer block. Blocks cannot overlap, but they can contain smaller blocks within, and further blocks within that – we say they can be 'nested'.

► Pascal is a block-oriented language, which forces the programmer to program in a logical way, suitable for later translation into machine code.

This feature helps to create naturally 'structured' program code. Sometimes, some of the more free and easy practices found in languages such as BASIC can seem easier to use, less formal and less restricting. However, such constructs, by their very informality, breed bad habits in programming, and do not naturally force a formal and easily comprehended form to the code. The aim of Pascal, and other structured languages, is to allow ease of comprehension, natural documentation, a standard structure, and easy transfer from programmer to programmer. It is also worth mentioning that later dialects of BASIC are very structured indeed, but unfortunately they still contain the historically unstructured elements in order to make them largely compatible with earlier versions. This gives the programmer the option as to the structure – Pascal prohibits such freedom, and breeds well-structured programming from the start.

Input and output
Once the program parameters (between round brackets at the start of the program) contain the word 'output', then reserved words such as 'write' and 'writeln' can be used to print information to the screen. Without 'output' at the start, this output channel would not be available, and use of 'write' and 'writeln' would simply cause an error. Again, you see how the initial declarations control all that follows.

'write' is used as follows:

```
begin

    write ('This is a line of text to be printed to the screen.')

end
```

► Note that a semi-colon is not used before an 'end', nor is it used before an 'else' in an 'if' statement.

Here, we assume that the declaration statements are in place, and we have skipped straight to the main program block. As you can see, the reserved word 'write' must be followed by round brackets within which appears the information which is to printed to the screen. When the computer comes to execute this, it notices the reserved word, looks at the head of the program for the declared program parameter, and knows that what appears between round brackets in the 'write' must simply be echoed to the screen. In this case it is a set of characters bounded by single quotes. The following appears:

This is a line of text to be printed to the screen.

The 'write' statement can contain several things to be printed, separated by commas, including variable values:

write('The answer = ', sum)

If the variable 'sum' contains the value 96.456, then the following would be printed:

The answer = 96.456

Notice the use of an extra space following '=' within the single quotes – this neatly prints the space needed to separate the '=' from the answer.

If another write statement appears after this one, the screen print just continues on the same line. For instance:

```
begin

        write('The answer = ', sum);

        write(' and this is the only solution.')

end
```

would produce:

The answer = 96.456 and this is the only solution.

Again, notice the use of extra spaces. These may appear to be details, but the subtlety of output is crucial to the way in which a program appears to the user – it must look neat, easy to use and logical. Also, this shows you how accurate you must be when programming.

Another important reserved screen output word is 'writeln'. This does the same thing, but has the subtle difference that further output to the screen will appear on the following line. For instance, writing the last example using writeln would be:

```
begin

     writeln('The answer = ',  sum);

     writeln('  and this is the only solution.')

end
```

the effect would be:

```
The answer = 96.456
 and this is the only solution.
```

(Why is the second line indented further than the first?)

Each output from a writeln statement appears on its own separate line. Note, as usual, how statements end with a semi-colon – except the one just before an 'end'. In fact, use of such a separator allows several statements to be typed onto the same line, without confusion. For instance, the following would be perfectly valid (if trivial!):

```
begin

     x:=15.6; writeln('answer = ',  x); write('program ended')

end
```

Often, it is more difficult to read a program which has too many statements on the same line, but this is up to the judgement of the programmer.

As you can see, there is some leeway in the exact syntax throughout the language – the trick is to know what is possible, and what causes an error.

Before looking at an example program, we will look at how the program can be annotated with comments for ease of reading later.

Anything written within curly brackets, or asterisks within round brackets, will be ignored by the computer, except that it will be faithfully reproduced as comments within the program. For instance:

```
{THIS IS A COMMENT}
```

and

```
(*This is also a comment*)
```

These will be ignored during execution, but reproduced within the program listing. We will see how this can be used in the example of a simple program containing a loop (see the box below). It is important to stick carefully to the use of the brackets, or the computer will fail to ignore it, and try to execute it, with consequent multiple errors. Anything can be written within the comment – there are normally no prohibited symbols.

► Syntax: grammar. The exact way in which words, punctuation marks and other symbols can be combined in a program.

The following program uses the constructs described above, along with a new one which allows the program to loop. It should be self-explanatory. Before reading further, examine the program and find three deliberate errors of syntax. Also, see if you can describe the process of the program, and write out the exact form of the output on the screen.

A simple program containing a loop

```
{NOTE: *** THIS PROGRAM CONTAINS THREE SYNTAX ERRORS! ***}
program add10 (output) {this is a simple example program}

{the following are declaration statements}

const
        max = 10;

var
        j, sum : integer;

begin {now we begin the program proper}
        sum:=0 j:=0;
        while j < max do {this is the start of a loop}
                begin
                j:=j+1;
                writeln(j);
                sum := sum+j
                end
        writeln('the sum of the first 10 nos. is ' sum)
end
```

As you can see, the program is called 'add10'. Its basic aim is simply to add ten consecutive integers, starting with 1, print them to the screen, and end with a message and the final sum. It starts with a warning which is in the form of a comment, and as such is ignored during program execution. There then follows a 'program' statement which includes the program name and declares the output channel which causes write statements to print to the screen. The statement does not end with a semi-colon, which is the first syntax error. Note that the same line contains a comment within curly brackets, which has nothing to do with the program statement. The line should read:

program add10 (output); {this is a simple example program}

The next declaration statements define a constant, 'max' set equal to 10, and two integer variables 'j' and 'sum'. These are followed by the block containing the main program, as the comment makes clear.

The first statement in the program is an assignment which sets the variable 'sum' to the initial value 0. Unfortunately, it is not ended with a semi-colon – which is the second error in the program.

It is followed by another statement on the same line, which initializes j to 0. The correct form of the line is:

sum :=0; j:=0;

Now we enter a 'while (condition) do' loop. Essentially, while the condition is true, the block following 'do', delimited by 'begin' and 'end' is performed over and over again. When, and if, the condition fails to be true, the block is not executed, and the program passes on to the statements following the block. Note the correct absence of the semi-colon before the 'end'.

Here, while the value of j is less than max (which has value 10), the enclosed block following the 'do' is executed over and over again. The block's statements start by incrementing the value of j to 1. The next step writes the value of j to the screen, without any message. The value of j is then added to 'sum', which starts as 0, and now becomes 1. As the following loop, described below, executes, the variable 'sum' will gradually accumulate the sum of j's values from 1 to 10.

The loop then brings the program execution back up to check the condition after the word 'while'. You can see that j (equal to 1 ath the start) is still less than 10, and so the process repeats. It continues to repeat until the value of j is incremented to 10, printed and added into 'sum' for the last time. Then, checking the 'while' condition produces a false answer and the loop block is not executed again.

At this point, the program execution passes on to the statements following the loop block. There is only one statement there, which is to print the message, and the final sum. This is where the third syntax error may be found. There is no comma separating the message characters from the variable 'sum' within the writeln statement. The correct form should be:

writeln('the sum of the first 10 nos. is ', sum)

The full output would look like this:

1

2

3

4

5

6

7

8

9

10

the sum of the first 10 nos. is 55

Explain why the use of a 'write' instead of a 'writeln' in the last statement would make no difference to the output. What general difference would it make if the first 'writeln' were to be replaced with 'write'?

This program shows how blocks become naturally nested – there are two blocks in the program, one within the other. You can also see how the block structure is used to enclose a set of statements which form their own submodule, as it were. Without a block structure, the 'while ... do' would not know how much of the following code to execute while the condition was true.

Conditions and Boolean variables

As you can see, the condition in the 'while' statement has an outcome which is true or false. These are called 'Boolean values'. 'Boolean' is simply another data type such as 'integer', 'real' and so on. In addition, in some languages a variable can be set equal to this type of value, for instance:

```
outcome := (k = 34)
```

The condition within the round brackets is a Boolean expression. The variable 'outcome' has the value true if k=34, and false otherwise. The variable 'outcome' can actually be used as the 'condition' in a 'while' or 'if' statement, or anywhere else that a condition is needed. Thus, the following would be perfectly valid:

```
if outcome then write('outcome is true')
else write('outcome is false');
```

This allows the **IF** condition to be constructed, perhaps using a complex logical 'calculation' elsewhere in the program, and then simply applied where needed in this shorthand form. Note the lack of a semi-colon before the 'else'.

Special Boolean functions such as **AND**, **OR**, etc. can be used to

---

Boolean conditions can also be constructed using the comparison operators:

= 'equals'

> 'greater than'

< 'less than'

>= or => 'greater than or equal'

<= or =< 'less than or equal'

<> or >< 'not equal'

For instance:

```
K >= 3
```

has the value true for K equal to any number from 3 upwards, and false otherwise, and:

K = 3

has the value true only when K has value 3.

---

combine these to produce complex logical expressions suited to any requirement. For instance:

(K < 10 and K <> 0)

is a conditional, or Boolean, expression having the value true for the numbers: 9, 8, 7, 6, 5, 4, 3, 2, 1, –1, –2, ... In many ways, these logical constructions, and decisions based on them, are at the very basis of the way in which humans think. Such functions and variables are used in the study of artificial intelligence (AI), and some languages specifically cater for this type of construction, using mostly words, in order to allow logical sentences to be constructed.

Input and simple file handling

If the 'program' statement at the top of the program contains the parameter 'input', as in:

program name (input, output);

then the 'read' and 'readln' statements can automatically be used to take input directly from the keyboard. A typical 'read' statement would be:

read(z)

This would wait for the program user to type in a number of the correct type for storage in 'z'. In this manner, values can be passed to the program from the user. If the variable 'question' has type char, then the following would allow the user to type in a letter:

read(question)

The variable 'question' would then contain the letter typed in at this point. It might be used in the following manner:

read(question);

if question = 'y' then writeln('yes');

if question = 'n' then writeln('no')

else writeln('try again!');

This starts by waiting for the user to type in the letter 'y' or 'n'. Then, depending upon the outcome, it prints 'yes' or 'no'. If anything else is input, the message 'try again!' is printed, and presumably the program will be made to loop back to the 'read' again to give the user another chance.

If the input is to be taken from a file of data, the same basic constructs are used. Suppose there is a file of numbers called 'oddnos', containing the following numbers, stored one per line:

1

3

5

7

9

11

Before this can be used, the file must be declared in a program statement at the top of the program, which we shall name 'odd', as follows:

program odd (oddnos, output);

If there is to be input from the keyboard as well, then the following would have to appear:

program odd (oddnos, input, output);

The program segment itself would be something like:

```
begin
readln(oddnos, x);
    y := x*2;
    writeln(y)
end
```

This reads a line, which contains a single number, from the file 'oddnos' and stores it in the variable x. The variable x is then doubled, and stored in variable y, which is printed to the screen.

Note how the specific file being used is named within the 'readln' statement to distinguish it from any other file, and indeed from keyboard input.

Storage to a file is just as simple. The following is the storage counterpart to the above:

writeln(oddnos,m)

Here, the value of m is stored onto a single line within the file oddnos, which also needs to be declared in the program statement in the same way. Effectively, the files being handled here should be regarded as pieces of paper on which data is written in the same way as it is written to the screen.

Other special looping constructions

Looping, or iteration, is one of the most important concepts in program writing in procedural languages. The whole ethos of such languages is the sequential execution of statements, sometimes over and over again in a loop.

There has been a move, over a long period, to control the concept of iteration, and program structure, by providing iteration keywords which allow the program to be logically modularized, or contained within separated routines. We have seen this in the 'while' loop where a block of statements contained within a block is executed in a loop.

Other looping constructs are 'for' and 'repeat ... until'. 'for' is similar to 'while' in that it heads a block of statements contained within delimiters 'begin' and 'end', whereas 'repeat' and 'until' are used as the delimiters themselves. If a block of statements is to be performed k times, a neat way of achieving it would be using something similar to the following example:

```
for j = 1 to k do

begin

        program statements;

end
```

This produces a loop through the statements for all values of j from 1 to k, and then ends. An alternative would be to use:

```
j:=1;

repeat

program statements;

j:=j+1

until j=k
```

► Iteration keywords/loop keywords: while, for, repeat ... until.

This is more cumbersome for the same result. Note that 'until' is another of those reserved words which does not need to be preceded with a semi-colon. Here, the value of j must be initialised, and then specifically incremented to achieve the same result. However, 'repeat' is useful in other contexts such as:

```
repeat

read(text, letter);

if letter = 'z' then writeln('last letter')

until letter = 'z'
```

This reads the contents of a file called 'text' character by character (not line by line because read was used and not readln). Each character is written into the char variable 'letter', and then checked to see whether it is the lower case letter 'z'. If it is not, the repeat continues until it is so. When 'letter' is equal to 'z', the message 'last letter' is printed, and the program segment finishes. As you can see, 'repeat' and 'until' are replacement delimiters for 'begin' and 'end'.

There are equivalent constructions in BASIC, which is not a block-oriented language. Thus, each of the BASIC equivalents of the

► Loops in BASIC.

above looping structures needs its own special block delimiters. For instance, the 'for' statement in BASIC looks like this:

```
for i = 1 to 15

j=i*32/7

print"j = ",j

next i
```

Here, the 'for' statement loops for all values of i from 1 to 15, executing all statements from the 'for' down to the 'next', which are, therefore, the delimiters in this case. In BASIC, the 'print' statement does the job of 'write', and uses double quotes without the round brackets. There are no semi-colon endings to statements either, though usually colons are used to separate statements if they appear on the same line.

Modern dialects of BASIC have 'while' statements, and various others have iteration statements, all with their own way of delimiting. In addition, BASIC can be made to jump to (or **GOTO**) a given line, just like machine code, but this is considered dangerous as it produces badly structured code.

Structured and object-oriented programming

The above has been concerned with the provision of iteration functions which helped to keep loops within modules. The opposite of this is found in programs which use the BASIC **GOTO** statement. This can send program execution all over the place, making it difficult to follow the logical strands. In addition, documenting this type of tortuous flow is difficult.

▶ BASIC's 'GOTO' statement gives unstructured programs.

Full structured programming is a science in itself, and there are special standards which are applied to the way in which program writing is achieved.

Modularization is an important element of structured programming. The other important element is the 'top down' method of constructing solutions to problems. This implies that a problem is attacked by starting with the highest level of solution logic, and then breaking it into smaller and smaller modules, until the level is reached when it can be coded directly into computer language statements.

▶ Modularization and the 'stop down' approach.

For instance, suppose we wish to produce a program to collect and sort the returns from a school census, and produce an alphabetically sorted list of the pupils, plus the number in the school. The following might be a suitable top-level solution, with the various tasks confined to five separate modules:

Input the names of all pupils

Sort the list alphabetically

Count the names

Print the names in order

Print the total number

This is the general approach chosen for the solution, but cannot simply be typed into a computer verbatim. The tasks must now be described in a manner which can be broken down into computer statements as in the inset.

Module 1:

    Input a name

    Store on a file

    Input the next name

    (and so on until the names are exhausted)

Module 2:

    Sort the file of names

Module 3:

    Read a name from the file

    Increment a count

    Read the next name

    Increment count and repeat until file exhausted

Module 4:

    Read a name from the sorted file

    Print the name

    Repeat until all names printed

Module 5:

    Print the total number of pupils counted

    End

As you can see, we have made rather a meal of this simple task, but it illustrates how the process is split into modules, and goes from the top level of solution and down to the next with more detail. To see the next stage in constructing the program, here is the first module above in more detail, and written in a form which could easily be converted into a running Pascal program:

{NOTE: THIS IS MODULE 1, where names are input from the keyboard in any order, and stored in a file called names}

declare 'names' as a file and 'namech' as a 'char' variable

write ('Input names one by one, ending each name with a full stop. Finish the final name with an exclamation mark instead.')

repeat {do until end of set of names – i.e. '!' input}

► Note that if you analyse this process you will see there are two loops nested together. The inner loop just inputs and stores a single name, character by character, including full stops and exclamation mark. The outer loop repeats this process for name after name until the last name has been input, which is denoted by the presence of an exclamation mark.

```
while namech <> '.' and namech <> '!' do

{read in a name, character by character, storing on a single line,
until you reach the end of the name, denoted by '.', or the end of
the last name, denoted by '!'}

    begin

    read(namech);

    write(names,namech)

    end

start new line in names

until namech = '!'
```

 Draw an algorithm for module 1 of this program to show the nesting loops.

The other modules would be similarly converted into program elements, and the whole program written in final form and tested.

Note how the comments document the program to make it easier to follow. There is an art to documenting programs as they are written, and it takes experience to achieve this important task effectively.

As you can see, the logic of the above five modules is a little tortuous. The printing of the names and the counting of the names, for instance, could have been included in the same routine. This long-winded format is, therefore, just for illustration purposes.

 Assuming that modules 1 and 2 are complete, write out modules 3 and 4 as accurately as possible in Pascal, but including both counting and printing together – i.e. combine modules 3 and 4. Include the necessary declaration statements.

The advantages of structured programming

The format described above is typical of a structured program. A clever programmer will be able to collapse the whole of this routine into a single module, and for such a simple example this might be considered perfectly acceptable. However, structuring the process into modules provides an easily readable procedural form which is also, again, self-documenting and easy to edit and change for future requirements.

Another crucial advantage of structured programming and structured specification is that a team of programmers can be employed, each working on a separate module of the final program. Each team must know the definition of the 'interface' variables and files, that is the variables and files which are to be passed between them, but they need only be concerned with their own piece of the program. This approach might be used, for instance, to write a complete spreadsheet program, or a large suite of accounts software.

The logical extension of a structured programming approach is that of 'OOP' or object-oriented programming. In OOP languages, the program splits naturally into completely separate modules, with carefully defined universal interfaces which allow any module to be used by another programmer at any time. An overall plan for a complete programming task is designed, and split into modules. These are either constructed from a library of previously written modules, or are specially written from scratch. This again caters for teams of programmers working separately on a piece of software, and also ensures that when a given module is written, it is available to be 'plugged' into any other program at a later date.

▶ OOP – object-oriented programming: preconstructed modules can be selected from a library and combined. The important matter is the way in which one module will interface with others to fit.

Subroutines, procedures and user functions

Modularization can be achieved even in the simplest languages using concepts such as 'subroutines' or 'procedures'. In BASIC, for instance, certain parts of the process are written as a series of separate little, or even large, programs, called 'subroutines', and stored at the end of the main program. The main body of the program simply proceeds by calling subroutine after subroutine, and passing variables back and forth between them. This is a particularly fruitful approach for a program which needs to repeat a given type of process over and over again. A subroutine is written just once for the process, and it is called again and again.

▶ Subroutines.

Pascal uses 'procedures' for this purpose. They are described and declared at the start of the program, and used in the subsequent main program.

Technically, a subroutine is a piece of code which resides in a set labelled position within the body of the program, and is called by its label. It manipulates variables which are universally available to the main program, and not distinguished in any way. A procedure, on the other hand, is called by name, and the call includes the definition of a certain set of 'interface' variables which are used to pass information in and out of the procedure. Any other variables used within the procedure are local, and not generally available elsewhere. This restricts the passing of data in and out of the procedure to a more formal and well-defined interface. It helps in structuring programs.

▶ Procedures: PROCS.

A typical procedure or subroutine would be an alphabetic sort routine for files. This might be called each time a file is constructed from keyboard input. Similarly, a routine to feed in a given set of data from the keyboard could also be written as a procedure (or PROC), and called each time that input is needed. Use of procedures and subroutines can reduce the size of a program significantly.

▶ User-functions.

Finally, 'user-functions', as mentioned on page 197, are routines which allow the programmer to make up new functions. Such new functions are available for use in exactly the same way as the standard functions provided. That is, they are written into mathematical, or other, formulae directly. When encountered within a program, the compiler searches around for a body of program which is headed in a prescribed manner with the name of that function, and evaluates the function, using the values available at that point of the program.

As you can see, the main point of all of these structures is to confine a given process to a separately written module. This can be used in a fully structured manner to split a problem into small, easily digested pieces.

Although special programming languages exist to allow OOP, it should be clear that given the structures mentioned in this section, as long as the interface variables, along with their exact form, are defined completely, an object-oriented approach can be simulated using almost any high level language. The trick is to regulate, with care, the way in which subroutines and procedures communicate information to and from other parts of a program.

Program conversion

After the high-level program code has been written in full, as a body of text, it must be stored in a file, and then converted into machine code. To run this program, the processor's program counter must then be set to the memory address at which the machine code starts.

This is achieved using a compiler, as we have seen. The text form of the program, the source code, is turned into object (or machine) code. Then the programmer runs the program.

A programming language package consists of several parts. In full, it may contain the following parts, among others:

> An editor – which is used to write the program text
>
> An interpreter – to execute the code in an immediate manner
>
> A compiler – to convert source into object code
>
> An execution module – to cause the object code to be run
>
> An error checker – to help the programmer to correct mistakes
>
> A debugger – to give the programmer high level aid during correction

An editor is simply a wordprocessor which allows the high-level program statements to be written out in full. An interpreter does the same thing, but can be used to run the program, or parts of it, immediately. An interpreter does not convert the whole source code into an object code file, it converts part of it as required for execution of the current part of the program. It allows a program to be developed and run immediately, so that the programmer can see and correct bugs. However, it is slower, and less efficient than a file of object code.

An execution module is used to take the object code file, and present it at the right place in the processor's address map for execution.

The error check and debugging modules, if they are supplied separately, will print up specific information as to mistakes in the program 'at run time'. That is, during the running of the object code itself. Some packages have quite sophisticated debugging software which allows the program to be run in a special simulation mode, with the state of the variables, etc. displayed as the program runs, at slow speed. In this manner, the inner workings of the program can be examined, and problems sorted out.

A given language package does not always include all of the above elements, but enough is always present to write and run a program in the given language. The manual for such a package usually contains a scientifically accurate definition of the language package, so that there is no confusion as to the exact use of all language words. There is also often a primer to teach the language to a new user. Unfortunately, manuals can let you down in either, or both, of these aspects, and it is often necessary to look at a book written by an external author who has done the job of going through the package, learning it, and then describing it in a more comprehensible manner. There are many such books available. Books for particular programs, if not in stock at your local book shop, can be ordered for you from the publisher.

OTHER APPROACHES TO COMPUTERIZING

This chapter has dealt with the 'procedural' approach to problem solving so far. It is a natural approach, but may not be efficient for some classes of problem.

► Three approaches:
• procedural
• declaratory
• neural network.

The main rival to the procedural approach is that catered for by the 'declarative' languages, and we will look at this shortly. However, there are other completely different approaches which do not even try to write programs to solve problems. One of these is the 'neural network' where, in a sense, the problem writes its own program! A whole set of known standard solutions is presented. The network learns and adjusts itself accordingly, and when new data is presented, it is able to make a good guess at the answer to the new problem, 'from experience'. This is akin to the way in which our brain solves problems.

Declarative languages

All the programming mentioned so far has been procedural – that is, lists of instructions are executed, chronologically, by the processor. In general, you should be clear that processors, at their lowest level, always work in this way. They just execute lists of machine code in sequence.

However, by writing suitable programming language packages, it is possible to simulate completely different approaches to programming at the higher levels.

One example is the declarative approach. Very broadly, in this approach, it is the specification of the problem to be solved, rather than the actual method of solution, which is provided by the programmer. For instance, information about a set of objects might be supplied, along with the definition of a problem using that information. This problem definition, written as a program in the declarative language, would then be compiled and run. The resulting solution would be presented without the programmer having explained any of the steps needed for that solution.

Essentially, much of the work goes into defining the characteristics of the problem, rather than a sequential method of finding a solution. This is somewhat opposite to the procedural approach where careful descriptions of the method of solution predominate.

This happens to be ideally suited to database applications, where a large body of information is stored, and queries are made of the database.

Declarative languages are also useful in a related branch of computing called 'expert systems'. Here, a base of information called a 'knowledge base' is constructed about which questions can be asked in a very high-level manner.

For instance, a vehicle-engine manual is a knowledge base. It contains specific information about a given engine, and instructions as to how to disassemble and repair each part of the engine. If this were to be stored appropriately in a knowledge base, a screen system could be constructed, using that information, to find out how to remove and replace any given part of the engine, and how to maintain it in general.

Any computing language can be used to produce such programs, but a declarative language makes it into a natural process. SQL is an example of a declarative language specifically designed to query a database. Another, more general, language is called Prolog. It allows problems to be expressed in a mathematical logic form, and deals largely, but not exclusively, with text data.

As an example of how this approach works, we will consider the following table of information:

ITEM	QTY. IN	REORDER_QTY.	POSITION	COLOUR	COST	PRICE
G/1003	100	50	MAIN_AREA	GREEN	32	41
A/7842	1000	100	MAIN_AREA	ORANGE	54.2	65
C/3581	567	150	SUB_BASE.	BLUE	4.9	8
S/3367	39	80	SUB_BASE.	WHITE	5	7.2
S/3367	45	80	SUB_BASE.	YELLOW	5	7.2
S/3367	92	75	SUB_BASE.	LILAC	5	7.2
F/7583	129	120	MAIN_AREA	GREEN	12.3	16.8
G/9964	206	25	SUB_BASE.	YELLOW	15	19
O/2098	39	150	WAREH.2	WHITE	28	42
O/2098	49	125	WAREH.2	ORANGE	28	42
O/2098	66	125	WAREH.2	GREEN	28	42

This is a small stock file of products stored and recognized by a standard ITEM code, which appears in the first column. The next column is the quantity in stock, followed by that level of stock below which an order for restocking should be issued. Then comes the place where the product is stored: MAIN AREA, SUB BASE-MENT, WAREHOUSE NO. 2. Then comes the colour, followed by the cost and selling prices. In the table, each attribute and data item is restricted to being a single word or number, hence the use of the lower 'dash' to join otherwise separate words together.

This is a standard database file, with records and fields. If we wish to construct a list of all products which have to be reordered, a declarative approach would simply state the problem:

list all records with REORDER_QTY. > QTY.IN

The output table (solution) thus produced automatically would be:

ITEM	QTY. IN	REORDER_QTY.	POSITION	COLOUR	COST	PRICE
S/3367	39	80	SUB_BASE	WHITE	5	7.2
S/3367	45	80	SUB_BASE	YELLOW	5	7.2
O/2098	39	150	WAREH.2	WHITE	28	42
O/2098	49	125	WAREH.2	ORANGE	28	42
O/2098	66	125	WAREH.2	GREEN	28	42

If the reordering is to be restricted only to product found in the sub basement, something like this would be required:

list all records with REORDER_QTY. > QTY.IN and POSITION = SUB_BASE.

The output list would be:

ITEM	QTY. IN	REORDER_QTY.	POSITION	COLOUR	COST	PRICE
S/3367	39	80	SUB_BASE.	WHITE	5	7.2
S/3367	45	80	SUB_BASE.	YELLOW	5	7.2

These are very simple applications of a query system for a database, and you can see that once the database is set up, the task of selecting a list just comes down to defining the problem, and not telling the system how to do it.

A full declarative language is more concerned with relationships, than tables of data. The table of data above can be written in terms of the relationships between things in the following manner:

ITEM_WHITE_S/3367 HAS_QTY.IN 39

ITEM_WHITE_S/3367 HAS_REORDER_QTY. 80

ITEM_WHITE_S/3367 IS_IN_POSITION SUB_BASE.

ITEM_WHITE_S/3367 COSTS 5

ITEM_WHITE_S/3367 SELLS_FOR 7.2

The whole point is to define the characteristics of each unique item in the list. Note that the item has to be made unique by joining in its colour. Once the complete table has been defined in this manner, complex relationships can be invoked by formal logical constructions. These are basically equivalent to asking for all items with specific relationships between certain attributes. For instance, finding all items which need reordering, or which are in the main area, and so on.

Standard relationships exist in such a language, such as 'less than', 'equals', etc. The programmer's task is to supply a base of knowledge about specific relationships. Use of the information is by a human language, or a formal logical language, which defines problems carefully, without worrying specifically about the mechanics of the solution method itself. You should now understand what is meant by concentrating on defining the problem, rather than how to solve it.

Neural networks

A rather different approach from that of the many examples above, is that of the self-learning system. This is an attractive approach, it suggests that programs do not have to be written, with the attendant complexity of constructing algorithms, coding, testing, maintaining, and so on. The idea is to let the computer do all the work, and end up by presenting a finished working system.

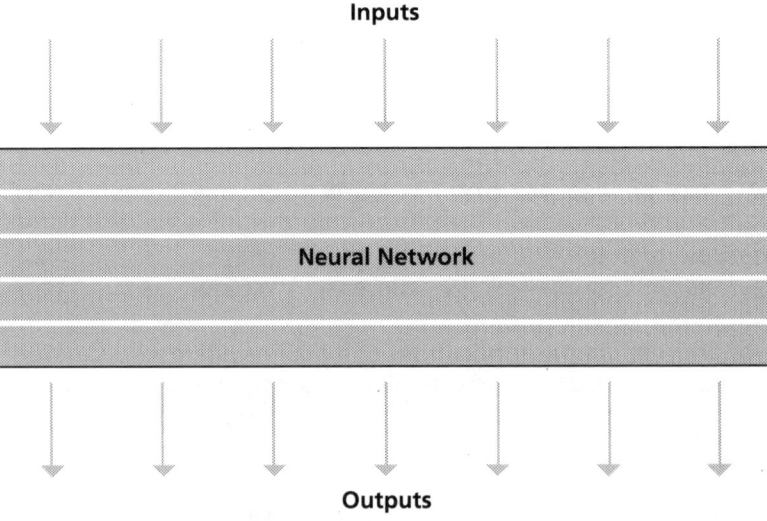

Figure 10.3 Neural networks from the outside

Figure 10.3 shows the outward presentation of a neural network. It appears to be a 'black box' with inputs and outputs. The inputs and outputs can be numbers, electrical impulses with varying amplitudes, or anything for which the black box is set up. The black box, for instance, could be a fast electronic circuit taking input from a set of weather sensors, and outputting the probability of rain over a given period. Alternatively, the black box could be a piece of software reading in-data stored within the records of a file. Each record, for instance, could have a set of fields containing the results of a scientific process. The outputs would contain the processed solution for each applied input record.

The neural network ('net' for short) is first put into a 'learning mode'. While in this mode, each time a set of inputs is applied, the correct outputs are also supplied so that the net can 'adjust' itself to this information. This process of applying learning data is repeated until the net seems to have learned enough.

The next step is to place the net in 'problem-solving mode'. In this mode, applying inputs to it causes the stored 'experience' to produce an output set. After learning, a set of test data is applied to ensure that it has learned correctly. Finally, completely new data can be applied with a degree of certainty which comes from trial and error.

The neural network is simply a transfer function from input to output which is defined by standard trial data. Some indication of the inner workings of a net is shown in Figure 10.4.

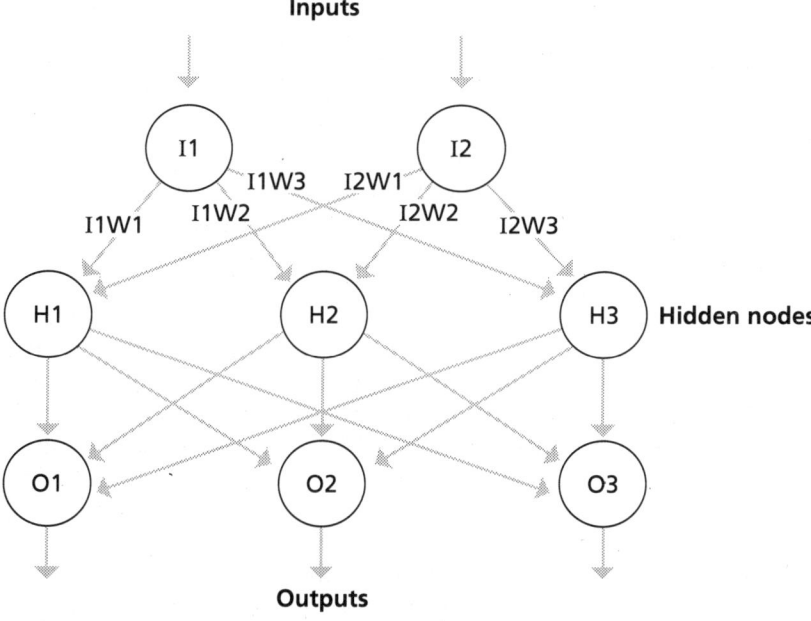

Figure 10.4 Inside a neural network

The inspiration for this approach came from examining the human brain. The basic cells of the brain, the neurons, were observed having many connections to each other. It was also observed that as the brain formed a habit, i.e. learned something, lines of tissue would grow across neurons, providing new connection possibilities.

In Figure 10.4, for simplicity, a two-net is illustrated with just three outputs. Each input and output is connected to a node, and there is a 'layer' of 'hidden' nodes, which are not connected directly to the outside of the black box. The way in which information transfers across the net is as follows.

Each input node is connected through to every hidden node, and each hidden node is connected onwards to every output node. For simplicity, only the nodes and the first layer of connections are labelled.

When a numerical value appears at the input of a net, in problem solving mode, a separate mathematical formula is applied to it for each of the connections from that node to the hidden layer. For instance, when a value appears at I1, it is 'modified' using formulae I1W1, I1W2 and I1W3. These are 'weighted' numerical transforms which are 'combined', as shown, with all the other values appearing at the hidden nodes. For instance, at H2, the values of the formulae I1W2 and I2W2 are 'combined'.

The actual formulae used for modification and combination through the net are calculated during the use of the learning mode. Their mathematical structure is beyond our scope here. However, you should be aware that each time a learning set is applied, the net software, or electronics, adjusts all the weights and formulae to allow for the new information.

By this means, the inputs are modified and combined and produce output values which can be read directly at the output end.

As you can see, once a net has been set up, and assuming it is efficient, the rest is easy. The background structure of neural networks has been worked out mathematically, and by experiment, and it is possible to purchase a standard neural network, with a simple front-end processor so that you can experiment for yourself.

The problems with neural networks stem from choosing a suitable learning set. If the set is not wide enough, then the experience of the final net values is not wide enough to produce accurate results. If the learning set is contradictory, the net cannot learn properly, and so on.

A neural network is good at discovering the underlying patterns which exist in bodies of data. If there is no pattern, it will have nothing to learn. In general, nets are applied to situations where fast output is required without the attendant sequential processing which goes with a normal program. They are also good for situations where the user does not know the underlying pattern, and has not the time or the energy to learn it. The net learns it automatically, and applies it without the operator's ever knowing how.

Neural networks are, in many ways, the future of general computing. They are already being used in many technical and scientific settings, and are being applied to make predictions in the complex financial world. They do not need to be realized using software in a normal computer to simulate the activity. The whole network can be built using dedicated electronic logic and memory elements. This does not need to run a program, with all the attendant facilities to slow it down. It simply learns electronically, and applies that electronic system directly to the applied problems. This makes for an extremely fast, and effectively customized computing machine.

Parallel computing

In the past, speed and complexity were attacked by making the processors run much faster, and speeding up memory components. However, the same effect can be achieved by splitting problems into parts which can be processed simultaneously, or in parallel.

There are special processors which 'plug' together to share electronic data, and act on different parts of a program at the same time. However, even a simple accounts system, sharing the same files, will be able to run parallel activities on separate computer systems.

In other words, parallelism can be achieved either at the processor level, or at the system level. However, the problem is the software. How, for instance, can two systems share a single file of accounts data? Suppose that the first system was writing new data to the file at the same time as the second system also wanted to modify that file – which version of the file would be valid? In any case, such clashes can be fatal. The answer is to use a special operating system to control the clashes, perhaps by locking out the second system until the first is finished, or by apportioning separate time slices to each, and so on.

At the processor level, special computer languages have to be developed to allow a natural splitting of a program into parallel segments, which are then applied to a set of processors in a logical and efficient manner. An example of a parallel language is OCCAM which has been developed to run the Inmos 'Transputer' parallel processors. Any number of such devices, each with its own internal memory area, can be strung together, and the OCCAM program apportions task segments accordingly.

The increase in speed possible by parallel processing is arbitrarily large, as long as the process can be split up. Speeds equivalent to the fastest super computers can be reached, for a fraction of the cost. Again, the overhead is on the software.

Parallel computing is good for processing problems where the inputs and outputs naturally split up. For instance, the world's weather system, split into cells, each evolving under the laws of nature, and interacting with its neighbours, can be split into programming cells, each communicating with neighbouring ones in a standard manner. As you can see, this is very akin to object-oriented programming, and lends itself well to a structured approach.

Parallel computing is an expanding branch of IT, and it will be found more and more in the larger problems which are being attacked in everyday life.

Chapter review

- Procedural languages use sequences of steps to solve problems.
- A sequence of such steps is a program.
- Systems analysts analyse systems and problems, and specify programs.

- Programmers code programs.
- Systems engineers install and maintain systems.
- A program should contain error checking and error messages.
- A program should be properly documented for ease of comprehension and maintenance.
- A flow chart can be used to aid algorithm construction.
- Debugging is the process of finding and correcting program errors or 'bugs'.
- Assignment statements use the '=' sign, and give values to variables.
- Decisions are taken depending upon conditions, or conditional expressions.
- Looping, or iteration, is the process of repeating a given part of a program.
- MIS (management information services) is concerned with producing reports and analysis for management to help control the business.
- Analysis of a business system examines documentation, data storage and business methods.
- Systems analysis defines I/O, filing and algorithm.
- SSADM – structured systems analysis design methodology – standardizes systems analysis.
- High-level languages are generally used to write business systems.
- Data types include integer, real, string, Boolean.
- Arrays are indexed tables of variable values of any data type.
- Program statement types include sequential, decision, loop.
- 'True' and 'false' are the Boolean values.
- A Boolean variable or expression only takes the values true and false.
- A condition in a decision statement is a Boolean variable or expression.
- Well-structured programs are modular, and loops are confined within modules.
- Construction of structured programs is 'top–down' a problem is defined in general terms, and then made more and more specific.
- OOP – object-orientated programming – programs are written in modules which communicate via a standardized interface.
- Subroutines, procedures, definable user-functions help to modularize a program.
- An editor is used to write a high level program, the output is called 'source code'.
- Source code is turned into object, or machine, code by a compiler.
- An interpreter allows a programmer to write and immediately test a program without compiling.

- A declarative language does not use sequential statements, the problem is defined without a specific solution method.
- A neural network learns from a set of given input/output patterns, and can then be applied to a new set of inputs.
- Parallel computing combines several systems or processors to work simultaneously on separate parts of a given problem.

► **Now that you have completed this chapter, look back to the objectives at the beginning and check that you have accomplished each of them.**

 # Communications and networks

Chapter objectives

By the time you have read this chapter, you will understand:

∎ why communications are important

∎ the meaning of parallel and serial communications

∎ how asynchronous data is transferred

∎ the speed of data communications

∎ the way in which data flow is controlled

∎ how communications errors are detected and corrected

∎ the meaning of synchronous data transfer

∎ how different protocols work

∎ The OSI model

∎ how the telephone system operates

∎ the meaning and use of local and wide area networks

∎ various popular types of local area network (LAN)

∎ the following key words: link, fibre-optic, cable, serial, parallel, protocol, handshaking, asynchronous, transmitter, sender, receiver, block, frame, mark, space, bps, BAUD, full duplex, half duplex, simplex, buffer, error check, parity, Hamming code, BCC, LRC, CRC, carrier, FSK, FM, modem, DTE, DCE, synchronous, OSI, layer, common mode, multiplex, MUX, TDM, statistical MUX, packet switching, PSTN, LAN, WAN, ring, star, token, broadcast, tap, CSMA/CD, collision, base band, spool, server, peer to peer, Teletext, Viewdata, Videotex, The Internet, ISDN, electronic mail, record locking, file locking.

▶ **This chapter is about the way computers and peripherals communicate with each other. The first part describes the main methods and characteristics of data communication. This leads to consideration of the large national and worldwide network of telephone systems, as an example of the largest kind of communications system, and of other network systems.**

COMMUNICATION OF INFORMATION IN THE MODERN WORLD.

As you read through the details of the various methods of communicating data, never forget that it is information which is being sent. This might be a letter, or even a photograph, through a fax machine, or down a digital link. It might be a telephone check on the state of your bank account when you try to pay at an automated shop till. It includes the conversations you have by phone, the TV pictures you receive at home, and the telemetry of information from a submarine exploring the ocean depths.

Your bank balance is nothing more than information which can be communicated to you by letter, automated teller machine, or over a bank counter. What you earn may well be transmitted automatically to your account, and then paid out automatically by standing order or direct debit. No money need change hands, just information over communications links. This is becoming more and more important – most people do not handle even a fraction of the money they earn. In a sense, most of the time, your money only exists as the information of its ownership which is kept within large networks of computers, and communicated around the world as it is needed. As we move towards the cashless society, this will become more and more true. It is the communication of the information which gives value to its existence, and if those communication links break down, it can be lost.

Slowly but surely, the breadth of communications channels capable of sending information is continuously increasing. We already have the worldwide telephone network, the worldwide satellite communications network, personal and public broadcast radio and television networks, several different cell-phone nets, fibre-optic and wire cable-TV which is now used for other data, and so on. Even the National Grid will be used as a further channel of communication, in addition to electricity, and the rail network is already used by the railway companies.

You will probably have come to realize the insidious nature of the way in which information on us can be shared in so many different ways. It is perhaps up to us all to keep these matters in full view, and to know as much as possible about the technology so that we can call for its proper control as it evolves. Some legislation also exists, as we shall see later when we look at the Data Protection Register in Chapter 12.

 Before reading on, write down a list of as many different media for the communication of data that you can think of.

TYPES OF DATA COMMUNICATION

When you buy a computer program, it usually comes on a set of floppy disks, or a CD-ROM. The disks are recorded by the program publisher, and carried by you to your machine. They are inserted, and the program set up, and perhaps copied to a hard disk. This is a simple but convenient method of communicating information, in the form of program files, from a publisher to a user.

A more immediate method of data communications is via an electronic link whereby data can flow directly from one machine to another. There are many different methods of sending data, and these fall into two main categories: 'serial' and 'parallel' data transfer. Each of these main categories has many different definitions of the way in which data is transferred, and each such definition is called a 'protocol'. Also, for each protocol, there are many electronic 'media' for the information to flow physically along. These might

▶ Electronic links can be serial or parallel.

▶ In this context, protocols are the rules or instruction sets governing the way data is transferred.

include copper wires, fibre-optic light guides, radio channels, micro-wave and satellite links, and so on.

When you buy a peripheral which has to send and/or receive data, the manufacturer will describe the protocol(s) under which the peripheral communicates. For instance, you might purchase a printer for hard copy output from a computer. Its manual will inform you as to how it must be connected to the computer, and which communications protocols it runs. Normally, this will be a parallel protocol, though printers often support both parallel and serial protocols.

It is important to ensure the protocols supported are ones which your machinery can understand. It is no good, for instance, buying a peripheral which takes serial data if your computer can only provide parallel output. You must ensure that all equipment is fully compatible. To do this, you will need some understanding of the meaning of communications protocols.

Whatever the protocol, computers normally communicate by transferring a file of BYTEs from one machine to another, probably with some further BYTEs sent for error correction and general communications control. The communication medium and protocol is completely independent of the nature of the data being transferred. Data can consist of programs, text, business data, graphics, even real-time conversations and video pictures. The protocol and medium simply perform the transfer, slavishly, BYTE by BYTE, for any purpose.

Parallel and serial

Most microcomputer printers are connected to computers via a parallel interface, even if they can also support a serial one.

The difference between parallel and serial communications

A parallel interface will transfer all eight BITS of each BYTE along eight data lines simultaneously.

A serial line will transfer the separate BITs of each BYTE, one BIT at a time, in a serial stream.

Thus, serial communications can, theoretically, be transferred along a single physical line – a single fibre-optic fibre for instance, or aerial to aerial radio link, while parallel communications need at least eight such lines, one for each BIT. In fact, parallel communication uses more than eight lines in order to allow for the control of the communicating interfaces. The control lines perform a function called 'handshaking', which is a method of allowing two machines to 'agree', BYTE by BYTE, that the transfer has occurred correctly. For this purpose, the receiver of the data must be able to talk back to the transmitter. It is this 'feedback' which allows the two to confirm the integrity of the communication.

Handshaking

Handshaking of some kind occurs in all situations where two machines are coupled together for dedicated communication. For instance, facsimile (fax) machines handshake over the telephone network to ensure that data is sent and received correctly. Errors in transmission can be detected and signalled to the sender to allow correction. The same is not true, however, for generally broadcast information. For instance, television-based Teletext communication does not handshake with the receiver in your home, or everyone would have to be connected back to the TV transmitter.

The handshaking described below is a hardware concept, but we will see that handshaking can also be performed in software – as is necessary, for instance, over the telephone network.

▶ Handshaking: a method of allowing two machines to agree that data transfer is happening correctly. There is more on handshaking on page 229.

Parallel communications

Figure 11.1 shows a simple example of a parallel communications set-up – it omits a number of less important control lines, but illustrates the main attributes of the 'Centronics' parallel interface protocol. This is chosen here as it is currently the most common method of outputting data to a printer, and you will see it mentioned in most computer and printer literature.

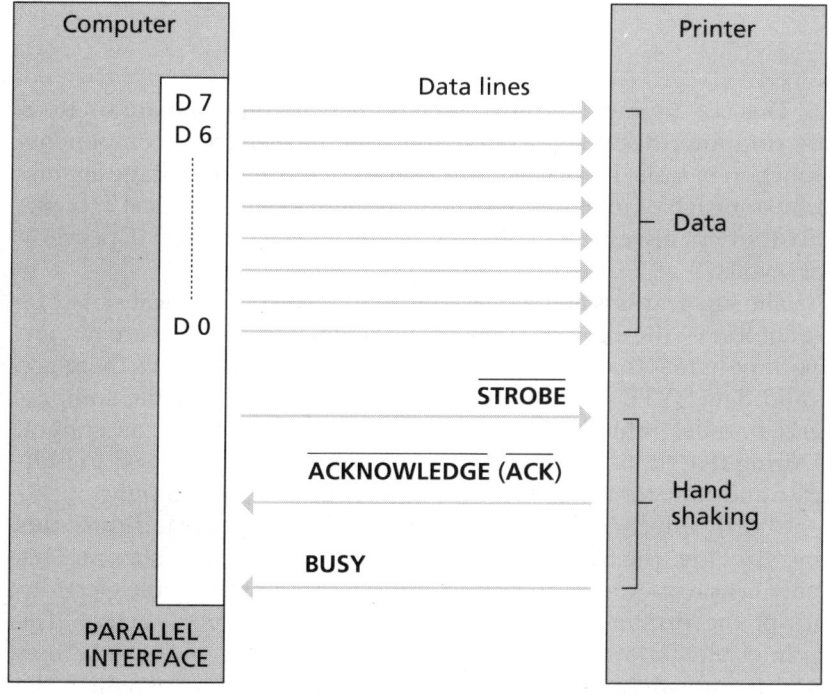

Figure 11.1 The main attributes of Centronics parallel communication

As you can see, there are eleven lines in all, of which eight are data lines, labelled D7 to D0. The next three lines are control lines. They are labelled STROBE and ACKNOWLEDGE (or ACK for short), both with lines or 'bars' above, and BUSY, without a bar.

A bar above a line's label denotes that it is active when it contains a 0, while the lack of a bar denotes active when it contains a 1. For instance, when the printer is busy, it activates its BUSY line – holding it at a 1 level, probably +5 volts. The way in which these three control lines work gives a good example of the concept of handshaking. Figure 11.2 shows the sequence of events.

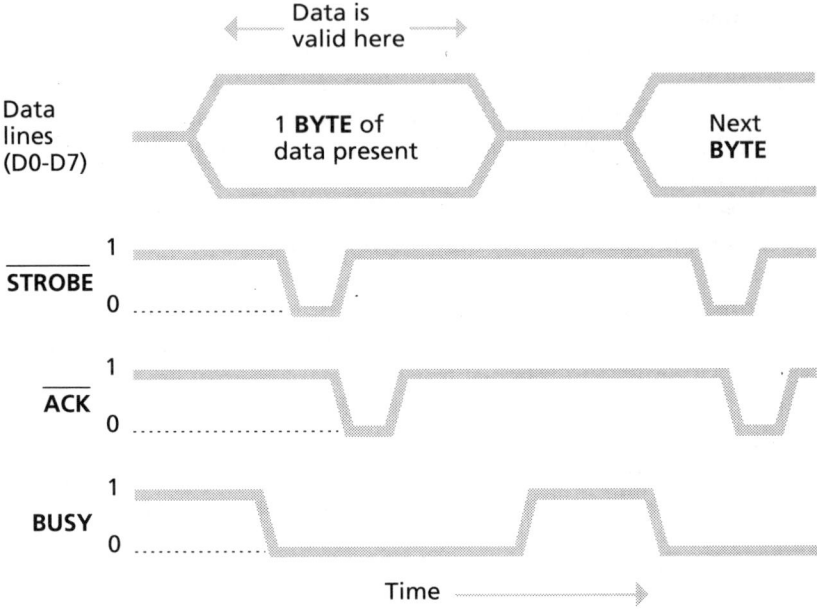

Figure 11.2 The sequence of events in parallel communication

This is a 'timing diagram' and it is the main type of diagram used by computer designers to describe how the electronic components function in time. It is essentially a series of graphs of voltage against time for each of the lines indicated. A high level is a logical 1, possibly (but not always) +5 volts, and a low level is a logical 0, possibly at 0 volts.

The top graph is actually a representation of the logical state of a set of lines – the eight data lines. The actual logical states are not important here – that is software. However, at certain times there is a valid data BYTE present on the lines, placed there by the computer's parallel interface, and denoted by an envelope, as shown. During that 'data valid' time, certain control lines are used to indicate and transfer the data BYTE. Time runs from left to right.

Shortly after the data becomes valid, the computer indicates this by 'strobing' the STROBE line active – down to a 0, as shown. This only lasts a microsecond or two, but is long enough for the electronics of the printer to note that the STROBE has gone active. The printer then knows that the next BYTE is available on the data lines and it can safely take it in, and print the character for which the BYTE is the code.

To ensure that the computer knows that the printer has actually accepted and used a data BYTE, the printer pulses its ACKNOWLEDGE line low, again for a few microseconds. The computer can then set up the next BYTE for transfer, safe in the knowledge that the printer will not confuse it with the last BYTE presented. To prevent confusion, no actual transfer occurs until the STROBE and

► The strobe and acknowledge cycle is a complete cycle of data transfer, BYTE by BYTE.

ACKNOWLEDGE cycle is complete. At the same time, the computer monitors the BUSY line from the printer, and will not try to pulse STROBE low until BUSY is also low (inactive) to show that the printer is ready and willing to accept data. If the BUSY line is held permanently low (inactive) the STROBE and ACKNOWLEDGE cycles will just run on at whatever speed they wish, without interruption.

The BUSY line is used by the printer to suspend the whole operation if, for instance, the printer runs out of paper. This requires external assistance before any further data can be transferred for printing. However, since printers are often slower than the data communications itself, the BUSY line might well be continually suspending data transfer, and thus slowing it down to the printing speed.

Thus, handshaking is used to make data transfer occur fast and efficiently, and at a speed which suits both sender and receiver. In this case, it is not actually involved in the validation of the data being sent, just the synchronization of the transfer activity. In a more sophisticated setting, the data is actually checked to ensure that there are no errors, and handshaking only occurs if the data is correct.

► Handshaking regulates the speed at which data is transferred.

Data is transferred by the above method in a manner which can be described as 'asynchronous'. That is, there is no permanent background time-frame which decides when each BYTE is transferred. The speed of transfer varies as the receiver commands its BUSY line, and thus is able to slow the transfer to a speed with which it is comfortable.

► Asynchronous parallel transfer.

We will discuss in the next section how asynchronous serial data is transferred. All things being equal, serial communications methods are inherently slower as only a single BIT is physically transferred at any instant instead of, say, eight in parallel. However, the increased complexity of parallel cabling and channelling only makes it appropriate for devices which are physically close together. It would not be possible to send data in parallel along the telephone network, for instance. In practice, therefore, serial communications are used for well separated sites. In fact, the increased physical simplicity of serial communication finds it being used for network communication too, even between computers which are close together. This is not exclusively true, however, and some fast networks are implemented, at least locally, using parallel lines.

 Use the text above to note down the main differences between parallel and serial transfer, and the circumstances under which each is most likely to be used. You can add to these notes as you read on.

Asynchronous serial communications

The best-known standard of serial communications is called 'RS232'. It comes in several forms, but the description below describes the basis of the protocol. In fact, although it is a serial protocol, some of its implementations have many lines for a variety of hardware controls, which can be rather confusing. The protocol was developed in the days of mechanical teletype machines which required certain special control lines to work them. Some of the original controls have survived, but many are rarely used. In fact, RS232 is still used by some printers, and most computers and packages allow printing to be performed either by a parallel or a serial interface.

Imagine a copper wire down which a whole business letter is to be sent to some remote site. The first problem is to make each end of the wire agree to the transfer. The sender must be sure that the receiver is listening, and the receiver must ensure that it deals with the characters of the letter as they are received. If the receiver is a printer, and the serial communications are being sent very fast, the printer may miss some while it is printing others. Similarly, if the receiver is receiving the characters within a program which has many other things to do at the same time, it will need to inform the sender to slow down. This is achieved by handshaking – either in hardware or software. In other words, the sender will only send if it has been given 'permission' by the receiver in some manner.

As serial communications occur BIT by BIT down a single line, it is useful and efficient to package up the BITs into blocks of some length. A complete block is then sent every time the receiver gives it permission. It would be wasteful for the receiver to acknowledge and control every single BIT, and it would be no good if it were only acknowledging complete business letters – a happy medium must be struck. There are normally two levels of packaging. First, approximately BYTE-sized packets of BITs are formed, and then blocks of BYTEs are packaged together.

> Start and stop BITs: control BITs which mark the beginning and end of BYTEs being transferred. BYTEs are transferred within 'frames' of ten to twelve BITs (eight data BITs plus control BITs).

Each BYTE-packet is started and finished with at least one control BIT – these are called 'start' and 'stop' BITs. In addition, extra BITs are added to allow for error checking and correction. In all, each BYTE may be included within a 'frame' of ten or twelve BITs to send and receive it correctly.

These BYTEs are often further packaged into larger packets called 'blocks', and the receiver might be expected to acknowledge each block it receives, for maximum security. The sender would not send the next block until the previous one had been acknowledged.

The aim is to make the communication as error-free as possible, and also allow the communications to proceed asynchronously – that is, at a speed which varies according to the needs and capabilities of the sender and receiver. In general, blocks of BYTEs are used for communications between computers, or 'intelligent' peripheral systems. For communications with a local printer, the data is not packaged into blocks, but simply sent BYTE frame by BYTE frame.

Character of serial data

Figure 11.3 shows a frame of BITs which could be sent along a serial communications line.

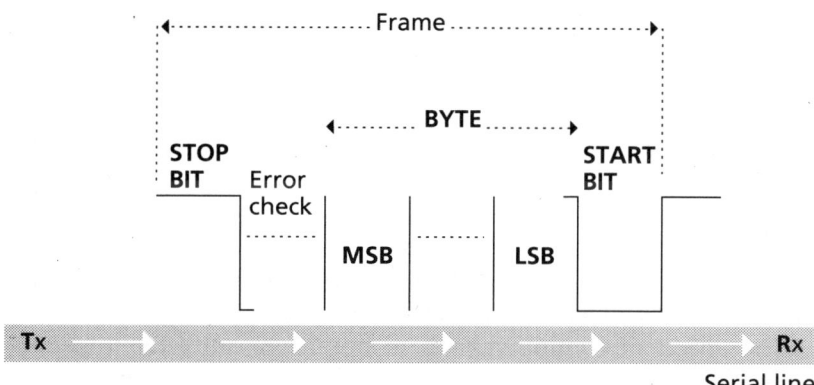

Figure 11.3 A frame of BITs which could be sent along a serial communications line

This figure shows a stream of BITs making their way from the Transmitter (Tx) to the Receiver (Rx). Time here goes from right to left, and the start BIT is shown at the front of the stream, on the right. The figure implies that a start BIT is a low level, or 0. The actual electrical level which is used to signify the start BIT is not important, as long as Tx and Rx agree. However, we will refer to it as a '0', which is conventional. The next BIT shown in this stream is the first BIT of the BYTE, which we have assumed will be the least significant BIT, or LSB. Then comes a further seven BITs, ending with the most significant BIT, or MSB. Then comes one or more BITs devoted to error checking, and finally a '1' which is the stop BIT. The stop BIT is designed to ensure that even if the frames are streaming down the line end to end, there will be at least one BIT time at level '1' before the next '0' start BIT arrives – this helps to achieve physical separation of the frames, and ensures that the electronic 0 level signifying the start of a frame contrasts with the previous level of the line.

Note that though the frame packets are sent and received asynchronously, within the frame, the receiver and transmitter are completely synchronized – but only for that short time. Each BIT sent occupies a specific time slot within the frame. This ensures that the receiver reads the correct logical value (1 or 0) within the correct time slot. Otherwise, a data BYTE such as 11111111, which simply looks like a constant high level between start and stop BITs, would be difficult to separate into eight 1s.

► You might like to check this description of transfer with Chapter 6 on binary code.

Between frames, when the transmitter is waiting to send the next frame for some reason, the communications line is held in the '1' state, which is thus the quiescent, or inactive, state of the line. This is sometimes referred to as the 'mark' condition. A '0' is called a 'space'. A new frame (starting with a space) can only be sent after the line has returned to the mark condition at the end of the previous frame. Thus packets are properly separated, and may occur as and when it is appropriate.

The exact nature of the BIT stream is decided by the hardware of the Tx and Rx. Any number of data and control BITs can be placed within the frame, as required. In general, for asynchronous communications, at least one start and one stop BIT is included, and often

► Tx – transmitter; Rx – receiver.

at least one BIT for error checking – a 'parity' BIT is most common, and we will look at how this works on page 232.

Speed of communication

► Speed in BITs per second (bps or BAUD) or BYTES per second.

The speed with which information is sent can be stated in two basic ways. Either the number of BYTEs per second, or the number of BITs per second. The latter is more common, and the units used are 'BITs per second' (bps), often also called 'BAUD'. In straightforward two-state digital communications, BAUD and bps are identical, and will be used as such in this book.

The speed of communication in bps comes directly from the width of the time slot used for a single BIT. Thus, if the time slot for each BIT were one milli-second (1ms) long, then there would be one thousand BITs sent in a second, and the speed would be 1,000 bps, or 1,000 BAUD.

RS232 communications usually occurs at one of various special speeds such as: 110 BAUD, 300 BAUD, 600, 1,200, 2,400, etc. up to 19,200, or more. The higher rates are given units of K BAUD, or Kbps. Thus, for instance, 9,600 BAUD might be written 9.6K BAUD, or 9.6 Kbps, and so on.

Data speed depends both upon BIT rate, and how many BITs are included within the frame. For instance, if the frame contains a seven-BIT data part, one start BIT, two stop BITs, and one parity BIT then the total number of BITs sent per frame is eleven. If the BITs are sent at, say, 110 BAUD (bits per second), then you should be able to see that these eleven BITs are sent in a tenth of a second – ten times this amount are sent each second at 110 BAUD. In fact, this speed was quite common in the days of the mechanical teletype, and the frame above was a common format, which neatly sent ten characters per second in seven-BIT ASCII.

► Considerably higher speeds than these are used by sophisticated communications systems, and even in a typical computer network 10 MHz (10 million bits per second) are normal. This latter speed would transmit data 520 times faster than at 19,200 BAUD. In other words, the typical book mentioned here could be sent in a little over a quarter of a second!

More common now is a frame containing eight data BITs, plus one start and one stop BIT, giving a frame of ten BITs. Error checking is performed by block, rather than within the frame itself. Thus, for instance, at 2,400 bps, this would transmit 240 characters, or pieces of data, per second. At the high speed of 19,200 BAUD, around 2K BYTEs of data are sent each second. This would, for instance, transmit a typical 180-page novel of about 65,000 words in three or four minutes. A more normal 'high' speed of 9,600 BAUD will be encountered in even the least sophisticated machinery, which would take six to eight minutes to transmit the book. However, this assumes that the information is stored digitally – one character per BYTE. If the information were being scanned and sent between fax machines, the patterns on a piece of paper would have to be digitized, and sent in fax code. This takes longer.

Duplex and simplex

When you speak on the telephone, you are usually experiencing 'full duplex' communications. Both of you can both speak at the same time, and be heard, just as if you were face to face. If you were on a telephone line which was in 'half duplex', you would both still be able to talk to each other, but not at the same time. Some overseas calls are in this mode. You cannot hear the other person while you are talking, because you have taken over the line completely. The person at the other end must wait for you to finish before speaking. This is also the way in which most personal two-way radio communications proceeds. That is why you generally say 'over' when you have finished what you were saying, and thus invite the other person to press a key and talk back.

If a communications line is in 'simplex' mode, then it can only communicate in one direction – the public radio and television companies transmit in simplex mode into your home. Also, telemetry applications, where a computer is listening for, and collecting data from, a sensor of some kind, may well be in simplex mode. However, most of the common computer communications applications you will encounter will be in full or half duplex.

▶ Duplex: you can talk at the same time.
Half duplex: you can take turns to talk.
Simplex: one-way communication (television, for example).

More on handshaking

It is all very well to organize the data into frames and blocks, but the main problem in general is to ensure that the receiver is ready for communication when the transmitter suddenly tries to send something. This is where the start BIT comes in. Fast dedicated hardware in the receiver waits for the start BIT, and then wakes up the rest of its machinery for the communications.

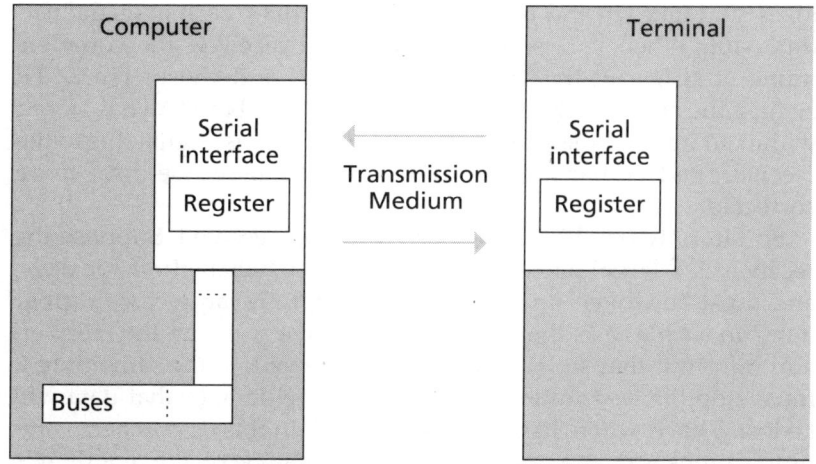

Figure 11.4 Communications set-up between computer and terminal

Figure 11.4 shows an example of a communications set up. Here, a computer is communicating with a terminal. This could just as well be two computers, a computer and a printer, or anything else. There are two lines shown running from both computer and terminal, giving full duplex, but a single line could be used, operating first in one direction and then the other, to provide half duplex communication.

In this case, the computer has a serial communications interface which is connected to its internal busses. This means that the serial interface will have an address within the memory map of the machine. When the computer has a series of BYTEs to communicate, it will, essentially, feed the first one into an internal register of the serial interface. It then commands the interface to proceed with the business of actually sending the data. The computer waits until the interface indicates it is ready for the next BYTE, and then stores that next BYTE into the interface's register, and so on.

Each time the serial interface has a BYTE to send, it adds start and stop BITs, and perhaps error check BITs, and converts it into the correct type of electrical, or other, signal for transmission down the line to the receiver. This might use copper wire and electrical signals, it might use light along an optical fibre, microwaves to a satellite, or even acoustic signals for transmission to a submarine beneath the sea.

Whatever physical method is used to send and receive data, it eventually arrives at the receiver as a series of electrical signals starting with a '0', or space, which differs from the quiescent '1', or mark, on the line. The receiver might not have had a communication for days, and will not necessarily be ready for it, even if it is switched on. How is this overcome?

The point is that the serial interface at the receiver must be switched on, and dedicated to monitoring the incoming serial line. This must be independent of whatever the receiver itself is doing, such as printing the previously received character.

When the serial interface in the receiver 'sees' a low level on the line, it immediately assumes this is a start BIT, and then synchronizes, and takes in and reads the incoming BITs, each in its defined time slot. When it is satisfied that it has received the complete frame, it strips off the start and stop BITs, and checks the BYTE against the error checking BITs. If all is well, the bare BYTE is stored within an internal register. If all is not well, it must signal this to the receiver, and perhaps to the transmitter, to allow the error to be corrected.

So far, only one BYTE has been sent and received. Suppose the receiver is a large machine which has been switched off for days, and must be woken up and restarted before it can receive further data? In such a case, the serial interface must wake up the receiver, and inform it that serial data is being received, at the same time it must stop the transmitter sending any more data, or that data will be lost. This is where handshaking is used. In this case, where communications is over a remote line, which may be of any length, it is not possible to include a separate control line between transmitter and receiver, as with the BUSY line in the parallel interface described earlier, to stop and control the transmitter.

▶ Handshaking by software.

The handshaking in this case is by software. There is an infinite number of ways whereby software can be used to handshake. The essential point is that special control characters are sent backwards and forwards to control the flow of data. For instance, in this example it would be appropriate for the receiver to immediately send back a special code, called an 'XOFF' character, which has a specific ASCII code. The sender must be running a program which recognizes this when it appears in its serial interface, and must not continue sending until this is resolved. When the receiver is ready for another character, it might send an 'XON' character, again a specific ASCII code, which the transmitter receives and takes as permission to restart its transmission. If the receiver is slow, it will be sending back XOFF characters continually, between BYTEs, in order to slow the transmitter.

This is a simple and rather slow method of software handshaking. It also does not allow for any actual error correction. To allow for error correction, the receiver must send back a special code to ask for the communication to be repeated until it has been received correctly. Again, this is simply in the hands of the program running the two systems.

Speeding up handshaking

In the above, higher speeds can be achieved if the XON and XOFF characters are generated by the interface hardware, not involving the computer or terminal machinery itself. This allows the computer, for instance, to be processing other work, and looking from time to time at its serial interface to see whether it is ready for the next BYTE. The interface itself will have dealt automatically with the XON and XOFF characters it has received. Similarly in the receiver.

Further, if the receiving serial interface has its own memory, separated from the receiver itself, it could take in a large block of data automatically, without worrying about the speed with which the receiver will eventually use it. Such a block of memory is called a 'buffer', and printers commonly have such blocks of memory. Typically, a computer can send a complete document down to a printer's buffer at high speed, and then go off and continue with its own work. The buffer electronics then control the feeding of the data to the printer, at an appropriate speed for printing.

▶ Buffer: in a printer, a block of memory which allows data to be received quickly, and then supplied at an appropriate speed for printing, i.e. like a storage tank for data.

Even faster handshaking can be effected if there are a couple of control lines connecting the transmitter and receiver. Typical control lines used are 'RTS' and 'CTS' – 'request to send' and 'clear to send', respectively. When the transmitter is ready to send its next BYTE, it sets its RTS line active. The receiver notes this, and if it is ready it sets its CTS line active. The BYTE is then sent, and this hardware handshaking begins again – very much as with the parallel interface. This is a faster method of handshaking than using software where a complete frame of BITs must be sent, received, stripped, decoded and then used for the control. However, as mentioned before, these lines reduce the simplicity of the serial interface, and can only work in practice over short distances.

If the handshaking is confined to blocks instead of BYTEs, the control can be much faster.

For instance, if the receiver is capable of receiving a continuous stream of 128 BYTEs, then the transmitter simply runs these down the line and waits for the receiver to show it is ready for the next block, which is again sent at maximum speed. This block by block transmission saves many individual handshaking codes. Also, a special code can be reserved for a request to retransmit a packet if it has been received incorrectly. We will see on the next page how a receiver can tell whether a transmission is correct, or not.

▶ The bigger the packages sent, the less frequently handshaking codes have to be transmitted, hence more speedy transfer.

There are many other ways to handshake in software, but you should now have a grasp of the basic principles.

Error checking and correcting

There are two levels of error checking and correction. The lowest level is at the BIT-frame level, and the highest at the block level, if the data is being sent in blocks.

At the frame level, a common method of error checking, but not correction, is that of the 'parity' BIT. 'Parity' is the name given to the quality of being 'even' or 'odd'. Thus the number 5 has odd parity (i.e. it is an odd number), while 34 has even parity. The parity BIT is added to the end of the frame, just before the stop BIT, to ensure that the number of '1s' in the frame, including the parity BIT, but excluding the stop BITs, has a given parity.

For instance, if even parity has been chosen for a given transmission, each BYTE is checked, before it is sent, and the parity BIT set to '1' if the number of 1s in the BYTE adds up to an odd number (thus correcting the total parity back to 'even'), otherwise the parity BIT is set to '0'.

In this way, the receiver receives the data, plus some information as to whether the data has been correctly communicated. When a frame is received, the receiver's serial interface automatically counts the number of 1s in the frame, including the parity BIT, but not the stop BIT(s), and checks the parity of this number. If it is incorrect, the serial interface alerts the receiving machine, which then takes the appropriate action.

► Parity: odd parity – odd number of BITs; even parity – even number of BITs.

 The parity check is by no means foolproof and, before reading on, you should try to find a couple of ways in which the parity check can be fooled.

The first way in which the parity check could be fooled would be if, by a couple of errors, two 1s turned into 0s, or vice versa – this preserves the parity. Second, if the parity BIT itself were transmitted incorrectly, its value would give a false error.

Parity is a fast and simple way to aid in error detection, and will work most of the time on a good communications link.

It is also possible to transmit extra BITs which allow errors to be both detected and corrected without recourse to retransmission. Such a system could be realized simply by transmitting each data frame several times and, if there is an error, a majority verdict could be taken for the data frame. This is too wasteful, and as a compromise a few extra BITs can be sent within the frame, called 'Hamming codes', which give a measure of correction.

Without being too specific, extra Hamming code BITs, logically derived from the data BITs, are generated by the transmitter's serial interface, and automatically included within the frame. The receiver monitors these codes and uses them to detect an error. If an error occurs, it is possible for the receiver to logically recreate an incorrect BIT in any position in the frame by using the Hamming code. If

► Transmission is checked by parity to see if when an odd value of BITs was sent, an odd value was received.

► Hamming code BITs: control BITs transmitted to allow for the detection and correction of errors.

more Hamming code BITs are used, a greater number of error BITs can be corrected in any frame. This is a valuable approach, and can be treated entirely electronically by the serial interface hardware without ever being 'seen' by the receiver and transmitter themselves. Only a grossly incorrect transmission needs to be dealt with by the higher level functions of the two computers communicating with each other.

Block-level error detection and correction depend upon the block containing some extra BYTEs which are purely sent and received for error control. These are called 'block check characters' (BCCs). They are usually computed as the data stream is being sent and are immediately tagged on to the end of the transmitted block. The receiver is also performing the same calculation on the incoming data, and at the end of the block compares the result of its calculation with that of the BCC sent by the transmitter. If they do not agree, it is usual to request a retransmission, though in some cases fast correction is possible, as with Hamming codes. However, retransmission, which should be a rare occurrence in most cases, is the simplest and safest alternative.

▶ Block check characters (BCCs): extra BYTEs sent for error control purposes.

Examples of BCC calculations

There is an infinite number of ways in which a suitable BCC can be computed. One of the simplest is to transmit a block of, say, 128 frames, and as they go, simply regard the frames as binary numbers, and add them all together. At the end of the block, after the 128 data BYTEs have been sent, the result of the addition, the 'checksum', is tagged on as the last part of the block, thus forming a BCC. Meanwhile, the receiver will also have been adding all the frames together, and will have its own result to compare with the BCC. As long as the receiver and transmitter do the same calculation exactly, the actual details are almost irrelevant.

In general, such additions are not performed completely. The actual addition is allowed to overflow so that higher BITs of the sum are lost, and just the lower eight BITs, say, are used for the BCC. To understand this, look at the following two binary numbers:

1010 0011 = 163 (decimal)

1100 1010 = 202 (decimal)

If these two are added together, to produce the number 365, the eight-BIT frame of a single BCC would be exceeded. In fact nine BITs would be needed:

1 0110 1101 = 365 (decimal)

However, if the MSB is discarded, the result truncates to an eight-BIT number:

0110 1101 = 109 (decimal)

▶ BCC calculations:
• adding and checking binary numbers (checksum)
• checking the parity of all MSBs (the longitudinal redundancy check: LRC)
• treating whole block as one binary number and dividing by a constant (the cyclic redundancy check: CRC).

We say that the 'overflow' or 'carry' above eight BITs has been disregarded. As a BCC, the lower eight BITs are quite sensitive enough to indicate any errors which may occur in transmission, and the result is that the actual BCC is kept to a single frame, and has a constant length.

Another BCC calculation is to extend the meaning of parity to cover all BITs in a given position in all the frames. For instance, the number of 1s in all the MSBs of all the frames is found, and the MSB of the BCC simply contains a suitable parity BIT to turn this into an odd or even number. The same goes for all the other BIT positions in the frames, to make up the BITs of the BCC. This is called a 'longitudinal redundancy check' or LRC.

One of the most common BCC calculations is called the 'cyclic redundancy check', or CRC. This involves treating the whole data block as one very long binary number, and dividing (in a special way) by a constant. Only the remainder is sent as the BCC. Most changes to the stream of BITs produce a change in the remainder, and thus causes the receiver-calculated BCC to be wrong.

Most of the above calculations can be done automatically in hardware, and thus never involve the higher functions of the computers and peripherals which are communicating, unless a retransmission is required. The error checking is designed to be performed in the background. The CRC error check method is also generally employed in applications such the verification of data being communicated to and from the magnetic surface of a disk.

Carriers and modulation

Over short distances, say a few metres, it is possible to send the 1s and 0s from Rx to Tx by simple +5 volt and 0 volt levels. Over greater distances, these voltages are increased to overcome interference and distortion. They are often changed to +12 volts and –12 volts to give a large 'signal to noise ratio' – that is to swamp any noise which may occur.

However, over a remote link, these electrical signals are more difficult to send and receive, and it is more appropriate to use an oscillating electronic signal, called a 'carrier', which is transmitted all the time, and simply varied in some way as 1s and 0s are sent. This is because even a weak oscillating signal can be detected and distinguished from the noise. Also, oscillating signals can be transmitted through space – from an aerial – and can be 'modulated' or manipulated in sophisticated and efficient ways.

For instance, if a radio link is to be used, a carrier signal is transmitted and modulated, or changed, in some fashion to distinguish between the sending of a mark (1), and a space (0). Similarly, if a long wire is being used, it is electronically more efficient to send an oscillating electronic signal, than to send two electronic voltage levels for the 1 and 0 states.

▶ Carrier: oscillating electronic signal for carrying information over large distances.

If the frequency is simply changed from high to low to signify 1 and 0, this is called 'frequency shift keying' (FSK) – it is a basic form of 'frequency modulation' (FM). In addition, if a high frequency carrier is used for the purpose, it is possible to send many channels at the same time over the link – the higher the frequency, the more channels. Thus, if you know anything about light, you will appreciate that a fibre-optic cable is able to send a very large number of separate channels at the same time, because light has a very high frequency.

NETWORKS

The telephone network, modems, DTE and DCE

The best-known transmission medium between remote computers is the telephone network. This network has several different media types carrying data, but the user just sees a wall socket, and a simple electronic cable. In order to transmit data over the telephone network, it necessary to change digital data into FSK signals as the entry into the network is for voice-type information, and not simply for digital electrical levels. The digital data is used to modulate a carrier, and the device which is used to perform this task is called a 'modulator/demodulator' or 'modem' for short. Many computers have them built in, others require a separate electronic modem box which connects to the serial, usually RS232, socket in the back of a typical computer. Any type of data can be sent in this way, once it has been digitized, including text and programs, video pictures, voice, fax, and so on.

Data communications equipment (DCE) and data terminal equipment (DTE)

There are thus two types of equipment used in communications. There are devices such as modems which are physically connected to the ends of communication lines, and there are machines which use or originate the data being communicated. The communications equipment, such as a modem, is given the term 'data communications equipment' or 'DCE'. (This is also, occasionally, referred to as 'data circuit-terminating equipment'). The computer, printer, terminal, etc. which connects to a DCE is termed 'data terminal equipment' or 'DTE'. Figure 11.5 illustrates an example situation.

▶ FSK: frequency shift keying, a type of frequency modulation (the FM you are familiar with on the radio).

▶ Modem: short for modulator/demodulator. Converts digital data to FSK signals (and back) for transmission down a telephone line.

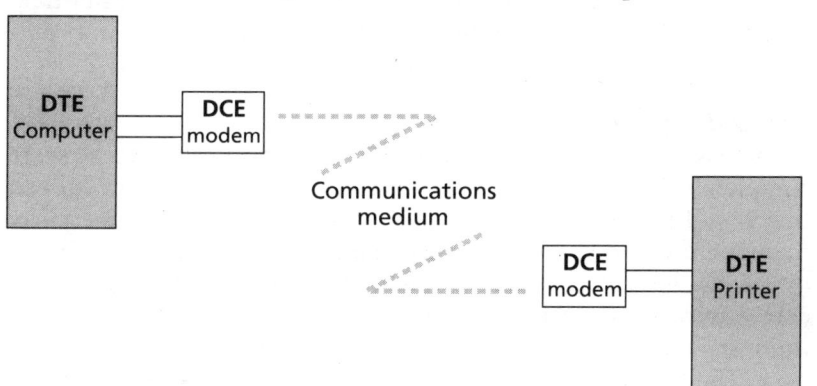

Figure 11.5 A computer (DTE) communicating with a printer (DTE) via modems (DCE)

In this figure, a computer (DTE) is communicating with a printer (DTE) over a communications channel, using modems (DCE) to effect the actual interface to the communications medium – which may be a telephone wire. Two DTEs need two DCEs for remote communications. The DCE may be any other machinery which takes the raw binary data from the DTE and conditions it correctly for the communications medium. The exact line drawn between the DTE's serial interface and the DCE's electronics may be a little blurred on occasion, but the main principles should be clear.

Synchronous communications

The next step in communications is to synchronize the receiver and transmitter continuously, and not just within the frame. Basically, the communications link is kept live and working all the time, even if there is no data to communicate. This is achieved by continuously sending and receiving special synchronization codes called 'SYN' codes. The exact electronic way in which this is achieved is not important here.

When data is to be sent, it is placed on the communications link according to the specifications of the link, and received without any slowing down of the transmitter during the transfer. Between transmissions, the two ends of the line are kept synchronized by the transmitter sending SYNs continuously. Data transmissions can be very long, even without all the usual start and stop BITs, and if synchronization is lost due to electronic interference, the result can be disastrous. Normally, some SYNs are sent every now and then to ensure that synchronization is kept established.

When real data is sent, the receiver takes these data in, and uses or stores them in a buffer immediately, without delay. If there is an error, the receiver can still send back retransmit requests. There are many ways of achieving synchronous communications, and these, as before, are called protocols. There are attempts to standardize protocols, and one of these is the OSI model, which we will look at below.

The basic point to remember is that a synchronous communications link has a life of its own, like a conveyer belt. It is always live, and no start or stop BITs are needed. The data is simply placed on the conveyer belt, in appropriate time slots, and appears at the receiver where it leaves the conveyer belt. This makes for faster data transfer, and is used for all fast communications systems, and particularly around computer and communications networks.

The OSI model

▶ OSI: open systems interconnection – a standard for computer communications.

In the past, communications protocols for computer networks were completely different from manufacturer to manufacturer, indeed this is still partly true. This makes it very difficult for third party manufacturers to produce general equipment and software to run on a large variety of systems. The move recently is to standardize communications, particularly for computer networks, so that many more standard devices and software can be written for a large audience. The International Standards Organization has developed the

OSI (open systems interconnection) model for this purpose. Older, non-standard systems can be referred to as 'closed systems' – just as the Apple Macintosh was designed as a closed architecture system, while the IBM PC standard has always been an open architecture system.

The OSI model is a 'layered' model. Its 'upper' layers describe the high level software of the communications, and the lowest levels deal with the hardware of the communications equipment. The aim in a layered model is to decompose the definition into easily managed and simpler parts, and then standardize everything from the highest level of software to the lowest level of hardware.

The lowest layer is the 'physical layer', it describes exactly how the BITs are handled by the communication. We have seen an example of part of such a protocol – RS232. The hardware of the synchronous protocols are also described in the physical layer of the model. There are standards for each of these physical protocols, and as long as they are fully agreed by all the communicating devices, any of these standards can form the physical layer of the OSI model – it is not restricted to just one of them.

There are seven layers in the OSI model, shown in the box:

The seven layers of an OSI model

7. Application Layer: which the user sees in his applications

6. Presentation Layer: deals with data formats between terminals and computers –e.g. facsimile, ASCII, etc.

5. Session Layer: provides for an organised method of communication between users – decides synchronisation and control, whether full or half duplex, etc.

4. Transport Layer: acts as the interface between the upper three layers, and the lower three – deals with the arrival of messages at destinations

3. Network Layer: deals with switching and routing of messages by establishing and maintaining connections – X.25 and 'packet switching' (both defined shortly) are included here

2. Data-link Layer: deals with errors, transmission speeds, synchronisation and reliability of communications

1. Physical Layer: deals with electronics and mechanics, and thus ensures the correct physical conditions exist for communications – RS232, for instance, is included here

---

When information is to be sent over the link, it must be 'transported' through the layers from the top level, all the way down to the physical layer. It then appears on the link, arrives at its destination, and then climbs back up the levels to the receiving user, and so on, backwards and forwards.

▶ A full definition of these layers is beyond our scope. If you are interested in pursuing this further, you should consult a book on networks which deals with the protocols and standards of the communications itself.

238 Chapter 11 *Communications and networks*

▶ Serial interface protocols.

Some physical communications protocols

To return to the business of actually communicating BITs, we will look briefly at some of the physical characteristics which you will meet for serial interfaces in standard equipment. The main parallel interface has already been described in some detail, and the majority of networks and other communication applications which you will meet are connected using serial lines.

We have looked briefly at RS232 (see pages 225–6), and this is where we will start. Figure 11.6 shows some of the physical characteristics of the interface.

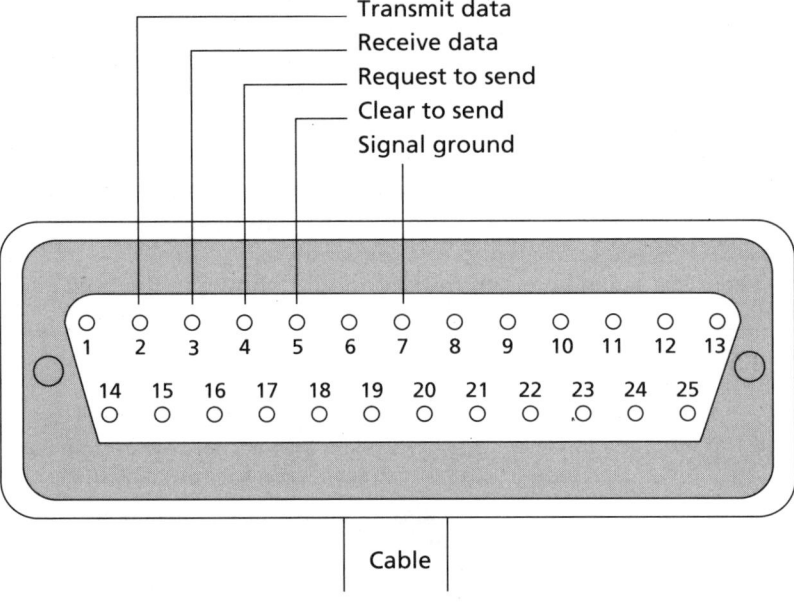

Figure 11.6 The physical characteristics of an RS232 Interface – a twenty five pin D-type connector

This figure shows a plug, or socket, which is physically polarized – it only fits one way round, and has twenty-five pins. It is described as a 'D-type' connector, because the profile is like a capital 'D'. There are definitions for most of the twenty-five pins, but only those mentioned above are included here. The other pins are designed to allow the DTE to control and communicate with the DCE.

On the back of a typical computer, printer or terminal, you will probably find a connector for this type of plug – its use is to allow communications via an RS232 interface of some kind.

▶ This is a serial interface so only a few of the pins are connected through the communications medium itself.

Serial communications usually use a small subset of the pins shown, and indeed some serial devices, such as a mouse, will use a smaller D-type connector, which will then require an adaptor to the twenty-five-pin socket shown in the figure.

The usual type of RS232 interface used in computer equipment is described as 'RS232-C' which includes an electrical definition for the logical levels. The '1' level, or mark, is represented by any voltage in the range –3 to –12, and the 0, or space, by a positive voltage between +3 and +12.6.

The above definition is one where the voltages are all referenced to an 'earth' or zero volt line which must be connected at least between DTE and DCE. This is said to be 'unbalanced' in that the signal voltages appear on a single line – the transmit line. This has the drawback that if there is interference on the line as it threads its way from place to place, the noise generated will appear as a signal, with respect to earth, at the other end of the line.

For instance, if the transmit line is sent around a factory, and passes heavy machinery, it may pick up unwanted voltage spikes, with respect to earth, and the receiver will confuse these extra signals with frame BITs. A more sensible approach in such environments (apart from changing the medium itself to, say, fibre-optics) is to send two lines, next to each other, from transmitter to receiver, with the signal being sent as a voltage referenced between them, rather than with respect to an earth. Any noise picked up by one of the lines will generally appear on the other one too, as long as they are physically very close. This type of common noise is irrelevant as only the relative voltage between the lines is significant. This system provides what is known as 'common-mode noise rejection'. The 'RS422' interface is an example of a balanced system.

▶ interference on unbalanced systems.

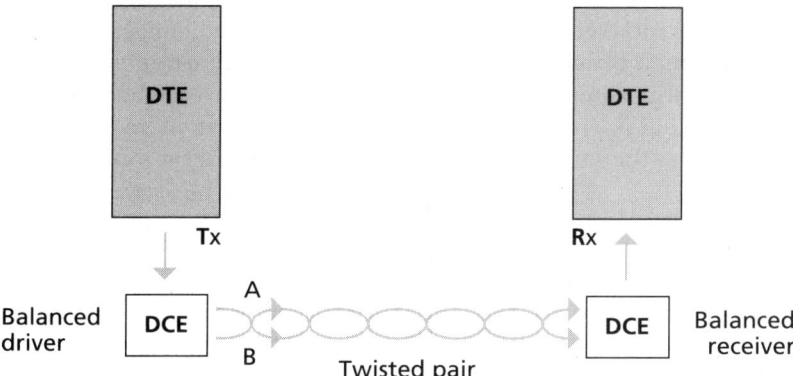

Figure 11.7 is a sketch of a balanced system. This shows a transmission link from the DTE on the left to the DTE on the right. It would only allow simplex communications, and the same again would be needed in the other direction for full duplex.

Figure 11.7 A balanced transmission system

▶ Balanced systems reduce the problem of interference.

The principle is that the DTE on the left transmits to the balanced line driver acting as its DCE. This transforms the frame into voltages which vary so that for a '1', line A, say, is at a higher voltage than line B, and vice versa for a '0'. No other reference is needed, and the wires are physically twisted around each other to ensure that where one goes, the other must also go. A noise voltage appearing at A, and also at B, leaves the relative voltage at that time untouched.

The actual form of the data is independent of these considerations. This works just as well for asynchronous frames as it does for any of the synchronous protocols.

Another important protocol which you will meet in equipment in common use is that of 'V24'. It also appears as a socket at the back of a computer and other machinery, and has a characteristic electronic definition which includes much of RS232, but extends it somewhat for more sophisticated communications. Another protocol, called X21, on the other hand, has much fewer control lines, and

▶ The V24 and the X21 protocols.

uses a fifteen-way socket. However, this standard allows for a very sophisticated communications protocol, both asynchronous and synchronous, and the exact state of the communications medium is defined by timing diagrams which ensure that comparatively intelligent control can be maintained. The X21 protocol has not been taken up as commonly as the others mentioned above, but will be encountered from time to time.

Multiplexing

A line is said to be 'multiplexed' if it carries data for several DTEs apparently at the same time. To multiplex anything simply means to use it simultaneously for more than one thing. 'Multiplex' is sometimes shortened to 'MUX'. For instance, you might say that the space around us is multiplexed (or MUXed) as to public broadcasts – there are many dozens, or hundreds, of transmissions passing through our immediate environment all the time. We only know they are there if we have a receiver tuned and decoded in the right way to receive any given transmission. In the same way, the telephone network sends many conversations down a single line, and to the human observer they all appear to be occurring simultaneously. A large computer system is being multiplexed when it runs a multi-tasking operating system and appears to run many terminals and users at the same time. The list of applications for multiplexing is endless.

A simple way to MUX a copper wire, or a fibre-optic cable, is to send many different data channels down the line on different carrier frequencies, very much as radio transmissions are made through space. The decoder, or 'demultiplexer' at the end of the line tunes out the different carrier frequencies, with their own data intact, and hence information channels are separated. This is called 'frequency division multiplexing' (FDM), as it divides the available frequencies able to be sent on a given line into separate channels, each carrying its own data.

Another method of MUXing is 'time division multiplexing' (TDM). This divides the time on a given line into separate 'slots', as shown in Figure 11.8.

▶ There are many other communication protocols. If you are interested in the details of others you should consult a text on communications theory.
▶ A multiplex line carries data for several DTEs at once (MUX).

▶ Multiplexing includes frequency division multiplexing (FDM), time division multiplexing (TDM) and statistical multiplexing.

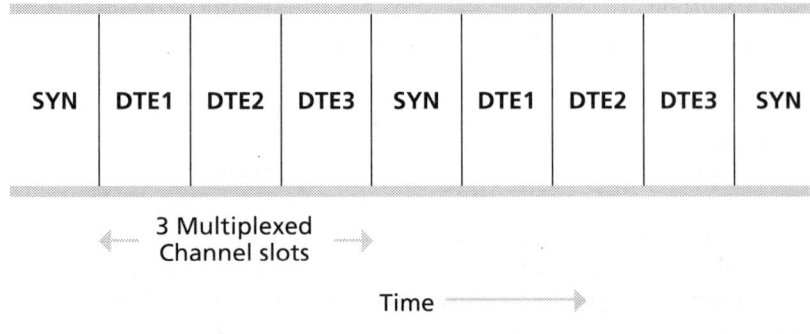

Figure 11.8 time division multiplexing (TDM)

Three pieces of equipment, DTE1, DTE2 and DTE3, are using the line at the same time to communicate to other remote equipment. Time on the line is split into clocked portions, or slots, and the MUX equipment takes in the data from each DTE, and shares it out as shown. A SYN character is sent to keep the remote receiver synchronized, and then a portion of DTE1's data is sent. After a given time interval, its slot comes to an end, and it is DTE2's turn, and so on. Finally, another SYN is sent, and then the next part of DTE1's data, and so on.

As you can see, the line itself is a sort of bottleneck. It collects communications channels from three DTEs, and sends the data from the three lines down a single line. This works only if the communications lines of the DTEs are working at a slower rate than the multiplexed line, or data can back up and overflow. In general, a given DTE's time slot is immutable, if it has no data to send at that time, its slot remains empty – the format of the communications remains a constant so that it is always ready to communicate anything produced by the DTEs feeding it. The data rate of the MUXed line is approximately equal to the sum of the data rates of the feeders.

The next step in MUXing is to use a more intelligent multiplexer, and demultiplexer, which can dynamically allocate time to DTEs as they require it, rather than sending lots of empty slots if nothing is being sent. This is called 'statistical multiplexing'. This method is particularly useful for systems containing DTEs which use the line infrequently. The data rate of the MUXed line can, in fact, be less than the total data rates of all the DTEs, and usually this works out fine. However, on the odd occasion that all DTEs demand full capacity, the statistical MUXer contains a memory buffer to hold the overload for long enough to smooth out these occasional events.

▶ Statistical multiplexing/statistical MUX.

This is a very efficient method of using a line. It allows many more channels to be MUXed onto a single line than would otherwise be possible, by using the spare time which most of its feeders provide. The complexity of this process requires a fast dedicated microprocessor control system, within the MUX equipment.

To understand how the statistical MUX sorts out what it should be transmitting at any time, we must look at a typical system, and the character of the communications itself. This leads into the concept of 'packet switching', and computer-controlled networks in general.

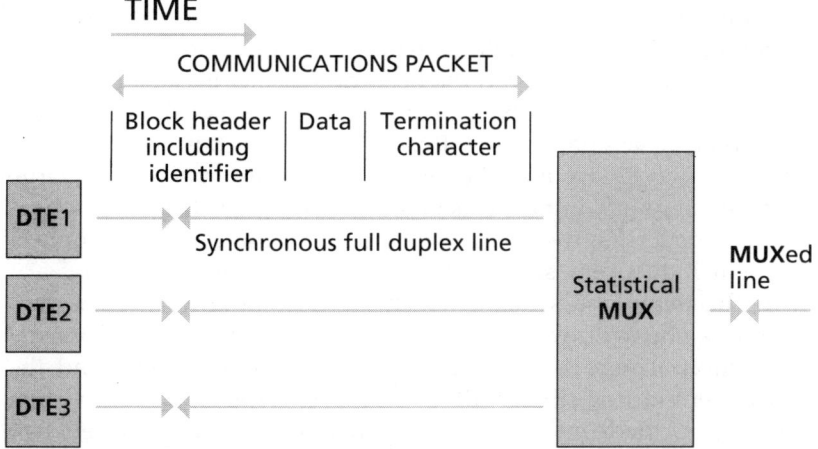

Figure 11.9 A computer (DTE) communicating with a printer (DTE) via modems (DCE)

► Packets.

Figure 11.9 shows three terminals, computers, or whatever, acting as DTEs, connected to the statistical MUXer over full duplex synchronous lines. Each terminal sends a block header first, containing an identifier unique to itself. This serves to identify the DTE, and tell the MUXer that a packet of information is now ready to be sent. When the data part of the packet is complete, the MUXer must be told this by a termination character. This allows the MUXer to free the line for something else to use the spare time. The deMUXer at the other end uses the control data to correctly decode and send data to the appropriate channel.

Digitization and packet switching

Much of the data sent and received on public telephone networks, and others, is sent in the form of variable length packets, at irregular intervals. Think of the telephone calls we all make. We use our telephone line irregularly, and for any length of time we like. It would be very wasteful indeed if part of the telephone network were time-dedicated to a given line, whether it was in use or not. When we dial out, we take control of a portion of the network for the time of the call, and no more.

► A/D–C – analogue/digital converter.

A voice channel can be turned into fast digital data by using an analogue to digital converter, and as such the type of communication which is sent is no different from that of computer data, or any other data, for that matter – it can all be digitized for long-distance communication. Furthermore, a lot of the actual electronic signal of a telephone call is redundant, and data compression is employed to send just enough information to ensure that the phone call sounds acceptable. The same is true of video pictures, for instance, and even though the digitization of a complete moving video picture is quite complex, it can be compressed considerably. This saves time in transmission, and allows more users to use the network at any time. Another benefit for video phones, for instance, is that more compressed pictures can be sent each second, and the picture quality and its movements better reproduced.

However the data is derived, it is sent in 'packets', as introduced above, and we will now look at a couple of definitions for packet switching itself. You will see below why the telephone system is sometimes called the 'public switched telephone network' (PSTN).

The terminal identifier in the head of a packet is called a 'logical channel number', or LCN. The statistical MUX is called a 'packet assembler/disassembler', or PAD. The connection which exists between two DTEs may be made over many parts of a large switched network, but the exact mechanics and electronics involved is of no concern to the users, or operators of the DTE. This connection which the users 'see' is called a 'virtual connection' (VC).

In the telephone system, which is one of the most important networks you will ever meet, there are two main types of virtual connection. There is the 'switched virtual circuit' (SVC) and the 'permanent virtual circuit' (PVC). The SVC is the temporary virtual connection, made in any way which is expedient, between two users. A PVC, on the other hand, is a dedicated line leased from the telephone company for permanent private use. PVCs would be established, for instance, between the head office of a large company and its outlying subsidiaries if much sensitive data had to be sent frequently. The advantage of a leased line is that it is electronically 'cleaner', and is always instantly available.

An example of a large packet switched network is shown in Figure 11.10.

▶ In telephone systems:
SVC – the connection you make temporarily when you use the phone;
PVC – a dedicated line.

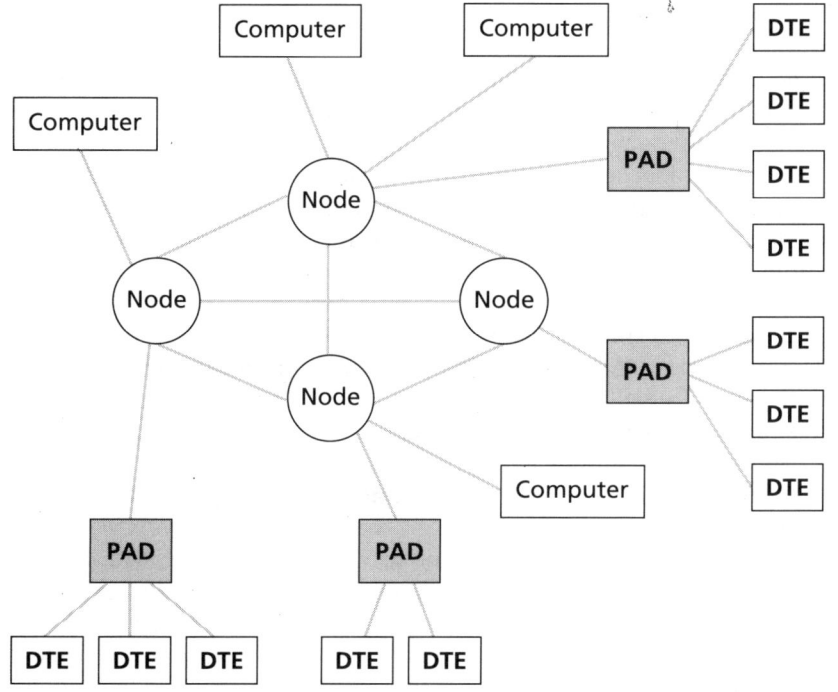

Figure 11.10 A large packet switched network

Here, packet switching nodes concentrate many communication lines together, and send them out along an appropriate line to other nodes to establish the most efficient connection between users. The nodes are connected to PADs, computers, and so on, and the PADs are connected to various terminals. Interconnection between nodes is designed to shorten the path of any data packet.

Figure 11.10 is a rough sketch of the system for communication networks where data is sent and received in packets. There are standard protocols for packet switching, and the most common is called 'X.25'. This protocol defines the packet, with its LCN, its start and end characters, and many other attributes of the packet and its communication. The telephone system generally adheres to X.25, and it is sufficiently internationally standard to allow much equipment and software to be produced for a wide variety of applications.

The above paragraphs have given an introduction to the concept of national and worldwide networks for the general communication of data. The next step is to look at the local area network or 'LAN', which you will come across in most medium-sized applications in all walks of life.

▶ The usual protocol for telephone systems is X.25 which defines the packet, its LCN, start and end characters and so on.

Local area networks (LANs)

▶ The telephone system is an example of a WAN (wide area network). LANs (local area networks) are systems of computers and peripherals linked in a relatively small area.

A LAN is simply a collection of computers and peripherals bound together by a communications system, within a comparatively small area. This might be a single room, a single factory, or even a closely situated collection of buildings. The opposite of a LAN is a 'wide area network' or WAN, of which the telephone network is an example. A LAN is usually fast and relatively noise free, but small. A WAN can be national or international, is often slower and more noise-prone. A LAN, or several LANs, can be connected together through a WAN. For instance, a telephone connection might be used between two LANs situated at geographically separated sites.

Historically, when most companies employed only mainframes, a single fast machine would be multitasked to provide centralized computing facilities to a large number of users, apparently simultaneously. The problem was that no matter how powerful the main computer might be, it would slow down as more users required support. Also, and more importantly, these facilities were top heavy, and expensive. This made them inflexible, and denied computer access to small enterprises, and to personnel for personal use. The revolution of the so-called personal computer has changed all that, but there still remains a problem for even the small user – that of sharing information and resources.

Sharing information is a basic need for any business. It is true that many small concerns can make do with a single machine, and thus all resources are fully shared, within itself. However, when several machines are needed – one in Accounts, one in Sales, one in Stores, and so on, the need to communicate data becomes acute. Of course, people can 'shout' the information to each other, or pass memos, or rely on manual recording systems, and multipart stationery. However, all this completely misses out on the main power of the computer – its ability to handle all your information – which you will remember is the main commodity of business and finance.

An example of a local area network

Salesco sells knitting patterns and accessories by mail order. It has 10,000 product lines, and two sales staff sitting at the end of telephones all day, taking orders, and dealing with queries. The accounts department has a full-time book-keeper, who also doubles as a secretary, and the stock room has a full-time stock controller and a packing assistant.

Many orders come in by telephone and mail each day. The business has to know exactly what it has in stock, and has to be able to allocate any of that stock to a specific customer, immediately, and not sell it to anyone else, in case it sells the last piece of stock again. Stock must be reordered well in time. When a set of items is sold, it must either be despatched immediately, or held until a cheque clears, or payment is made by some other means. At the same time, the business accounts must be kept fully, and automatically, up to date to allow for inspection by the tax authorities, including Inland

Revenue, Customs and Excise, and the Department of Employment. Finally, the business controller must be kept fully informed of the progress of the business on a day-to-day basis.

Salesco is a small business, not a large concern. In the past, all systems would have been manual, which would be slow, inaccurate and expensive. All of the above information tasks can be handled by a few microcomputers, which are able to share fully all information, and communicate it at will throughout the system. This saves writing and reading multipart stationery, saves manual ordering of goods, saves looking through stacks of files, which two sales people will find cumbersome and awkward, and so on. The savings are quite large, and the increase in efficiency unattainable at a reasonable cost manually.

The system which would fit this company is sketched in Figure 11.11.

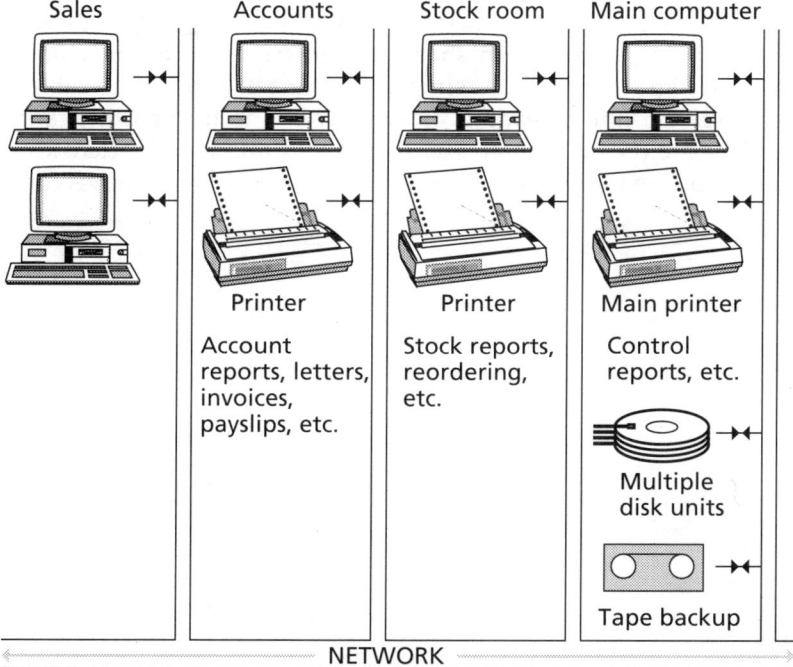

Figure 11.11 A computer network suitable for Salesco

As you can see, there are five computers here, plus a few printers and peripherals. The main disk storage is concentrated at one place, and shared over the whole system. However, much more importantly, the information on the main disks is shared around. For instance, when the sales staff receive a query about a given order they need access to the customer's ordering history. The accounts staff must produce invoices for account customers – they also need access to ordering history. The stock room must actually pack the knitting accessories – they also need access to that information. And so it goes on. This sharing of information is fundamental to many business organizations, and a local area network of computers and peripherals satisfies the needs of all these departments.

There are many variations which could be applied to this example. For instance, it may not be necessary for the majority of computers on the network to act as much more than just screens and keyboards – terminals in fact. The main processing could occur at the main computer. Alternatively, all the processing could occur at the terminal computers, thus distributing the processing power. Again, a central disk stack could be replaced by distributed disk systems, perhaps with some repetition of data to allow for disk crashes. There could be more or fewer printers, depending upon the throughput of hard copy at each station.

Without a network to allow information to flow wherever it is needed, the whole system would grind to a halt. A LAN is needed to bind the machines together. Again, there are many different physical set-ups for LAN technology, and we will look at some of these now.

LAN types – ring and star

One of the most important variables in designing a LAN is to decide on its 'topology' or pattern shape. For instance, all the machines shown in Figure 11.11 could simply be connected in a large cabled ring, with the link threading its way from one to the other, and round in a circle. Alternatively, they could all be connected to a single hub, like the spokes of a wheel, and so on. The machines con-

▶ The system must be constructed to be cost effective and efficient. it is the task of the systems analyst to specify a system which achieves the correct balance between these qualities.

▶ Topology: pattern shape. The term is derived from so-called 'rubber-sheet geometry' where general patterns are identified.

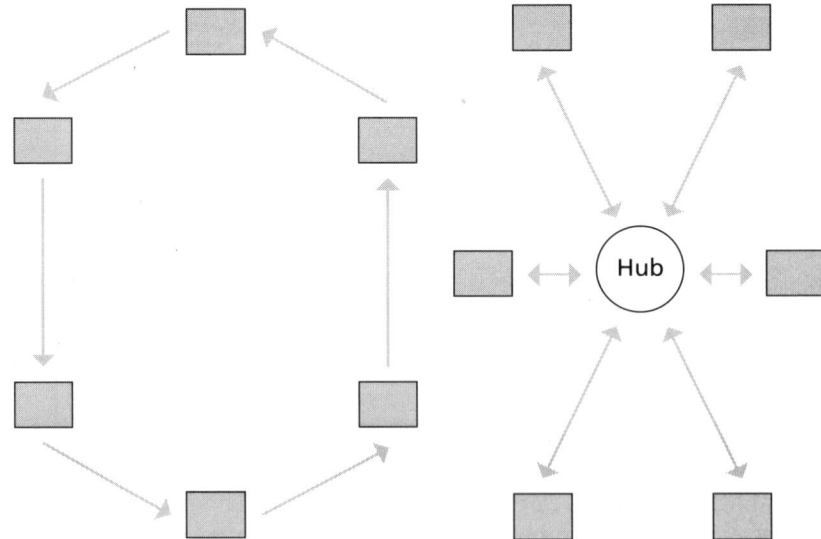

Figure 11.12 A ring plan local network (left) and a star plan local area network (right)

nected to a LAN are given the general name of 'nodes'.

Figure 11.12 sketches these two main patterns – the ring plan and the star plan.

The first of these topologies is usually realized by the 'token passing ring' or simply 'token ring' system. Here, each component of the LAN, whether it be computer, tape unit, printer, etc., is connected in a ring. All information passes in the same direction, and thus sometimes one component must send its data right round the ring to a neighbour on the 'wrong' side. Also, all components take in all the data, and retransmit to the next in line. If a link goes down, the whole ring is useless. There are moves to improve this situation with automatic bypasses, but this is not entirely satisfactory.

► Token passing ring.

The token passing ring works as follows. When there is no data being communicated anywhere, a special BIT pattern called a 'free token' is passed from node to node. When a given node has some data to relay, it receives the token, and changes its code to a 'busy token'. It then adds a frame of data containing its own address and that of the destination, and finally adds the data itself. Each node receives and retransmits the data and busy token until the destination is reached, where the information is copied, and then retransmitted again. Finally, the originator receives and recognizes its own transmission, clears the frame, and starts a free token going around again. While a node is transmitting to a destination, and until it receives its own frame back again, it is in full control of the ring.

This system is one of the best for handling fast high density traffic. However, nodes are much more complex, as is the software, and the system is more prone to systemic failure following a local crash.

► Star plan.

The next topology is that of the 'star'. As its name implies, the nodes are all connected to a single hub whose job it is to connect any two nodes together who wish to communicate. Variations on this theme can be very fast indeed. If the hub were a single computer bus, confined to a large cabinet, and the nodes were implemented as boards plugged into the bus, the speeds of communication between these physically close components can be immense. Connection to the users would be via slow communications links, from the bus-boards to 'dumb' terminals, which reflect the comparative slow human response to screens and keyboards. However, this is not, now, a common form of network topology, though it has some application in the field.

Ethernet

► Ethernet is a broadcast network.

A common and expanding topology is that of the broadcast network, of which 'Ethernet' is the most common standard. Figure 11.13 sketches this system.

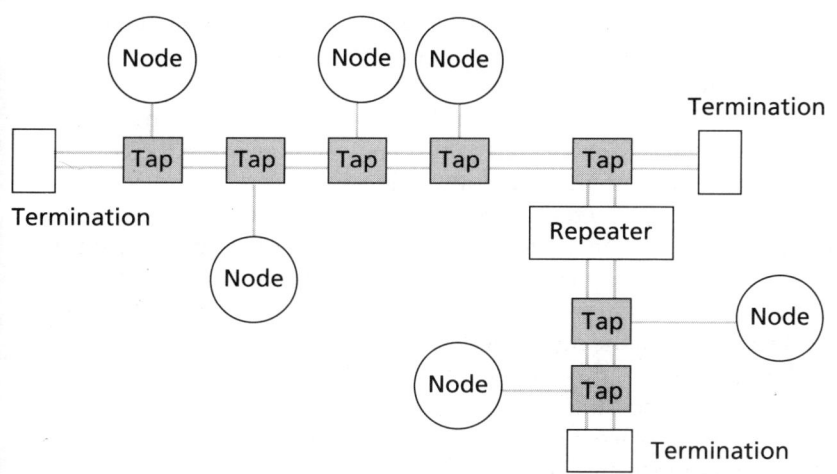

Figure 11.13 Ethernet

Ethernet was designed and specified in the late 1970s by three giants of the then emerging small computer field: DEC, Intel and Xerox. As such, its standard has been as irresistible as IBM and the ubiquitous PC. Ethernet is a reasonably efficient and fast protocol, and in the present era of cheap integrated circuits, quite cost effective, even for small installations.

Essentially, an Ethernet network consists of a coaxial cable into which nodes are connected anywhere, through physical connectors called 'taps'. The taps are not intelligent – they just interface electronically between the node electronics and the cable. Segments of cable can be connected together via taps and repeaters, which just amplify and preserve the signal between cables. The ends of the cables are terminated in a special way to prevent electronic reflections from occurring as data is fed onto the cable, which might otherwise interfere electronically. The speed of data transfer over the cable is 10 Mega BITS per second (or 10 MBAUD) per second, which is fast compared to any of the communications systems we met in the previous sections. Also it is a 'base-band' system – that is, the actual digital signals are placed on the cable, and not a modulated carrier. The opposite type of system to this is called a 'broad-band' system.

There are a few rules which must be observed when laying a large Ethernet network. No cable segment may be longer than 500m, the cable is marked at 2.5m intervals, and can only be tapped into at these positions, and so on. In fact, with the various rules in place, a maximum Ethernet length of 1,500m is possible, and up to 2,500m with special types of repeater.

There is a move towards using Ethernet protocols with other media, and the rules can be changed dramatically under these circumstances.

When a node has data to communicate, it attempts to feed it onto the cable, with destination address included to ensure only the correct receiver collects it. If there is no other node using the cable, the data is simply 'broadcast' onto the cable system – it goes everywhere, and is absorbed at the cable-end terminations, as well as being taken in by the appropriate receiver.

CSMA/CD – *carrier sense multiple access with collision detect*

▶ CSMA/CD – a feature of Ethernet.

If the cable is already in use, the node backs off to wait for the current user to finish. The protocol governing this activity is termed 'CSMA/CD' – carrier sense multiple access with collision detect. It provides a good example of the problems of managing the communication medium in this type of topology.

To make the main terms above clear, the 'carrier' means any electrical activity on the cable, as caused by a node communicating – this is a thoroughly confusing use of the word 'carrier', because there is no carrier in use, but it is now set in the definition. The word 'collision' means the attempted actual use of the cable by two nodes at the same time – this can occur due to transmission delays. If two nodes look at the cable and think it is clear, and if they are far apart they may both place data onto the cable, and it will only be later that the signals meet and interfere. This interference can be detected, and the tap will send a signal to the two nodes so that they know the communication has been abortive.

The basic rules of CSMA/CD

1. If a node looks at the cable and finds no carrier, it may communicate, and thus gain control of the cable.

2. If a collision occurs, both nodes cease communication and start the process again.

3. After a collision, to prevent both starting again at exactly the same time, and recreating the collision, each uses its own random delay algorithm to decide when to try to communicate again.

Typical node applications for a LAN

Now that you understand the idea of a LAN we will look at the types of application and device which it is useful to have on the network.

Obviously, computers and printers are useful. Many machines can share a single, or a couple of printers if this does not cause a bottleneck, but the network operating system must be able to buffer or 'spool' print jobs in case more than one is requested at any time. In addition to shared printers, some computer stations may also have local printers, which they alone connect to. This would be needed, for instance, in the accounts department, for invoices, perhaps.

Another important node is that of the 'file server'. This is a term given to a fast computer system controlling the network's shared disk system. Files to be shared around the network can be stored there for general access. This concentrates the storage in one place, and is perhaps cost effective in keeping individual machine costs to a minimum. Larger disk systems are also faster in access time, though the need to communicate over the LAN may reduce the effectiveness of this aspect. The file server may have a supervisory role in the system, reducing the need for any sophistication at other computer nodes. It may also control a fast high quality printing system, and its spooler, as well as tape backup. There may also be a dedicated 'printer server' for the printers alone, and so on.

Another aspect of the LAN is the use of electronic mail. Terminals can usually send messages to other terminals at will, in order to send internal letters and memos around the company. Similarly, general broadcasts can be generated by management or personnel to all users. This extends the concept of the internal phone network.

An important term in general use today is that of the 'peer to peer' network. The implication is that terminals are all on the same level of priority, and data can be processed and shared at any station. This term is used for small accessible systems connecting similar computers together.

▶ The Ethernet protocol is carefully constructed to allow for the full vagaries of the use of baseband coax. It is not an ideal medium, but is in wide use, and thus cost effective.
Ethernet can go seriously wrong if too many nodes are sending long frames of data, and the theoretical maximum density of traffic to keep collision at a minimum is around 50 per cent of the full theoretical capacity.

▶ File servers: system controlling a network's disk sharing.

▶ Electronic mail (E-mail).

▶ Peer to peer networking.

► Data security and passwords.

Another important consideration of a network sharing information is that of data security. Most network operating systems include the ability for a master password to be used by a controller, and other, lower priority passwords to be used by others. Thus, the user of the accounts computer in a company would have to have access to all the confidential files on employees' pay, but would not need technical information of a sensitive kind. Each user would have a tailored password, in an ideal system, but the truth of the matter is that most systems are wide open to information theft, and abuse. This is an aspect of computing which is still evolving.

Proprietary networks

► Teletext, Prestel, Minitel, Viewdata, Videotex, ISDN.

In addition to the switched telephone network for general communications, and the LAN for local data, there are several proprietary networks and network services. You may already be familiar with the broadcast network of Teletext. This broadcast utilizes the spare TV lines at the top of the picture, which you do not generally see. During this time slot, digital information is transmitted, free of charge, for public use. This includes news, business information, TV guides, adverts, entertainment information, weather, subtitles to TV programmes, and so on. There are many hundreds of pages of data available, but the colour graphics are very basic, and the system is irritatingly slow.

Another network is that of Prestel. This is a wide-ranging information provider reached by modem through the telephone. You pay telephone charges, plus other usage charges for some types of data. Full financial information is available, plus types of specialized service. Other services are reached through the telephone network, including many 'bulletin boards' where individuals place information, including programs, on a centralized database for anyone to read and copy. A more up-to-date example of such a network is The Internet. There are potentially many millions of computers and users on this planet-wide network providing and sharing information of every kind.

An interesting public network, telephone based, is that of the French 'Minitel' system. Some years ago, the French telephone company decided that it would be cheaper to give all its customers free keyboard/screen terminals instead of publishing and updating phone directories continuously. All subscribers were thus sent, free of charge, the terminal. The subsequent success of this system has led to many offshoots such as telephone banking, armchair shopping, access to information of any kind on entertainment, confined to the smallest local area, and so on. As a means of mass dissemination of interactive information, Minitel has been a major success.

The more general term for Prestel and Minitel is 'Viewdata' or 'Videotex', which simply means gaining information from centralized databases through the telephone system, and interacting with it by screen and keyboard.

Another public network service becoming important in the UK is that of the expanding Integrated Systems Digital Network (ISDN).

This service is carried by the public switched telephone network, but requires a specialized dedicated interface to be fitted at the user site. It effectively allows a company to build its own LAN between separate sites, as well as communicate any type of data much faster and more accurately than normal. An ISDN interface can be installed cheaply, and be used for everything from normal voice communication to video conferencing, and any other digital data.

 Investigate The Internet. What does it transmit? Who is it useful for? How do you get access to it and with what hardware? How much does it cost?

Network operating systems

So far, we have considered the hardware, and low level control of networks. However, within an installation, the users will only see the screen-handling characteristics of the network, and will never appreciate the finer points of the media or the electronic signals.

▶ In a network the operating system will have to give several users access to the same files, and allow them to run applications without conflict or confusion.

The operating system, and applications software, will have to be capable of giving several users access to commonly held files, without conflict. Also, some system to allow users to communicate between themselves should be available – this is sometimes called 'electronic mail'. Other functions include shared use of peripherals, and so on. In general, such networking functions are not provided by the average small computer operating system. However, upgrades to common packages, and OSs, allow the various attributes of a network to be used in full.

A crucial function of a shared resource system is that of 'record locking', or 'file locking'. Imagine two people working at different terminals on a network, each running the accounts package of a business. User 'A' is calling up a given customer's invoice in order to correct a mistake, and user 'B' is recalling all invoices from the same customer in order to chase payment. Suppose B calls up an invoice at just the same time as A does – there is an immediate conflict. Further, suppose A is actually writing a change just as B wants to read the information – which version of the invoice will B be given – the original invoice with its mistake intact, or the corrected version? The conflict becomes even more acute if both A and B are actually writing at the same time, this causes untold problems in a system, and can cause it to lock up completely, requiring a low level reset, and even loss of data.

▶ Record/file locking on networks to avoid conflict or confusion between users.

Essentially, the software (OS or package) must ensure that only one user is given full access to a given record within a file at any given instant – others must be locked out. This is called 'record locking'. The system is even safer if 'file locking' is employed, thus locking all but one user out of the whole file at any instant. This could be important in the case where files are being updated, and their length and order being changed.

In general, a network system will run under a piece of network-control software, and be able to run normal versions of popular software without modification. For instance, if several computers are networked together, it should be possible to run a familiar wordprocessor on one or more of them, a spreadsheet on others, and so on. These are separate copies of the program, each working on its own computer. This is the simplest level at which a network can be used, but conflict may well arise if two users try to access the same file. It is usually safe, however, for each user to use completely separate files on the central disk units. Of course, it can be argued that this hardly gives an advantage over a set of separate single-user machines anyway.

The best solution is to use the correct network-compatible version of any software being used, and not try to upgrade existing systems and software to a network. Setting up a network in a given situation is always a specialized business, but if it must incorporate existing systems too, the problems which arise can be many times more difficult and expensive to solve than simply starting from scratch.

Chapter review

- Communication of information is becoming central to the modern world.
- A parallel interface (Centronics) is most common to printers.
- Parallel means communication of many BITs at once through multiple wires.
- Serial means communicating each BIT of data along a single line.
- Asynchronous means a data frame can be sent at any time.
- RS232 is the most common asynchronous serial protocol.
- In RS232, frames start with a 0 start BIT and end with at least one stop BIT.
- Synchronous means that each data frame occupies a preselected and fixed time slot.
- OSI is a standardised communications protocol model.
- Handshaking is used to allow Rx and Tx to control data flow.
- Serial data is sent in frames of BITs, and blocks of frames 'mark' = 1 and 'space' = 0.
- Duplex means communications in both directions, otherwise simplex.
- Parity BIT is set to keep the number of 1s in the frame either even or odd.
- BCC – block check character for error control in blocks of data.
- DTE – a terminal of some kind.
- DCE – a modem, for instance, for connecting the DTE to the communications link.
- RS422 is a balanced-line protocol for common mode rejection of noise.

- Multiplex (MUX) means using a single line for multiple channels.
- Frequency division MUX keeps channels apart by frequency of carrier.
- Time division MUX (TDM) keeps channels apart by assigning them fixed time slots in the serial stream.
- Statistical MUX allocates time to a channel only when it needs it.
- Statistical MUX is used in packet switching on the telephone network.
- Packet switching commonly uses X.25 protocol, e.g. to send digitized speech.
- WAN – wide area network, e.g. telephone network.
- LAN – local area network for geographically compact resource and information sharing.
- LAN topologies, e.g. token ring, star, broadcast.
- Ethernet common broadcast network protocol using CSMA/CD.
- A file server is a large fast computer on a network controlling memory and printers for the whole network.
- Print jobs can be spooled together for printing on a shared hard copy device.
- Conflict can occur in networked files unless records or files are locked against multiple use.

▶ **Now that you have completed this chapter, look back to the objectives at the beginning and check that you have accomplished each of them.**

12 Practical computerization

Chapter objectives

By the time you have read this chapter, you will understand:

- how computers are introduced into the workplace
- why computerization sometimes fails
- the basic steps in installing computer systems
- how the workforce can be affected
- the need for computer maintenance
- some rules for the layout of a system
- the need for security within a computer system
- how to combat computer viruses
- how data can be encrypted
- protection of individuals' data – the Data Protection Register
- the following key words: DP, documentation, user friendly, installation, commissioning, maintenance, backup, security, virus, hacking, password, public domain, encryption, cipher, clear text, substitution, transposition, DES, key, Data Protection Act.

BRINGING A COMPUTER SYSTEM INTO THE WORKPLACE

Imagine that you are involved in the job of bringing in a computer system, starting it up and helping to train the users. In a large installation, you may be part of a team of installers, whereas when you have sufficient experience, you may be working entirely alone on a small system.

Criteria for the successful introduction of a system

If the system has not been specified or conceived correctly, the outcome is likely to be a disaster.

Hopefully, the system you are about to install will be:

- directly applicable to the business, as per a full specification
- well-documented
- easy to use and learn
- cost effective, and preferably cost saving

► This chapter discusses the practical business of introducing computers into a workplace, and looks at topics such as security and data protection.

- up to date

- acceptable to the workforce

- expandable

– and probably many other things too. However, if several of these criteria are missing, you will have an uphill job, with a quickly hostile staff, and a disbelieving customer.

Common reasons for difficulty in introducing computers

Before proceeding with the main discussion of installing this system, we will look at some of the all-too common reasons for the absence of the above criteria. Unfortunately, every year many customers are irritated, or worse, by the incorrect application of what should be their best step forward in the modern world – namely computerization. The reasons for this are plentiful, but experience of working in the field will quickly introduce you to some of the following reasons for failure, and probably many others (not necessarily in this order):

- a greedy sales force, interested only in the largest commission

- inadequate, or inexperienced specification preparation

- poor documentation, particularly for any customized portion of the system

- poor attention to those aspects of computerization which will save money, or allow greater productivity

- too complex a system for the problem, with attendant difficulties with learning and using

- inadequate consideration given to the workforce who will use the system all the time, and perhaps even be displaced by it

- customer's unwillingness to spend adequate sums of money to purchase sophisticated enough hardware, software and support

- lack of allowance for expansion

- customer has purchased equipment from a high-street electrical shop which is unprepared to offer the right advice and backup.

As you can see, the onus is not entirely on the shoulders of the system provider – the customer must understand how important it is to buy correctly, and spend money on specialist help for installation, training and later backup.

However, most systems seem to fail because they have not been properly specified and documented, and then not phased in carefully and sympathetically. Backup after the initial purchasing decision must be emphasized very strongly to any new users. They cannot possibly be expected to pick up a system, take it out of its box, read a manual, and then start to solve all their problems by computer.

▶ In Chapter 10 we gave you nine steps in introducing a computer application:
1) Analyse the problem
2) Define the data, its storage and I/O
3) Produce program specification
4) Construct algorithm
5) Code algorithm to machine-readable form
6) Produce and test program
7) Debug
8) Install
9) Maintain

This chapter deals with steps 7 to 9.

▶ Most systems seem to fail because they have not been properly specified and documented and are then introduced without care or sympathy.

Unless the customer is computer literate, all will be lost when the computer simply does nothing, after switch-on, while it waits for instructions as to which packages are to be run. Manuals for packaged software are notorious for their inadequate descriptions at the right level for a new user. Explanations either start so simply and pedantically that they quickly become terminally boring, or they begin at the level of a postgraduate degree in computer system architecture. Even systems which have their own tutorial modules are only as good as the 'teacher' who wrote the training program. Even if the material is good, many packages have training programs which leave out large amounts of the package facilities, so recourse to the manual is essential.

It is true that systems are becoming more and more 'user-friendly', but if a new user receives a set of boxes containing a network of computers with specialized software for a given set of applications, there is little chance of the system being put together quickly and efficiently for immediate use, or indeed of being put together at all!

Computer installation

▶ For the earlier steps in introducing computers see the order processing business example in Chapter 10.

Assuming that the correct level and type of system is being installed, your jobs, in order, are broadly as shown in the box.

Task list for computer installation

1. Unpack all equipment, and check that nothing is missing.

2. Switch on equipment one subsystem at a time, and check it works.

3. Tie the complete system together, if more than one machine is being installed, and check it is all functional.

4. Bring up the applications software which the user will see, and check it.

5. Interface with (i.e. talk to) the customer, and find out who will be using the equipment.

6. Explain how to switch on the machinery, and how to start the applications programs.

7. Perhaps train staff on the use of applications programs.

8. Institute correct data backup procedures.

9. Install general procedures of 'good practice', e.g. Never switch on a machine with a floppy disk loaded in case it is damaged, Power-up in the correct sequence, etc.

10. Check that the users can contact you, or someone, at any time for advice as to problems and queries.

There are many other functions which are required, but these form a background structure from which to work.

Installation is a matter of knowing the system which is being brought in sufficiently well to fix problems as they arise, and being confident in most, if not all, aspects of the running of the system.

Installation is at the end of an important sequence of events which should culminate in a system which can be splined in to the workplace without undue difficulty. The main barriers should already have been surmounted – installing then becomes a straightforward mechanical exercise.

An important aspect of installation is that of troubleshooting. It is often in the very early era of a new system that the main problems will occur. There is no substitute for a thorough knowledge of the system in finding the cause of errors. Of course, a naturally logical mind is also useful, but of no use if the basics of the system are not well-understood.

► There is more on troubleshooting later in the chapter.

Issues affecting the workforce

Introduction of a system to the workforce has already been mentioned. In some settings most members of staff never need to have any contact with the machinery, while in others there is a great deal of contact.

► See also Chapter 10.

We will look at two examples to illustrate both these cases:

Example 1 – Glassco

Glassco is a double-glazing firm, it has six salespeople who cold-call retail and commercial customers for orders. There are two surveyors who call on customers after they have made an order, and two fitters who actually fit the units at the customer site, when necessary. They measure up, and produce the basis of the window design for the complete job. Back at the factory, there are two indirect members of staff: secretary/book-keeper, stores manager/production controller; and three shop-floor workers who make the units. This makes fifteen members of staff, not including the owner of the business.

Computerization would comprise the following:

1. The basic packages of business accounts, wordprocessing for letters, and spreadsheet for the owner to predict the future financial requirements of the business.

2. Special customized software which takes in the basic measurements and specifications from the surveyors, and produces a list of stock items which will be needed for a job. This is called 'parts explosion' because it explodes a given product into separate stock parts. It then produces a list of jobs which can be given to the shop-floor staff to allow them to make up the order – this is called 'shop-floor loading'. In fact, this suite of programs gives a simple example of CADCAM – computer-aided design/computer-aided manufacturing.

3. Stock control to ensure that all parts and materials needed are always in stock.

Before reading on, write some notes on the human problems which may be encountered by the installation of computers in this example.

None of these packages need involve the salespeople, surveyors or shop-floor workers. The secretary writes letters, runs the accounts, including staff pay, invoices, etc., and sometimes feeds in the surveyor's reports. The stores manager also lends a hand feeding surveyor's reports when time is pressing, as well as running the stock control for the company. The same member of staff prints out the orders to the shop floor and the fitters, and the stores manager issues parts and materials. Some customers fit their own units, and simply take delivery of the units from the fitters, who also make deliveries.

As you can see, it is only necessary for two of the fifteen members of staff to be able to use the computer. This is not to say that it would not be worthwhile allowing others to use the system, but two would be enough. In this case, there are only two people to confront during installation and training, plus the owner of the business who may wish to use the system for everything, including spreadsheet predictions. The others will only notice some basic changes to the documentation which they are used to working with, along with an improvement to general efficiency and organization (hopefully!).

The system probably only has three screens, and a comparatively small storage system, plus a single printer. The owner of the business will have been made aware of the changes which will occur when the system is introduced, and should have prepared his two members of staff for them. The installer, and possibly a trainer, will introduce the details and practices which have to be followed, and in this case some of the training will be on a suite of customized programs.

At Glassco you should encounter very few human problems other than the normal ones of teaching non-technical staff a few new procedures, which will help to make the staff and business more efficient, to everyone's advantage.

Example 2 – Cutco
Cutco takes in sheet cardboard, paper and plastic, prepares cutting dies, and cuts the material into various shapes and patterns in high volume for industrial customers. It currently employs two technical salespeople, a stores manager, five people in the die-design shop, ten in the cutting shop, three in the finishing and packaging department, and two indirect staff. This makes a total staff of twenty-three, not including the owner.

The computerization will include:

1. Accounts, wordprocessing, spreadsheet, stock control, as for Example 1.

2. Complete computerization of the sales team, with screens next to telephone sales staff which can call up customers' details, state of their orders, date of despatch of product, and so on.

3. Complete automation of the whole manufacturing process. The system will take in orders from sales and assemble instructions to computer-controlled machines which will, effectively, make the cutting dies automatically. (This, again, is an example of CAM – computer-aided manufacturing.) The material will generally be fed into the machinery from continuous rolls, and be cut continuously. The completely finished product will be fully packaged and labelled by the machinery, ready to be picked up by an external delivery service.

 Before reading on, write some notes on the main human problems which will be encountered by this process of introducing computers and computer-controlled equipment into Cutco.

As you can see, a major change is about to occur in this company affecting a large proportion of the staff. The computers will have to be introduced slowly into the existing operation, unless production is stopped while installation and commissioning proceeds. Very few companies will be interested in shutting down, and so the automated machinery will have to be introduced side by side with the old sheet-fed manual cutting machinery.

As in the first example, the indirect staff will probably benefit from the computerization which they will encounter. The sales staff will also benefit from a much more streamlined system, which will help them to take more orders, and be more reactive to customer enquiries. The problems, however, come from the shop floor. Not only will many of them be put out of work, but they will have to assist for a time in the very automation which will take their jobs away. They will also have to continue to work the old system while the new one is being introduced. Some of the operatives can expect to transfer to the new machinery, but many will have to leave.

In a case such as this, a whole team of installation engineers will be working on this site for a period. Furthermore, there will be a regime, in the months following final commissioning, when maintenance will have to be overseen while the usual teething troubles surface. For much of this time, there is likely to be discontent directed at the installation teams, unless the management of Cutco has acted to offset these problems. Cutco will probably be aware that such problems can occur, but it is an important job of the installation team to discuss these matters before arriving on site. Of course, the resolution of such problems is not your job as a computer installer, but awareness of the problems can help you to be diplomatic and discrete, especially in the very early period of interaction with the customer.

> ### *Installation at Cutco*
> Installation has two main parts. The first is the standard computer equipment to run accounts, plus the specialized sales system. The more engineering-based installation of the manufacturing equipment is the other. The first should not be problematical from the human point of view. It is a standard training situation, using standard packages, and hardly differs from the first example of Glassco above. Human problems will occur with the second part. These problems may even spill over into the sympathies of the indirect and sales staff, and a certain amount of resistance to otherwise standard training and installation may be encountered. These problems are ones which any revolutionary industry must bear – they are the same ones which have existed since the start of the Industrial Revolution.

These two examples have been chosen to give you an idea of the way in which computers are introduced to an industrial situation. Assuming that the introduction has been successful, there are several other topics which you must understand and be able to explain to a customer. We will now look at these.

Maintenance and troubleshooting

Most clients are aware, from their experience with cars, washing machines, telephones, and so on, that hardware needs maintenance. Software maintenance, on the other hand, is a little more subtle, and harder to explain.

▶ Software maintenance.

In fact, most computer users will tell you that their hardware rarely, if ever, goes wrong – apart from the odd printer. Customized software, on the other hand, often has bugs and oddities which manifest themselves continuously. Even standard packages often contain subtle and irritating errors which only come to light as the system is used in more and more sophisticated ways. The software companies continuously publish new versions of their software, partly to correct mistakes, and partly to make the system run more smoothly, and these usually encompass more features. From time to time completely new versions of a well-known package will be published, and the previous one considered obsolete.

Versions of a package are ususally labelled in the form 'X.Y'. For instance, the current version of a package may be called 'SuperSoftware version 3.0'. A minor upgrade to this would be issued as version 3.1 (or V3.1 for short). Further minor upgrades would be V3.2, V3.3, etc. A major change would be called V4.0, and would probably be launched with some publicity. Subsequently, minor upgrades would appear as V4.1, V4.2, etc.

There are two main reasons for the need to maintain software:
- the correction of errors
- to improve the running of the software, and add new features.

With reference to the client's standard suite of packages someone should be continuously looking out for newer versions, and deciding whether it is worth updating. For customized software, it is crucial to appoint someone within the client company who is responsible for collecting careful, dated notes of all errors and problems which occur during the running of the system. At the same time, a collection of desired upgrade features should be kept. The supplier of the system will be given these lists on a regular basis, and make a decision as to which items are to be addressed free of charge, and which should be charged as being new modules. The supplier should have a system for automatic maintenance of the mandatory items, and for a quotation to be generated for the extras.

▶ The need for updating software.

Maintenance of hardware is simply a matter of providing, or buying in, on-site repair, and some preventative procedures such as cleaning out filters over cooling fans, and replacing ink and ribbons in good time. Some such maintenance can be undertaken in-house.

▶ Hardware maintenance.

When a problem occurs, a hardware and/or software engineer may be despatched to observe the problem, and read the recent error log. The engineer will then try to recreate the problem, and thus form an opinion as to the cause. If the solution is not immediately clear, a period of trial and error testing must occur, possibly with the entire system inoperative. This is serious to a manufacturing company, and some compensation may be due if a day or more of production is lost, and if the error is found to be caused by the supplier. This type of problem can cause a client to lose confidence in the system if it happens often, or if the engineers seem incapable of fixing problems quickly and efficiently.

A useful point to make is that the more the client is kept informed as to the problem, and the attempts at its solution, the better. This has two major advantages. First, it brings the client's staff into the process, and makes them feel that they can contribute, and that they are part of the troubleshooting team. The second crucial advantage is that they learn more about the technicalities of the system, and can then be considerably more useful in future in diagnosing and transmitting details to the supplier. The advantages of this aspect cannot be overemphasized – an intelligent and helpful client is a godsend in the difficult business of finding and repairing faults. Good troubleshooting is often dependent upon reliable and informed communication of the symptoms.

▶ Keeping the client informed.

System layout

Part of installing equipment is that of system layout. It is up to the client to decide where equipment should be sited, though a few simple rules apply.

Simple rules for layouts
- Keyboards and screens must be easy to view, and not strain operators' backs and eyes unnecessarily.
- Care must be taken to ensure that computer cabinets can take in and remove air for cooling. Papers, etc. must not be able to be placed over fan inlets, or cooling vents, for instance.
- Noisy printers must be cased, or kept in a room where the noise will not interfere.
- Cables must be run safely at all times – cables should not be able to trip anyone up, for instance.
- Printers should be sited so that it is easy to open them up to replace ink cartridges, or ribbons, and operate switches on their front panels. It should be easy to replace paper.
- Large disk units must be placed in a position where they are unlikely to be knocked by passers-by.
- The distance between machines on a network must conform to the network specifications.
- Large swings in temperature should be avoided.
- Screens should be sited so that they are easy to read – sunlight should not be allowed to fall directly onto their surface, for instance.
- Generally, consider the users carefully to ensure that they will find using the system pleasant and as easy as possible.

It is not always possible to follow all of these rules, and in any case there will be many others dictated by the specific installation itself. However, remember that correct siting and layout will contribute to the ease with which you will be able to install the system, and gain the help and confidence of the users, which will also make your job easier.

Backup, storage and security

Backing up information

▶ See Chapters 3 and 7.

The need to back up all data generated within a computer system has already been referred to. We looked at the methods and peripherals which could be used to store data, and how this is best achieved in previous chapters.

Part of the installation of a computer system must involve advice on systems for backing up data. The main operators must know how to store data onto a floppy disk for their own personal data security. Also, the system manager, or whoever fulfils this role, must know how to store dated and aged copies of all data, and even programs. Program storage is particularly important when customized systems are involved, which may be changing as they are updated or corrected. It is useful for previous versions of software to be stored on-site for future use in troubleshooting, or recreating a previous error state.

The medium on which backup data is kept depends upon the installation, but a small system will find it possible to store data on a few floppies, though even here a tape backup is useful. Certainly tape is crucial for a larger installation.

▶ Media for backups.

Other useful media include the removable hard disk cartridge, and the rewritable CD-ROM. The latter will become more and more common as a compact alternative in the future.

Another important consideration is where to keep backups. Storage off-site is preferable for at least some of the data. If a fire breaks out and destroys all the computer equipment, it will probably also destroy backup disks and tapes. If backup is performed every day, this could be duplicated so that one backup set can stay on-site, and the other be removed. A practical alternative may be to remove a separate copy once a week, or whenever possible. At least all would not be lost in a disaster.

▶ Storage of backups.

A company can be brought to bankruptcy by losing all their information of debtors (those who owe it money). However, if it burns down and the data and programs are safe, it is simply a matter of hiring some hardware, and continuing to chase for payments as if nothing had happened. Of course, a manufacturing company can also be destroyed by the loss of crucial equipment, and so on, but there is simply no excuse for failure due to the lack of a sensible backup system for software and data.

An alternative, or addition, to the storage of data off-site is to install a fireproof safe. This would be expected to keep the contents at a suitably low temperature for long enough for a rescue to be effected. However, again, there is no substitute for simply taking a copy away every so often.

 Write a short (one page at the most) section for a computer manual on specific procedures for backing up data for one of the two companies described in the above examples – Glassco and Cutco. Make your manual concise and give actual instructions to the operator.

Security
The subject of security is very wide.

Security problems

1. Possible loss of data through error, negligence or disaster – hopefully preventable by efficient backing-up.

2. Espionage – or the copying of sensitive information which may be useful to a competitor.

3. Confidentiality of information between levels and/or departments within a business.

4. The malicious introduction of harmful software. This could be by the accidental or purposeful introduction of a 'virus', or simply the more local problem of a disaffected or mischievous employee 'hacking' into the system and meddling with the data or software.

5. Security of communication over public and private communications links and networks – which is effected by scrambling or 'encrypting' data.

The first topic in the list of security problems requires adequate backup as a solution and this been adequately dealt with in the previous paragraphs. The remaining problems will be dealt with below.

Espionage and confidentiality problems
The main problem is that any system is conceived and operated by humans, who are both fallible and corruptible. This causes problems for the owner of a small company which are rather different from those of a large concern.

In a large company, there may be many people walking and drifting around the site, any of whom could be outsiders intent upon breaking into the system. In addition, the computer system of a large company will probably be connected to a telephone line to allow outworkers and others to access the facilities. All that is required is for someone to be given information by an internal employee, to simply walk into the offices, or be invited in for some spurious reason, observe a telephone number, and perhaps watch an operator using a password injudiciously. From that point, the system is wide open to abuse.

These are the main methods by which systems are tampered with – not, as in the popular misconception, by an eight-year-old computer genius cracking complex system codes over the telephone – though this does occur, of course. The simple truth is that the personnel in a large company feel cosy and secure, and do not continuously look over their shoulders at possible interlopers.

If the data being held is particularly sensitive, it will have to be held in a closed system, with no external connections, and access will have to be severely restricted. Any leak then immediately suggests inside help, and an enquiry is likely to identify those responsible.

In a small company, however, an extra person wandering around is obvious. Also, the owner of the company can more easily organize a very small and secure circle of people to guard against possible penetration.

An important consideration in security is its cost, both financially and in terms of loss of system flexibility. It is better to have a system which is open to all, than to jealously protect, at great expense, some slightly confidential data, which hardly matters.

Security systems should only be recommended if they are thoroughly cost effective.

► Security is expensive. It should be cost effective.

The classical method of separating information from some individuals in a system is via personalized passwords. Of course, there is the obvious danger of sharing of passwords between friends, and a client should be made aware of the possible flaws in the system. However, for light security, a system of passwords which gives each individual access to just the data required, is simple to operate, and cost effective to impose.

The next step is to incorporate hardware such as card readers, and give everyone their own personal card to carry. This can be used to give access to computer equipment, buildings, and even specific pieces of equipment. Such a system should generally be controlled and monitored so that the use of the card is also logged into a database. This would allow a controller to find all the uses which any given card has experienced, and allows a measure of surveillance security.

► Passwords and smart cards.

In fact, purely by using extra software, the complete history of each person's use of a system can be stored for future use, if required.

 Think about the information gained from the electronic logging of the use of a password or smart card. List the kinds of use to which such information might be put. For instance, it would be possible to check whether someone really was working hard at a given problem on a given day.

Encryption of data

While information is being sent from one place to another, it is always exposed to the possibility of eavesdropping. This may be irrelevant, or it may be a matter of great seriousness. For instance, scientific data which is being sent from a sensor to a main computer will probably be of little interest, and in any case be publicly available to all other researchers. Similarly, there is a wealth of software available through sharing facilities which is not copyright – it is said to be in the 'public domain'. Such information, by its very nature, is not sensitive to eavesdropping. However, personal health records transmitted from a central computer, or the telephone calls which we make to each other, are private. Eavesdropping is then a serious matter.

► Encryption – (secret) coding.

It is also simple to listen in on such transmissions, particularly if any of it passes by radio transmission. For instance, the cellphone network began with 'analogue', or voice-like, radio transmissions. That is, the calls are broadcast in the same form as that used by the public radio networks. In general, a cellphone call uses two radio channels chosen effectively at random by the main controlling computer system. One channel is used for communications in one direction, and the second in the other. This gives full duplex communications. However, to ensure that you can hear yourself in the earpiece of your own telephone, the communications appear on both channels at the same time. This makes it possible to hear both sides of the conversation on a single channel.

It is almost a sure bet, given the widespread availability and use of radio-scanning equipment, that any such call you make is being listened in to illegal though this maybe. Similarly for data channels using radio.

Gradually, the whole cellphone system is changing to a digital format. The analogue voice signals picked up by the microphone are changed by analogue to digital converters into binary data. This is then transmitted, and reconstructed at the other end by digital to analogue conversion (D/A–C). This makes it difficult for ordinary radio equipment to hear the conversations. However, as with normal digital data, all that is needed is a computer, with its own D/A–C, and a program to capture and store the data, and present it in some form.

▶ Scrambling and unscrambling.

The only solution to the problem of eavesdropping is to scramble the data in such a way that it is just too difficult to reassemble. Remember, however, that the eavesdropper has as long as is required to unscramble the data – it could simply be stored for later when powerful, but slower, programs work on it in their own time.

'Encryption' is the term used for scrambling digital data. The technique must 'encrypt' the data in real time into a form which the receiver can decipher just as quickly. No one else should be able to decipher it in any timescale.

▶ Encrypting/decrypting.

There are many methods of encrypting data. It is a fascinating and complex subject, and uses powerful mathematics for its implementation. Encryption is akin to the games you may have played where secret codes were used to change a message into unintelligible text, and then a key used to 'decrypt' it back into its original form.

As you can see, the process of scrambling is called 'encryption'. It produces 'encrypted' or 'cipher' text. The reverse process is called 'decryption' and produces 'clear' text.

Encryption by substitution

Games you might have played would probably have used a 'substitution' system for encryption. That is, the alphabet would have been scrambled around, producing a new alphabet with the first letter being something other than 'A', and the second not a 'B', etc. Every occurrence of 'A' in the clear text would have been changed to the new first letter, and every 'B' to the second letter in the new alphabet, and so on to produce the cipher text. Decryption is a matter of reversing the substituted alphabetic characters, using the scrambled alphabet as the 'key' to unlock the code.

This method of coding produces a completely unintelligible and scrambled version of the message. Trial and error would take an inordinately large amount of time to decipher the cipher text. In fact, there are 4 times 10 to the power 26 different scrambled alphabets (the number 4 followed by 26 zeros). Suppose a computer were to work through all of these, at one every billionth of a second (1 nanosecond), which is rather faster than any single computer can work today, it would still take nearly 45 million times the currently estimated age of the universe to complete the task.

A very secure code you might think! Unfortunately, this is one of the very simplest codes to break. It suffers from the fatal flaw that it does not disguise the format and character of the original text. For instance, the letter 'E' is the most common letter in the alphabet, and this will still be true for the substituted letter, whatever it is, and so on for the other letter frequencies. Also, letter combinations are preserved, such as 'in', 'an', 'the', 'ing', 'h' with 't' and 's' and so on. This gives enough clues to be able to discover the scrambled alphabetic key in rather less time than it takes to make a cup of tea, let alone many times the age of the universe!

Using fast programming, or even hardware logic devices, it is possible to create encryption by substitution every few minutes in a computer network, and this can help to make it difficult for the casual observer to decipher the information. As such, this method has some merit. It is crucial that the receiver knows the alphabetic 'key' which is being used at any time, but this can be arranged either over the network, or by other means. However, it is not secure enough for the country's national security services, for instance.

Another class of encryption method relies on 'transposition'. In this case, the original letters or data of the clear version are kept, but they are permuted, or transposed around until the information is scrambled. There are many methods available for such transposition, but an attempt has been made to standardize the methods for the best possible effect. A standard method is used in 'DES' or data encryption standard.

► Encryption through transposition.

In fact, DES uses a mixture of both substitution and transposition. It has been developed by the US Government in conjunction with IBM, and released for public use. It relies on a 'key', but in a rather different way from that described in the pure substitution above.

► The data encryption standard (DES) uses both substitution and transposition.

The key can either be a private key, which is known only to the sender or the receiver, or in fact it can be public, but only the receiver knows how to use it. A private key suffers from the problem of keeping it secret, as well as of communicating it to the receiver each time it is changed. A public key can be transmitted openly, but only unlocks the trick of decryption to the receiver.

► The way in which this style of encryption works is a little beyond our scope here, and if you are interested in the details you should consult a text on encryption.

The DES ciphering and deciphering algorithm can be built into dedicated chips and incorporated, for instance, into a telephone handset. With this level of technology, secure communications of any kind is available to everyone.

An interesting political angle has been suggested by some commentators, on the way in which DES works. It relies on a key which is essentially 56 BITs in length. This happens to produce an encryption level of prodigious depth, which should be uncrackable by its civilian users. However, it <u>can</u> be cracked by using the level of equipment available to the US Government.

If the key had been chosen, as originally suggested, as 128 BITs long, decryption would simply not be possible, currently.

It has thus been suggested that the US Government agency which produced DES was loath to allow civilian data to be indecipherable. The alternative would, perhaps, aid criminal and anti-state activity just that bit too much!

Data Protection Act

Quite apart from the problem of keeping communications private, there is also the problem of the ever-burgeoning activity of keeping files on people. The compilation of data on individuals for any purpose has its associated responsibility. If sensitive information is held electronically, it can be easy to use a fast system to select and print information which may be embarrassing to an individual. It is also irritating to some people to have their personal details available by machine. Criminals can find uses for our personal information, and some kind of control has to be maintained. In the UK this is administered according to an Act of Parliament which set up the 'Data Protection Register', with a Registrar who must be given details of almost all kinds of computerized personal record.

With a few exceptions, if you hold personal data on living people, you must register. This even applies to the simple keeping of people's names and addresses in a club computer. Registration is for three years at a time, and is for a given stated purpose. If you change the purpose or type of data you hold, you must inform the Registrar. It is ultimately a criminal offence not to register, or not to keep the registration updated as changes occur.

The goal of registration is to give individuals the security of knowing that companies which keep details on them are made to consider it seriously. In fact, registration also includes a mandatory code of practice whose principles are summarized in the box.

► Data Protection Act 1984.

The main points of the code of practice on data protection

Data must be:

- obtained and processed lawfully;
- held only for lawful purposes and as per the user's registration;
- disclosed only to the people described in the registration;
- adequate, relevant and not excessive;
- accurate and up to date;
- held for the minimum period necessary;
- accessible, correctable and erasable by the individual named;
- held under proper security.

This gives a backdrop against which all information about ourselves is kept. It gives rights to individuals, and ensures that if unlawful data is being held, it can be corrected.

This Act concerns a large fraction of the business community, most of which hold personal data of some sort. For instance, accounts, employee and customer details, statistical information, sales data, health and security information, and so on. A computer consultant should be alert to the possibility of registration in clients, and be ready to advise when the need arises. Although complying with the Act produces a small overhead on a business, there are few companies who find registration particularly onerous.

 List a few common computer applications which you know of from everyday life where the owner of the computer should have a registration. If you have time, contact the Data Protection Registrar, and ask to see the entry for one of these applications. This will give you some experience when advising clients as to their own particular application.

▶ An anomaly within the whole system of data protection is that a manual database does not need registration. Thus, the most personal, incorrect, even libellous information could be, and is, held by unscrupulous firms on old-fashioned card indexes, etc.

Free literature on the Data Protection Act is available from:
Data Protection Registrar
Springfield House
Water Lane
Wilmslow
Cheshire SK9 5AX
Telephone: 0625 535777

Computer viruses

In addition to the simple meddling within a given system by an individual, there are program elements which have been introduced for malicious reasons on a more public basis. It is possible to write a destructive piece of code which is hidden in the machine, and which is able to jump from machine to machine, infecting all machines it comes across. These are the so-called computer 'viruses'. They have all too many parallels with biological viruses. They are difficult to see, they have to have a host to survive, the more computer contacts you have, the more likely you are to succumb. They can multiply fast and overtake a machine completely, 'killing' all its data. Generally the user is unaware of infection until things start to go wrong.

Some viruses are harmless, and are meant to worry rather than destroy. The virus writer can make the screen and keyboard act in unusual ways. Typical examples include making all the characters on display 'fall' to the bottom of the screen, or suddenly displaying inexplicable messages on the screen. Some viruses are programmed to exhibit themselves on certain dates, such as a Friday the 13th, for instance. Other viruses are distinctly nasty – some are programmed to put up a message, lock up the system and then write rubbish across the entire disk system, erasing all the data. Others eat up all the spare internal and disk memory, preventing normal operation of the machine until the memory has been cleaned out completely. Other viruses are designed to 'live' in a network, infecting all the users who log in, and using up valuable space and computer time.

There are many ways in which a virus can be hidden within the memory of a machine. For instance, you will remember that disks are split into sectors, and each sector has, typically, 512 BYTEs. A given file may take up, say, ten sectors, or, ostensibly 5,120 BYTEs. However, the active information in that file may only be, say, 4,800 BYTEs in total. Thus, at the end of the tenth sector there is an unused portion of 320 BYTEs which are always transported wherever that file goes. A virus can be transferred within that region. The difficulty, for a virus writer, is how to start the virus program going – but a description of that process is probably best omitted here! Another common place to store the virus is in the unused spaces in the operating system – typically the very initial bootstrap part, or boot sector, which is always loaded and started automatically when the machine is switched on.

▶ Standard anti-virus programs are available to deal with the best-known viruses.

Most of the viruses making the rounds are well-known, and standard anti-virus programs exist which 'know' the tricks and can root them out. However, new viruses are being produced all the time, and anti-virus programs must be updated continuously to keep up.

▶ Virus infection is most usual through pirated game disks.

Probably the most common method of being infected is via games programs which have a suspect origin, probably having been copied illegally, and passed around quietly among friends. Any illegally copied software should be considered suspect, and the only way to try to ensure that your system does not catch a virus is to use original write-protected issue disks of software (but even this does not guarantee freedom from infection). Viruses purposely introduced into large wide area network systems produce multiple infections throughout the system, and are particularly dangerous. As such, they are considered to be a great prize by the originators.

Unfortunately, this practice of producing viruses is considered in some quarters to be 'fun' and 'up to date' in some way. This is simply not the case. As with biological viruses, much serious damage and worry can be caused by this childish practice. Indeed, in a health or safety setting, a computer virus can be life-threatening. Every computer professional has a responsibility to erode this 'clever swashbuckling' image of the virus writer. It is dangerous, irresponsible, expensive, and potentially lethal.

Eventually, it is hoped that completely virus-protected systems will evolve, but the complexity and 'newness' of systems in the current era make this impossible at present. If every BYTE of a given piece of software is 'known' along with the full details of a given system, nothing can 'creep in' without being noticed.

Protection against viruses takes many forms. Naturally, prevention is better than the need for cure, and there are some basic practices which can be recommended to a client.

Preventing infection by viruses

- Never allow users to bring in their own software – control all programs introduced into the system. Make it a dismissable offence for anyone to bring in personal games, or any copied software, for running on the system. If this rule is followed strictly, virus attack will be almost unknown.
- Run a virus check program regularly as part of maintenance, and keep the virus checker carefully up to date. Certainly run it each time new software is introduced.
- Keep a careful log of errors or strange occurrences, and mention them to the software engineer during maintenance.

These are the main precautions which can be taken against viruses. They will not, of course, prevent a determined malicious attack by an insider, and there is little that can be done against this type of computer terrorism. The main point to remember is for someone responsible to be in control of the use of the system at all times.

Even though a company may put in only two or three simple systems, they must be made to take security and maintenance seriously, or the investment in new technology could fail completely.

Chapter review

- Computer systems must be installed and maintained by trained computer experts.
- Computerization can fail if poorly specified and/or badly installed.
- Keep close to the customer during installation and troubleshooting.
- The introduction of a new computer system can disrupt the staff.
- Software needs maintaining just as much as hardware – indeed, often more so.
- Software maintenance consists largely of error correction, expansion and updating.
- A system must be laid out in a manner which is safe, efficient and comfortable to use.
- Data and programs must be backed up regularly, and a copy held off-site.
- Most systems are wide open to malicious tampering and unauthorized copying.
- Passwords can help to maintain privacy levels.
- Computer viruses can be avoided by preventing unauthorized introduction of software.
- Communications security can be achieved by encryption.

▶ Now that you have completed this chapter, look back to the objectives at the beginning and check that you have accomplished each of them.

- Almost all computer databases in the UK, containing information on living individuals, must be registered with the Data Protection Registrar.

(13) The future

THE FUTURE OF COMPUTING

Throughout the book, suggestions have been made as to the way in which the near future of computing is likely to look. However, this merely scratches the surface of the subject. We will look a little further in this final chapter.

► This chapter discusses future trends in information technology.

Advances such as the wider use of read/writable CD-ROMs for software distribution, faster processors and higher capacity memories are almost certain. The more important question to ask is what major advances are in the offing, or what advances are desirable. The difficulty is that this touches the topics of science fiction, and as such can generate predictions which are wildly wrong.

Future memory

At present, memory devices fall into three main categories:

- semi-conductor based, for fast internal RAM
- magnetic, for peripheral mass storage
- laser-read compact disk, also for peripheral mass storage.

This, in many ways, is a compromise. It is a pity that internal and peripheral memory cannot at present be integrated together into fast high capacity storage devices.

An important possible move in this direction is research into the 'molecular memory' approach. In this technology, single molecules are made to change state, storing one BIT per molecule. This is achieved using laser light to read and alter the states of the molecules, because, among other things, electronic connections between such small units would be rather difficult. Several molecules could be ganged together for each BIT, thus allowing for redundancy in case a single molecule should fail. Even so, the reduction in unit size is enormous.

► Molecular memory.

Molecules and atoms are already being handled with a device called the 'scanning tunnelling microscope' (STM) which can manipulate single atoms, and produce minute pits and bumps in the surface of a material many times smaller than the pits in a compact disk. In fact, in April 1990, Don Eigler, an IBM researcher, was able

► The scanning tunnelling microscope (STM) can manipulate single atoms to produce bumps and pits on a surface to encode information.

to write the word 'IBM' in letters five nanometres high – that is, five millionths of a millimetre high. The letters were written using just thirty-five atoms of xenon.

Using the STM to deposit minute blobs of gold on a surface can produce storage densities of the scale of 1 teraBIT (1,000,000,000,000 BITs) to a square inch. The complete works of Shakespeare would fit in a square with sides of 0.2mm. Furthermore, this all occurs at room temperature, and in air! The problem is to read and write fast enough to make a practical memory, let alone integrate peripheral and internal memory together.

It is true that the equipment for this technology is rather large and cumbersome at present, and perhaps an entirely new process is required to reduce the size. However, the possibilities for future memory devices on this type of physical scale would include credit-card sized computers with the data-holding and processing power of the largest supercomputer. But, even if you forget miniaturiztion, imagine the power that this could harness within the size of the present-day supercomputer!

Naturally, software would have to keep up with hardware, but there are plenty of problems which just need simple straightforward memory capacity, without greater computing power. For instance, how would you like the complete contents of all the libraries on the face of the Earth in your wallet? Or how about all the TV programs ever transmitted?

▶ Licensing and copyright problems.

The problems would become those of licensing and copyright. In fact, it is such problems which could seriously hold up the applications, and perhaps will only be resolved when money, and payment, become truly electronic.

Future styles of computer

With far greater densities of integration, it is possible to envisage miniature computers which could control all the functions of a car, including driving along roadways, avoiding accidents, and acting, essentially, as chauffeurs. This would dispense with the most dangerous component of the vehicle: the human driver. There is no technical reason why this should not be produced with current technology, but the machinery would be a little cumbersome, not to mention the software.

Greater memory and processing capacity in a small space will allow super powerful controllers to be incorporated into everything at low cost. We are only at the very start of this technology, and such concepts as the fully automated electronic home are not yet appropriate. However, one day this will be as natural as having a telephone and television in every home now seems.

Future pattern recognition

Current technology already produces machinery which can recognize human speech and human handwriting, but do not imagine that either of these problems has been fully cracked.

Scan the computer magazines and daily papers for examples of computers which claim to have transcended the simple standard keyboard and/or mouse input medium for information.

Recognizing spoken words is part of the general problem of pattern recognition, and it has not been fully solved. There are probably only two possible approaches to the problem:

1. Finding a set of universal algorithms which bring the spoken word down to a few basic defining variables which can be used universally to analyse and store those words in compact form. This would allow a simple program to recognize any spoken words by a simple matching process. So far this has eluded researchers.

2. Applying raw computer power – either in programming and fast hardware, or using powerful learning machines such as neural networks to analyse digitized voice patterns for later matching and recognition.

In the first case, someone discovers the mathematical make-up of human speech. The algorithm is used to analyse someone's voice while speaking every word in the English language. This stores the basic patterns involved, and is able to match these to anyone's speech, and thus convert acoustic speech into text on a screen. Of course 'understanding' this speech is another step entirely.

> ► There is a difference between converting speech and understanding it. For example, if someone smiles and says: 'I hate you', they mean something different from the dictionary definition of the words.

In the second case, the present line is continued until so much computing power is available in a small space that anyone can teach the machine to recognize their speech. Unfortunately, the machine will still find it difficult to apply this to the recognition of other speakers and accents. This is one of the main problems at present.

If recognition of speech, human faces, patterns of any kind, can be solved, the way is open for a massive increase in the efficiency of security, for instance. Even with current credit cards carrying a photo, the system is reliant upon a human being making the correct judgement as to whether the person offering payment is the owner pictured on the card. If this could be performed by machine, the system could be virtually foolproof.

> ► Pattern recognition and security: finger print, hand print, voice print, face recognition, for example.

Of course, you might also consider that a foolproof method of tying owners up with their credit cards could have some very serious effects on crime. A credit-card fraudster would no longer be able to practise the rather impersonal and merely irritating act of simply stealing some credit cards. The frightening concept opens out of extreme violence being threatened, as a matter of course, to force people to go into banks and shops, use their own credit cards and hand the proceeds over to the criminal.

You should always consider the social consequences of increased computer use. For instance, consider how all our lives will change as surveillance becomes considerably more efficient, as it surely will in the future, not to mention the increase in the storage of personal information, as mentioned on page 268.

(ACT) Imagine a great increase in the use of security video systems, linked to a pattern recognition program allowing individuals to be recognized, and then linked together so that individual movements through public spaces can be logged. What kind of arguments would some people use to justify the development of such a system, and what arguments would others use to try to prevent it being developed?

Intelligent machines

As you can see, everything is moving towards more and more intelligent machinery, but how is this to be achieved? We do not know how the human brain 'understands' so much, or indeed what the definition of 'understands' is! This type of discussion rapidly reverts to philosophy.

▶ Artificial intelligence (AI).

Current artificial intelligence (AI) is centred around such areas as 'expert systems' where a knowledge base of information is used, and cross-referenced, to make decisions. This essentially seeks to capture the knowledge and experience of an expert, and apply it automatically for anyone to use.

▶ Expert systems.

One of the most important goals of AI is the general pattern recognition problem. Other goals include the desire to make a machine capable of holding normal human conversations. On a certain level, this is already possible. Unfortunately, even dim humans can outsmart the cleverest such program.

▶ The Turing test for machine intelligence.

A famous British mathematical logician, Alan Turing, in the early part of this century, proposed an interesting test for machine intelligence. A machine and a human are set up behind screens, and anyone is able to communicate with either machine or human via links which are carefully made physically indistinguishable. If any human can come along and 'talk' to each without being able to determine which is the machine, then the machine has achieved artificial intelligence. This is not a bad working start in defining machine intelligence, and it is interesting to think of the questions and conversations which you might present in order to try to discover which is which. How about, for instance: 'What is the name of your mother, and where were you born?'!

Software of the future

There are systems at present which generate computer programs automatically, called 'program generators'. They do not have any intelligence, but just save the programmer from comparatively straightforward but time-consuming code generation.

▶ Program generators and CASE tools.

In the future, and again bound up with the basis of AI, it is possible to envisage machines which either generate their own code, or simply learn all the routines from a basic systems analysis, produced by a machine or human systems analyst.

The path to this goal, with current computing machinery, would be to systematize the analysis phase so that it always uses the same basic variables, no matter what the situation. This has been started with 'computer-aided software engineering' (CASE) tools. These attempt to systematize software development in order to produce a consistency across the industry.

Another problem with current software tools and languages is that a reasonable amount of study is needed before a computer-based routine (program) can be constructed. It is not possible for someone who has no experience of computers to pick up even a simple machine and immediately write a program for a simple routine. In the future, it would be possible to incorporate simple routine-generation into a GUI front end. The user would simply select the functions required, and the machine would string them together.

In general, however, it is difficult to imagine every one in the world wanting to write programs. Such activities would be confined to people performing technical tasks. While it is easy for engineers to use computer machinery for complex tasks, because their training probably includes familiarity with computer systems, it is more difficult, and less natural for, say, a psychologist or social worker to write routines to analyse experiments and patient information in a simple way. It is this level of function which could provide the greatest increase in the use of small computers in the future.

You can imagine a small universal notepad-sized machine, with a full display which is full of icons. A pointer system would allow icons to be chosen for all the standard tasks such as diary, WP, data storage, and so on but also have a section devoted to constructing new functions to be applied to input data, and providing answers quickly in a form which the user would prefer. This may sound simple, but all attempts to produce such universal systems have simply failed to interface naturally enough with the general user to be of much use.

The problem is one of analysing the psychology of the human–machine interface – a subject which has been studied for many years, but is still embryonic, as evidenced by the impenetrable nature of the manuals provided with even the most popular packages. The concept of 'context sensitive help' requires a complete overhaul in its application. Many packages have it, but it often supplies the help information in a form which is incomprehensible, or which produces more questions than answers. Again, the psychology of 'help' use, and how humans learn complex computer functions in an efficient and speedy manner, is a whole subject which requires a research program as far reaching as that of the ever evolving hardware advances. Until this is properly addressed, machines will remain in (albeit quite large) niche applications.

► The major problem lies in the psychology of the human–machine interface.

When members of the non-technical public can sit down and use a machine for their own specialized tasks as easily as they can use a piece of paper and a pencil, computing will finally have come of age. Perhaps this will only be possible in the far distant future when the interface between human and machine becomes almost telepathic, via a link directly to brain! In fact, the brain's function can be

► Computing will finally have come of age when ordinary people use computers as easily as they now use pencil and paper.

observed using a sensor called a 'SQUID' (superconducting quantum interference device). This can now map the minute magnetic effects of brain function, on a milli-second basis, and if refined considerably might form the basis of a complete link directly from (and to?) the brain in the future. Of course, such a sophisticated concept is doomed to failure if computers are as dim then as they are now – a quantum leap in machine intelligence will be required to keep up with such steps.

The future of graphics and visual display

▶ Display screens.

The days of the TV tube are numbered. The technology of a large evacuated tube, with high voltage supplies, and large power requirements must be dispensed with. The problem at present is the manufacturing technology of LCD screens. The yield of a large flat matrix containing millions of separate dots, each perhaps with its own activating transistor, is not high. Most screens manufactured have at least one dot, and often many more dots, inoperative. There is a move to provide redundancy within the matrix, but this is still in its infancy. These problems will be solved, either with current technology, or by a breakthrough. It is time that all screens were light to handle, and power saving.

▶ Presentation: animation and 3D.

Graphics presentation itself, apart from the display, is becoming more sophisticated. Complete animation sequences with computer-generated artwork can be produced. In the future, there should be an effective way to show full three-dimensional (3-D) displays without the need to use special glasses. This is a crucial step forward, and is as important as the cinema's move to 'talkies' or colour.

▶ In virtual reality applications the 3-D effect is produced by sending two identical but slightly offset streams of images to the eyes. The angle of view is determined by the movements of the wearer's headset.

The use of 3-D in such fields as CAD would be revolutionary. Already a 2-D representation of 3-D objects is offered by popular packages. Design of objects should be able to be performed as easily on 3-D objects as they can in 2-D. The next step would be to tie in an automatic modelling machine which would produce a prototype just as a printer or plotter produces hard copy. The final step (CAM) would be to transmit the information straight to the shop floor, itself fully automated, so that numerically controlled machinery could produce a final prototype, and after approval and modification, manufacture the object in bulk.

This is not far from the capability of modern technology, but requires a large financial and research investment for its practical realization.

▶ Data compression.

Another important and advancing field is that of data compression, and its application to the storage, retrieval and communication of complex moving coloured images. The applications of this include the ability to capture pictures from any source, and store them in small-capacity memories at high speed. However, memory capacity will not be the problem in the future. The real application for compressing data is in the field of communication, where high-resolution pictures, and any other type of data, can be compressed considerably to save communication time.

The smaller the data capacity required for digitizing graphical objects, the more likely it is that we can transmit full TV pictures along a telephone, or any other link, fast enough to use a video camera, or video player, over the phone in real time.

Among other things, this would open the way for premium, personally tailored entertainment channels. You might be able to phone a given number to be sent a complete film for real-time viewing, or storage on disk, CD-ROM or tape for later. As fast internal memory devices become available, the whole film might be stored within your own personal note-pad computer, for viewing on its full-colour high-speed display, or linked into a TV. The phone companies would be happy to be paid for the communications time, and they could pass a suitable fee to the service provider. After all, the telephone companies have two major assets: a worldwide communications network, and a highly efficient charging scheme. Films could be sent at high speed during the comparatively quiet night hours, for viewing later.

► Personal entertainment.

The distant future

To return to science fiction, as mentioned at the start of this chapter, there are many concepts which are merely wishful thoughts in computing.

► Friendly robots.

One such desire is to produce the truly intelligent mechanical companion, or robot. Isaac Asimov, in his celebrated *Robot* series of books, attempts to sketch out such a future. Some of his stories are also concerned with the ethical problems of such devices. If you are interested in this application of computers, you would be well-advised to read this entertaining series of books.

Before such a dream can come true, however, fundamental advances are required in a large number of fields.

 Before reading on, list the fields of technology which you think require a major advance before the walking, talking, companionable human-sized robot can be produced.

Apart from the computing advances needed, such as intelligent processing of voice and visual data, how about the power source? Modern batteries are so far beneath a suitable specification for robots, that an internal combustion engine, generating electricity directly, might as well be incorporated in the thing!

Then there are mechanical 'servos', or actuators, which produce movement when stimulated electronically, in a similar way to our muscles. There are no compact light actuators which have the sensitivity and accuracy of movement of muscles, and which run on such simple power sources. It is true that pneumatic servos are very good, and can be fashioned to act like muscles, but they require an air compressor constantly pumping air at high pressure for their power source.

Then there is the resolution with which the eye can see in full colour down to very low light levels, and even perform some of the basic pattern processing before passing it on to the brain. How can this be reproduced?

Advances would be required in power sources, servos, sensors, intelligent processing and pattern recognition, to name but a few. The age of the true Asimovian robot is still far off.

► Conversation.

Another interesting science fiction dream is that of the perfect weld of human and machine through physical contact. Typically, an operator holds a hand onto a sensitive plate, and 'becomes one' with the computer. They hold conversations, with the operator in full control of the machine, seeing everything that it sees through its own sensors, which may be at the bottom of a mine, or outside a space craft. The human–machine interface problem is solved at a stroke.

To perform a miracle such as this, we would, apart from everything else, have to find a suitable interface channel within our own bodies. The hand does not seem too suitable, and even sensors on or in the skull have only yielded gross contact so far. The field of neurology would have to advance in a very fundamental way before such contact would be possible. By then, computers will, no doubt, be intelligent enough to use this high-level interface.

► Computer predictions.

Another interesting field of endeavour which needs to be attacked is that of the complete prediction machine. This would, for instance, take in a complete history of the human race, down to small personal detail of all humans who have ever lived, plus all the natural, and other, events which have happened on Earth for as long as this information is available. The machine would then generalize this information, and predict the future path of every human being on Earth. The machine would keep itself up to date by taking in details on everyone and everything, and thus check itself continually. Long predictions would be difficult, but short ones quite efficient – rather like the weather forecast. This would be rather like a properly automated 'Big Brother' as in George Orwell's *1984*. We would probably all be thoroughly against it, assuming it is possible in principle.

► One of the difficulties with computer predictions in economics is that if they could be made, everyone would base their actions on them. The system would thus be changed and the predictions fail.

A more immediate application would be in the highly unstable field of economics. Prediction and control of economies has largely eluded us, to date. It is what is known as a 'non-linear' problem. In short, it seems that anything can happen, and new patterns are being generated all the time.

If there are underlying laws to be discovered, perhaps these could be found and applied by a super-neural network, acting within a computing machine thousands of times more powerful than the largest supercomputers today. The problems would then be confined to capturing data, and writing routines to analyse these data in a suitable manner.

 There are many other problems than those of pattern recognition, forecasting the weather and economics in everyday life – list as many as you can think of.

Final note

Two hundred years ago, our modern world was completely beyond comprehension, and the same must surely be true for our conception of the coming centuries. In the twentieth century, indeed, within the sentient existence of many of us, the computer has been both invented (in its present form) and shared out among everyone. After all, the transistor was only invented in 1947. What advances will occur over the rest of your lifetime, and beyond?

Chapter review
- Hardware and software are continuously advancing.
- Memory is becoming faster and higher in capacity.
- Personal computers, and hardware controllers will become more and more intelligent.
- Pattern recognition is not yet solved, it includes voice and visual recognition, among other things.
- Human–machine interface requires considerably more research.
- Data compression allows high capacity, fast storage and communication of complex objects.
- True robotics needs many advances in a diverse set of fields.

▶ Now that you have completed this chapter, look back to the objectives at the beginning and check that you have accomplished each of them.

Index